SOCIAL MEDIA LAW

IN A NUTSHELL®

RYAN GARCIA
Adjunct Professor of Law
University of Texas School of Law

THADDEUS HOFFMEISTER
Professor of Law
University of Dayton School of Law

WEST ACADEMIC PUBLISHING

The publisher is not engaged in rendering legal or other professional advice, and this publication is not a substitute for the advice of an attorney. If you require legal or other expert advice, you should seek the services of a competent attorney or other professional.

444 Cedar Street, Suite 700
St. Paul, MN 55101
1-877-888-1330

Printed in the United States of America

ISBN: 978-1-63459-354-0

ACKNOWLEDGMENTS

I dedicate this book to Sara, Besher, and Isaac, the most supportive family I could ever hope for. #yourock

Many people helped me along my social media law path but I would like to especially thank the following for their assistance in creating this book: Professor John Dzienkowski for introducing me to Dean Bobby Chesney and helping launch my Law & Social Media class at the University of Texas School of Law; Louis Higgins for his support and guidance; Jim Dudukovich, Mark Bisard, and all my fellow SMART colleagues who have guided so many of my social media thoughts; my Social Media and Communities (SMaC) colleagues at Dell who have helped shape these conversations by constantly innovating in their field; my co-author Thaddeus for his steady pursuit of bringing this book to fruition and his research assistant Marty Gehres; and to the entire staff of the Circle C Starbucks in Austin, Texas, who have provided me with writing space and, more importantly, caffeine enough to complete this journey.

RYAN GARCIA

This book is dedicated to A and Z.

I would like to acknowledge the efforts of my three research assistants Marty Gehres, Elizabeth Watson, and Ann Charles Watts.

THADDEUS HOFFMEISTER

OUTLINE

TABLE OF CASES

References are to Pages

SOCIAL MEDIA LAW

IN A NUTSHELL®

CHAPTER 1

WHY SOCIAL MEDIA LAW MATTERS

Social media has exploded into our culture and embedded itself into our daily lives. In 2006, Facebook first opened itself to the public instead of just college students and a few companies. Since that time, the platform has grown to over a billion users. While Facebook is the most dominant success story in social media it is far from the only one.

When social media established itself as a cultural phenomenon, the implications of this technological revolution were felt in virtually every industry. Marketing, sales, research, education, medicine, entrepreneurship, military—every aspect of our world has been impacted. The legal field is no exception. Social media has changed both the way lawyers practice and apply existing laws.

Social media law is less a distinct body of case law and statues such as copyright or employment but rather a manner of influencing or impacting existing areas of law. Every legal practitioner has had to accommodate social media, whether using new standards to search for relevant documents during electronic discovery or determining how to apply old marketing rules to new social media ad campaigns.

The social media revolution is still a new phenomenon and is rapidly evolving. Still, there are trends and patterns we can pull out from this new generation of network communications that provide valuable legal lessons to practitioners and their clients. This book explores the high level risks and concerns that social media raises and will provide a framework for thinking about these problems and potential solutions. But to begin this conversation we must first understand what social media means.

§ 1.01 DEFINING SOCIAL MEDIA

A. SOCIAL MEDIA IS ABOUT CONVERSATIONS

In order to discuss social media we must first define it. Many believe that social media is limited to the large social platforms: Facebook, Twitter, LinkedIn, and the like. The truth is that social media is far larger. These sites are social networking platforms and merely one part of social media.

Black's Law Dictionary defines social media as "Any cell phone or internet based tools and applications that are used to share and distribute information." At first glance this definition would appear to include any information connected to the Internet since distribution is the primary reason for putting information online. But there is one additional element that makes information, services, and sites fall under the umbrella of social media: conversation. The social in social media is the ability for communities to be formed and individuals to exchange content around the information that is posted. Conversation is the seed that has transformed the Internet and the World Wide Web into social media.

B. SOCIAL MEDIA IS BIGGER THAN SOCIAL NETWORKING

Social media is much larger than Facebook and Twitter, although those platforms alone are large and significant. Those sites are classified as social networking platforms and tend to include a particular set of functions (profile creation, content posting, ability to connect with other profiles, etc.).

Social networking is a huge part of social media, but it is still just one part. Social media is any technology that allows online conversations. This includes Facebook and Twitter but it also includes blogs, wikis, chat rooms, YouTube comments, and more. If you have visited a web page with a comments section, you have been on a social media community. If you have visited a community-run site where fans of a TV show collaborate to document every facet of their beloved televised world then you have visited a social media site. Similarly, if you browse a web page where a group of people are trying to raise funds to start a new business, interacting with their backers while trying to raise money, then you have spent time on a social media group. These are all examples of sites and pages that fall outside social networking but are certainly part of social media.

In fact, it is difficult these days to find a website or information service that is not social media. There are still older websites that simply present static information but the odds of a typical Internet user returning to that website, let alone remembering any of its content, are incredibly low. Instead, today's information consumers expect content to be interactive. Articles are expected to have a comments section and readers may view an article with skepticism if that comments section is disabled. Sites such as wikis that collect information around topics, both broad and focused, are expected to allow members of the public to make changes or corrections. Visitors to a site where a group is raising funds for a new product, a movie, or a community event expect to be able to ask questions of the people requesting money and may base their decision to contribute on the answer they receive. This is all social media. And it is very different from the previous generation of the Internet.

C. UNDERSTANDING SOCIAL MEDIA FUNCTIONALITY

There are hundreds of social media platforms and trying to list, let alone understand, all of them in a print publication is an exercise in futility. Instead, to discuss the impact on legal topics and the risks it carries, there are certain core functions that should be understood in relation to social media.

1. Posting

Central to all social media platforms is the ability for a user to post original content. This can take the form of a large or virtually unlimited amount of text like a blog (a word that derives its definition from people who started journaling on websites by creating a web log, later shortened to blog) or a small amount of text like Twitter's limit of 140 characters, sometimes referred to as a microblog.

Social media users can also post pictures or videos, whether captured spontaneously or prepared ahead of time. Instagram, a photo and video sharing service owned by Facebook, currently allows sixty seconds of raw or edited footage to be shared while services such as Periscope or Facebook Live allow live streaming of video from a person to other users around the world.

2. Hashtags (#)

While ordinarily a hashtag (#) is part of a social media post, its role is significant enough to call out separately. Hashtags in social media grew out of the first wave of Twitter users. Twitter, for the most part, is a single community of people not separated by topics or locations. Although Twitter users can choose to immediately see only content from accounts they follow, virtually all Twitter content is visible to all other users (the exception being protected Twitter accounts). This can make for a robust community to discuss certain topics. It can also make it incredibly difficult to follow a particular thread as users are presented with so many people discussing so many different topics.

Early adopters of Twitter settled on using the hashtag to mark certain topics and as a way of including a marker for people to follow a single conversation. This meant that if a group of Twitter users were discussing the latest full moon, they could include #moon in their tweets and then search by that hashtag to see the entire conversation by participants.

Hashtags had the extra advantage of allowing people to contribute to conversations without making their content explicitly about the topic at hand. It would be obvious to a reader that the tweet "This is the largest full #moon I have ever seen!" that the user was discussing the moon even without the hashtag symbol. But the tweet "That's the biggest one I've ever seen! #moon" might be undiscovered or misinterpreted without the accompanying hashtag.

Hashtags grew beyond Twitter and are now supported on virtually all social platforms. Not only do they serve as a way to search for specific topics or keywords but they also provide a way for organizations to interact with individuals. Commercials, advertisements, or general notices will now typically include a hashtag allowing individuals to interact around a brand or event no matter which platform they use.

3. Engagement

Because social media is about conversations, posting content is only the first step in creating a social platform. To have a dialogue of any kind there must be some kind of engagement with content posted by users. That engagement can range from simple one-click engagements to more complicated forms of content interaction.

a. One-Click Engagement

The simplest form of social media content engagement involves a single click or action. On Facebook, users can click the Like button to interact with text, photos, videos, or links. On Instagram, users can quickly double-tap on a photo to give it a heart. On Twitter, users can click a heart button associated with a tweet.

All of these engagements are indications that the user has seen the content and appreciates or recognizes it in some way. Yet the simplicity of the engagement can lead to complications based on its context. When a Facebook user posts that a parent has died, their connections may want to interact with that post but may not be willing to click the Like button on the announcement. For this reason, Facebook has expanded its simple engagement to include more than just Likes by presenting five additional simple reactions to content: Love, Haha, Sad, Angry, and Wow. Whether other platforms follow remains to be seen but it does show an increasing comfort and complexity social media users have when engaging with content.

b. Responses

More complicated engagement includes the ability to respond to a particular piece of content. On Facebook, users are typically allowed to post a comment to a piece of content. That response can include text, photos, or other graphics but the entire response becomes part of the conversation attached to the content posted by the original user.

On Twitter, LinkedIn, or other platforms, users can also enter a response to a piece of content. Some platforms display responses only when viewing the original piece of content. Other sites may allow the response itself to be seen independent of the original content—although the responses are frequently linked in such a way that another user can quickly visit the original content providing the context of the post.

c. *Tagging*

An even more sophisticated form of engagement includes Tagging. This occurs when one user of the social platform intentionally includes another user in the conversation or content. For example, User A could post a group photo and tag User B as also being in that photo. This may bring more attention to the photo by explicitly including User B and User B's connections in the conversation. Tagging can also take place inside comments or other social media activities as a way of intentionally connecting with other people and their networks.

4. Sharing

Sharing is what enables content to go viral on social media. A piece of content is initially visible to users who are connected to the original author—by sharing the content with their network a new audience can see the content and potentially share it with their own network as well. Social media is not just limited to an individual's network but also includes their network's network. Sharing is what allows the network of networks to distribute information. Facebook, for example, has a Share button which allows a user to post the original poster's content while also optionally adding their own comments.

Similarly, Twitter's Retweet button allows User A to share User B's tweet. User B's tweet will now be seen by people connected to User A even if those people are not connected to User B. This kind of sharing is what enables content to quickly spread from one network to another to yet another and it is this powerful feature that can allow a message initially seen by a few dozen to quickly be seen by a million or more people.

§ 1.02 WHAT MAKES SOCIAL MEDIA DIFFERENT

Before social media, the world went online and found information on the World Wide Web. Search engines and web indexes had come and gone. Emails were crossing the globe at the speed of light. Information was being exchanged on the Internet in a way never before imagined. Then social media came and changed everything by turning static information into a conversation.

The aspect of adding conversations to the information already online has fundamentally changed how we interact with online content. Whether as a by-product of social media functionality or as the core reason for its success, social media has created a different relationship between users and the underlying technology and information. This relationship both drives the social media explosion and also forms the foundation of various legal risks created by social media.

A. PERSONAL CONNECTIONS

Social media is deeply personal. Because social media is built around conversations, the first thing a typical social media user will do after setting up their account is to connect with their friends and family. In many cases, an offline request from a friend or family member is what brought a new user onto a social media platform in the first place. Once connected, the new social media user will consume content written by their friends, shared by their family members, or recommended by both. Social media is the ultimate dinner party and you don't even have to do dishes.

Because users are connected to friends and family on social media, users are drawn back to the platform to interact with these people. It is no longer a matter of arranging a time and place to meet face to face—social media users go online and are instantly connected with their friends and families. This brings users back. And back again. This is why the average American spent over 40 minutes a day on Facebook back in 2014. By 2016, that number was up to 50 minutes a day when counting Facebook, Instagram, and Messenger, all Facebook properties.

This connection with friends and family members also puts a personal perspective on the otherwise faceless Internet. Before social media, people interacted with soulless websites. Now users have forgotten about the technology itself and instead interact with people. It could be the stories they tell, the photos they've posted, or the articles they've shared, but each time an individual views a piece of information on their computer screen or smartphone they are not just interacting with a piece of data—they are interacting with the person who wrote that content. Every conversation is personal and much more impactful than the same information presented on a website without a face.

B. NETWORK OF NETWORKS

Another key component of the social media explosion is the network that it has created. A social media user has their own network of connections—people, interests (Movies, Reading, etc.), brands (Starbucks, Game of Thrones, etc.), and groups they have joined are all branches of their personal network (also called a social graph). By connecting to the particular people and subjects users want to see on their social platforms, every platform user creates their own private curated network of desired content. But each connection a user makes is not just a single source of content—that connection is also a network itself. Social media users are not hubs in a wheel with spokes connecting them to other people and topics—this visual implies that the connections stop after one step. Instead, those connections do not stop. Every social media user is a leaf connected to a branch with other leaves, a branch which is itself connected to bigger branches with more leaves, and all of those branches are connected to other trees with more branches and leaves.

This network of networks employed by social media has two enormous benefits. First, it keeps a steady stream of content coming to individual users which, in turn, encourages them to return to social media platforms over and over for more content. Second, it also allows information that originates with a single person to spread not only to their network of connections but also to the networks attached to their connections. When a piece of content spreads widely and quickly enough, we refer to that content as going viral.

In 1929 a now infamous theory posited the entire population of the planet was separated by only six degrees. In 2008, Facebook determined that 99.6% of its users were connected by only five degrees of separation. By 2016, that number had dropped to an average of 3.5 degrees of separation. But these are just numbers. The stories behind how information can employ these connections and go viral are far more interesting.

C. SOCIAL MEDIA CONTENT CAN GO VIRAL

Thanks to the personal aspect of social media and the network of networks, any piece of content posted on social media can go viral in minutes. Take, for example, the story of Stefanie Gordon. In 2011, Ms. Gordon was a former meeting planner for a non-profit organization. She was unemployed when she took a flight from New York City to West Palm Beach, Florida to visit family. While approaching her destination the pilot announced that passengers could see the space shuttle Endeavour launch outside of the plane (a very safe distance away). The normally impressive sight of a space shuttle launching into space was made even more significant by the fact that this was the second to last space shuttle launch, as the fleet was being retired. Stefanie readied her iPhone and watched as the shuttle appeared with a white trail breaking through the clouds. She caught several seconds of video and three still images of the launch.

When Stefanie landed she tweeted one of the photos, then proceeded to claim her bags and meet her family. Within minutes she reported her phone "going crazy" with alerts from the hundreds, then thousands, then tens and hundreds of thousands of shares, retweets, and messages Stefanie received. Major media outlets contacted her for permission to use the photo.

When Stefanie originally tweeted the photo and video she had 1,800 followers. By the end of the day the photo had been seen hundreds of thousands of times, her name had been mentioned on NBC Nightly News, her video had been shown on CNN, and several newspapers were set to publish the picture on the front page the next day. Stefanie took advantage of her newfound popularity to tweet out her LinkedIn profile and to say she was looking for a job.

While the personal connections keep users visiting social media sites more than the previous generation of Internet sites, it is the network of networks that allows information to spread faster and wider than ever before. These two elements make social media different and also create some significant legal risks.

§ 1.03 LEGAL RISKS FOR SOCIAL MEDIA

Social media law is less a discrete set of rules and cases that apply to social media but more about how the social media revolution has impacted the entire legal field. Every substantive area of law has been impacted by the rise of social media: electronic evidence, employment, free speech, marketing, and beyond.

While this book addresses many of the major areas where social media has created the largest legal impact, social media is both too large and too fast to cover it all. Instead, the co-authors intend for this book to give readers the tools to evaluate potential risks and a framework for identifying problem areas before they strike.

Just as two distinct features, viral content and personal connections, make social media different from previous generations of the Internet, so too do those two features give rise to significant high-level risks of social media across all topics. These high level risks can carry consequences ranging from regulatory breaches to brand or personal backlash but all of them show the power and danger of social media.

A. THE RISKS BEHIND VIRAL CONTENT

Having content go viral can be a thrilling experience for an individual or a brand. Having a person write a message or post a picture that is seen by thousands or millions of people can be an exciting adventure. Having a brand or organization post content for (almost) free that is then seen by more people than a Super Bowl commercial can be a huge success. Or can end up as a nightmare.

1. Personal Viral Nightmares

Justine Sacco worked as a public relations executive for a company that owned several well-known websites in 2013. For her winter holiday, she booked a trip to South Africa. Ms. Sacco was about to depart for her vacation when she sent the tweet "Going to Africa. Hope I don't get AIDS. Just kidding, I'm white!"

During the dozen or so hours Ms. Sacco was on the plane without Internet access, her tweet went viral. It ended up on the front page of most mainstream media news sources and on televised news as well. Her employer publicly distanced itself from her statement. Rumors circulated that she would be fired as soon as she landed causing a small group of Internet users to locate her gate in the Johannesburg airport. Another group physically went to the gate and waited to try and get a picture of the moment she was terminated. (They got the picture.)

While having a tweet like that go viral and carry such harsh consequences can be a nightmare, consider one additional point: Ms. Sacco had only a few hundred followers on Twitter when she sent the tweet. She was not an Internet celebrity with thousands or tens of thousands of fans waiting on her every post. She was just a regular Twitter user whose bad post made it to the front page of every US news site in a matter of hours. Having content go viral can happen to anyone.

2. Brand Viral Nightmares

While brands and organizations love taking advantage of social media so that their content may reach thousands or millions of potential customers they want that content to be positive. A single piece of negative content reaching that many people can have dire consequences for any organization. Take, for example, the case of Honda Eddie.

In 2009, Honda was set to release a new car model named the Crosstour. Early photos of the car generated intense negative buzz among Honda fans. According to the popular car website Autoblog, "81.7% of you feel the Crosstour should be killed with fire, and just 3.1% of you think it is good looking."

Honda decided to release some photos on its Facebook page to fans, perhaps hoping to generate some positive commentary from supporters. The result was the same as the Autoblog poll with numerous highly critical posts and negative responses about the new car.

Among the negative posts came one that was decidedly less negative. A user by the name of Eddie Okubo posted "Interesting design. I would get this car in a heartbeat. I may be the older crowd with my kids out of the house and still need some space and performance. Don't need anything big."

Within two minutes of Mr. Okubo's post came a response: "[S]ounds like you are trying to save your job at Honda?"

Approximately five minutes later came a second response: "Maybe you like it Eddie because you're the MANAGER OF PRODUCT PLANNING at Honda (light trucks in particular)?" This second response included links to Mr. Okubo's LinkedIn profile verifying his position as well as a link to an interview he had given to an industry publication about his role in the Crosstour launch.

Being optimistic for a brief period, pretend that Mr. Okubo, in his excitement over the launch of a product he was intimately involved with for years, simply forgot to mention that he happened to work at Honda and the Crosstour launch was part of his job. Unfortunately, that optimistic view looks the same on social media as the pessimistic view most experience when hearing this story: Eddie was trying to pull a fast one.

With social media providing greater access to information comes the opposing risk: that information can go viral and its impact is negative. In this case, when information is withheld from social media most users will assume the omission is intentional. The viral backlash against that content is then impossible to control.

The speed of such a viral backlash cannot be handled by any corporation or organization. Honda likely had no idea that Eddie was posting on their Facebook page. Less than eight minutes after posting his neutral-to-slightly-positive review, Eddie's post on the Honda Facebook page was a major news story.

B. THE RISKS BEHIND PERSONAL CONNECTIONS

The vast majority of content consumed and interacted with online comes from personal connections. Both the number of connections and the filtering algorithms used by major platforms ensure individuals are far more likely to see baby pictures posted by their friends than an announcement by a local store about a new sale. As users consume all of this personal social media content with sporadic commercial content, many people may find themselves thinking that they are participating in a platform populated solely by friends and family rather than a large community filled with co-workers and the press. This can cause social media users to lower their guard and behave as they would when out to dinner rather than at a large business meeting.

But in reality, social media users are participating on a platform filled with more strangers than friends. If a reporter for a major newspaper happens to see an off-color comment made by an employee on an online story, that employee (and their employer) can end up on the front page of the newspaper even if that comment never went viral. Similarly, an employee might make a scathing comment about their manager on a social media platform forgetting that they were already connected to their manager who may have just read it.

Social media's informal tone causes users to treat social media informally and behave a particular way on most platforms. This can directly impact individuals' use of social media on the job whether intentionally or not by exposing individuals and their employers to increased social media risk. The very element that causes people to come back and engage in social media can also turn its head and bite them with negative repercussions.

1. The Social Media Reply All

Anyone who has used email for at least a few years has encountered the reply all mistake. The problem begins when a group of people are emailed, then someone wants to make a private reply but instead accidentally hits reply all instead of reply. Hitting that one button can lead to embarrassing—or worse—consequences.

The social media equivalent of the reply all mistake can occur when people post content intended for a private audience but unintentionally post for a much broader audience. This mistake can happen even to professional social networking computer engineers. Take, for example, the case of Steve Yegge, an engineer at Google. After many years at Google, he decided to lash out against some frustrating mistakes he felt his company was making by writing a 4,500 word essay comparing Google to his former employer, Amazon. He intended to post the note to his fellow Google engineers but instead posted the note publicly for the world to read.

While Mr. Yegge may have faced initial embarrassment, he did keep the note posted publicly and it generated numerous responses—both from his fellow workers and other people outside the company. If this mistake can happen to a professional engineer who works on social networks, it can happen to anyone.

And while such a mistake can have embarrassing consequences, it can also have more serious ramifications. Take, for example, an instance in November, 2014 when the Chief Financial Officer for Twitter inadvertently sent a public tweet discussing how Twitter should buy another company and that they needed to be sold on the idea during an upcoming meeting. While the target company wasn't explicitly named, tech insiders quickly spread rumors causing larger issues for a Twitter user that certainly should have known better.

2. The Casual Good Day

Any social platform that allows status updates or quick notes will certainly contain posts by individuals expressing opinions about their day. Perhaps it was a good day because of the weather or bad because of the traffic. Being exposed to these kinds of notes can lead some people to share their own feelings about the day even when perhaps they shouldn't.

Gene Morphis was the Chief Financial Officer for Francesca Holdings Corp, a publicly traded company that owned retail clothing stores across the country. In March of 2012, Mr. Morphis presented his company's financial information to the Board of Directors in anticipation of their upcoming public earnings announcement. After the meeting he tweeted "Board meeting. Good numbers = Happy Board." While certainly a true feeling for Mr. Morphis, he was also the Chief Financial Officer of a publicly traded company and, as such, knew that the disclosure of financial results ahead of designated filings is not only a breach of securities regulations but also a breach of an officer's fiduciary duty to protect the company.

Mr. Morphis was fired from his job within days of the company discovering this and other social media transgressions. While Mr. Morphis did lose his job he kept his sense of humor, tweeting after the firing and subsequent press "There has to be an easier and cheaper way to create followers than that was. . ."

3. Jumping on a Trending Topic

Several social media platforms will identify topics or keywords that are currently being discussed by a large number of people. While these topics can be easy to identify just by their hashtag or description, sometimes the actual context of those trending topics may be hidden. If a company, brand, or individual incorrectly guesses at the meaning and wrongly inserts themselves into the conversation, the results can be incredibly harmful.

On July 20, 2012, Batman fans around the country flocked to movie theaters to see special midnight showings of the eagerly anticipated conclusion to the Christopher Nolan Batman movie trilogy, *The Dark*

Knight Rises. One showing in Aurora, Colorado ended in tragedy as a gunman burst into the theater with several weapons killing 12 people and injuring another 58.

As the attack took place at a late night movie screening many people first discovered the news when they awoke the next morning. Various keywords around the incident were trending on Twitter including the word "Aurora." An online fashion store, CelebBoutique.com, tweeted out a message early the next morning: "#Aurora is trending, clearly about our Kim K[ardashian] inspired #Aurora dress." The tweet also included an emoticon for a wink and a link to purchase the dress from their online store.

Amidst a flood of negative responses, the company later revealed that much of their public relations work is handled by an international company. That company saw the trending topic but did not investigate the origins of the topic and posted the controversial tweet. The company apologized repeatedly but the damage had been done—more people knew this company for its tasteless tweet than for any celebrity-inspired clothing.

And while the #Aurora tweet is a well-known example, the lesson it teaches has still not been learned by all major brands. In 2014, a video was released showing a famous professional athlete striking his then fiancée in the face. The release of the video made immediate national news and also triggered a series of discussions on social media concerning domestic violence. On Twitter, conversations for #WhyIStayed and #WhyILeft became a national trend as former and current domestic violence victims shared their personal experiences.

Amidst these serious and difficult posts on the topics came a tweet from DiGiorno Pizza, a company that markets frozen pizza and pizza products. Their tweet, "#WhyIStayed You had pizza," was inappropriate for the serious conversation. It was immediately called out and the tweet was taken down within seconds as the original poster realized the mistake he had made. Seconds was all it took for the tweet to be shared and copied. It continued to be broadcast long after the company had deleted the tweet. DiGiorno pizza later confirmed the mistake by posting a follow-up tweet "A million apologies. Did not read what the hashtag was about before posting."

A million apologies is only a slight exaggeration as the team behind the @DiGiornoPizza twitter account spent the next day personally responding to every tweet sent to their account. The responses were not a copy and paste of a generic apology—each response was customized. And if the individual responded back then DiGiorno kept the conversation going. One errant tweet, one fleeting moment, is all it takes today to force a major brand into hours or days of damage control by involving themselves in a conversation without understanding the context.

§ 1.04 HIGH-LEVEL RISKS VERSUS TOPIC SPECIFIC RISKS

These high-level social media behaviors can create a variety of risks for organizations and individuals in unpredictable ways. Beyond these high-level risks, however, a number of specific topics carry their own risks or concerns because of the social media revolution. Subsequent chapters in this book will explore these risks so that brands and users alike can avoid them or develop plans to address them if they occur.

CHAPTER 2

PLATFORM TERMS AND CONDITIONS

Let's be honest: almost nobody reads the terms and conditions for software before they use it. Even you, a reader who purchased, borrowed, or stole a copy of Social Media Law in a Nutshell are highly unlikely to have read the terms for Facebook, Twitter, or iTunes prior to using the software.

Users' failure to read the terms and conditions is not due to a lack of awareness. It is impossible to sign up for social media accounts or use most social websites without being presented with terms and conditions that impact individual use of the site. When individuals sign up for accounts, they are presented with links to the terms or they are given a large box of scrolling text that contains the terms. And still the vast majority of users simply agree to the terms by checking a box and clicking a button. If the scrolling box requires us to view all the terms before agreeing, then users may sigh in frustration and scroll as quickly as they can to the bottom before clicking the now-enabled button.

Individuals immediately agree to these terms and conditions despite knowing that they could be very important to our use of the platforms. And the same people increasingly know that these websites will host some of our most valued information including photos of our children, memories of our past, even private messages with friends and family members.

Why do the vast majority of social media users not care about the contract that dictates their usage?

This indifference may come from a lack of bargaining power. As an individual, nobody is free to negotiate these terms and conditions. New users are only presented two options: accept the terms and use the platform or never use it. Knowing there is no ability to change the terms, users may simply agree and hope the agreement isn't too draconian.

Another reason users may skip the terms is that they feel impossible to comprehend. Perhaps it is the length or density of the document presented to the user when all they really want is to watch a video of a kitten falling off a counter.

These terms are not impossible to understand. They are not even difficult to understand. They may take some time to review, depending on the number of topics and the length to which the platform chooses to discuss those topics, but all can be browsed quickly.

This chapter focuses on the topic areas that most social media platforms contain within their terms and conditions. While each may assign different names to these topics, the subject matter will be the same. Each area carries risk depending on how individuals or organizations are using the social media platform. In addition to the risk areas covered by the subject matter of the terms themselves, there is also some degree of risk in presenting or changing those terms to users.

§ 2.01 INSTAGRAMAPOCALYPSE: THE DANGER OF CHANGING TERMS

In December 2012, Instagram faced a tidal wave of negative publicity over some proposed changes to their terms and conditions. Celebrities and non-celebrities alike bemoaned the alterations to their beloved platform. CNN reporter Anderson Cooper tweeted "I may rethink using Instagram." The largest rallying cry came from reality television star Kim Kardashian who tweeted "I really loved Instagram :-(I need to review this new policy. I don't think its [sic] fair."

While social media users should take courage in Mrs. Kardashian's ability to read the entirety of Instagram's new terms and subject them to legal analysis whilst in the middle of composing such a compelling and thorough tweet, legal analysis of her position may not support her views. Unfortunately, her opinion on the content of those terms was as flawed as other celebrities' statements and even several technology publications' reports. The changes were wrongly described as allowing Instagram to sell photos on the service to third parties. The reality was that the terms allowed Instagram to utilize user content for on-site advertising similar to Facebook.

In fact, the changes to the terms and conditions brought the primarily photo-sharing service closer to Facebook's already existing terms and conditions. Facebook had recently purchased Instagram so many users were concerned Instagram would become another Facebook. Many of these Instagram users also had a presence on Facebook—yet the Facebook terms and conditions that Instagram now mimicked had not inspired a similar backlash. There was something about the new terms that made Instagram users concerned that the picture of their lunch could be displayed to their friends as a sponsored post.

Here, however, was the exact Instagram language that caused the controversy:

> Some or all of the Service may be supported by advertising revenue. To help us deliver interesting paid or sponsored content or promotions, you agree that a business or other entity may pay us to display your username, likeness, photos (along with any associated metadata), and/or actions you take, in connection with paid or sponsored content or promotions, without any compensation to you.

That does say the photos could potentially be included in advertisements. But the controversy was over the change in terms. Here were the Instagram terms prior to the change:

> Some of the Instagram Services are supported by advertising revenue and may display advertisements and promotions, and you hereby agree that Instagram may place such advertising and promotions on the Instagram Services or on, about, or in conjunction with your Content. The manner, mode and extent of such advertising and promotions are subject to change without specific notice to you.

The language that existed in Instagram's terms and conditions prior to the change covered the exact same ability for Instagram to use platform content in advertising. The newer version streamlined the language and then also added the words "without any compensation to you"—words that may not have even been necessary.

Perhaps that is the real lesson from Instagram's painful terms and conditions episode. Not that making terms easier to understand will bring them under fire but that small changes in terms and conditions can bring greater attention to existing terms and then lead to misinterpretation. Journalists are unlikely to write an article about terms and conditions that cover several pages. However, if only a sentence or two in the terms are changed and those changes can be (wrongly) interpreted in a scary or shocking matter, journalists may write about and propagate the misunderstanding. For social media websites, small changes can trigger major attention.

This episode is not unique. Facebook faced similar scrutiny in 2014 when journalists wrote about the Messenger app permissions and again in 2015 when minor changes were made to Facebook's terms. This is not to say the changes will never be significant and important, but oftentimes the media coverage of these changes misses the point entirely or is more interested in generating traffic than in accurately reflecting the impact of the change. This is why it is important to understand what these platform terms cover so that users can appreciate what, if any, risks these terms and conditions bring.

§ 2.02 PLATFORM TERMS AROUND CONTENT

Social media platforms exist solely to drive conversations around pieces of content. The terms and conditions around material submitted to the platform tends to be some of the most robust and the most applicable to individuals and organizations alike.

A. RIGHT TO POST CONTENT

A successful social media platform will have millions of users submitting billions of pieces of content over time. If that platform wishes to remain active, it cannot manually check each piece of content prior to posting. Even if such a review process were created, it would be difficult to maintain or staff. And even properly staffed, it is difficult to come up with a process that would allow any individual to recognize, for example, a photo being posted that actually belongs to another photographer. Ownership issues aside, theoretically, the group would need to know if the photo violates a court order or if the image is illegal under speech limitations in several different jurisdictions.

Balancing the ability for a social media platform to provide services to millions of people while also ensuring the posted content does not violate the law is a complex and sophisticated risk area. A risk area that is increasingly shifting away from the platform and onto the individual users posting the infringing content.

Social media platforms virtually always place the responsibility of determining whether content is permitted to be posted on the user. This burden is imposed through a combination of implicit or explicit statements about permissible content. In addition, language is used to indemnify the platform should a legal action be filed over content posted by the user.

1. Intellectual Property Rights and Posted Content

Social media platforms allow an individual to post a funny observation about the ticket line at a movie theater and instantaneously have that observation read by hundreds of their friends. Social media platforms also allow that same individual to share a picture of one of the movie posters hanging in the theater lobby with those same friends. Those same platforms allow that user to live stream the movie they are watching to their friends. The possibilities of intellectual property violations on social media are significant not only because of the ease with which content can be posted but also the speed of worldwide distribution and economic harm to content owners.

There are hundreds of millions of people with smartphones who can violate intellectual property rights with a quick video or snapshot. There are even more people with laptop computers who can copy and post other protected works. Using intellectual property laws to go after the individual violators can be a time-consuming and impossible task.

But there are only a few dozen social media platforms capable of distributing that infringing content in such a manner as to cause economic damage to the protected works. Social media platforms then are incredibly careful about and concerned over the ability of their users to post protected content. How these social media platforms protect themselves from intellectual property violations in turn creates or exposes legal risks for individual users.

There are several sophisticated machine-based systems for checking certain social media posts and preventing them from being posted in an unauthorized fashion if they contain protectable content. For example, YouTube has a program that can recognize copyrighted video clips or even copyrighted music played in the background of a video the moment the clip is uploaded. But even machine systems are not perfect—YouTube's video checking system sometimes has difficulty identifying copyrighted video if the visuals have been flipped left to right. While content owners and platforms attempt to use these systems to prevent posting, no system is fool-proof. Platforms must then attempt to address posts that might have protected content in other ways.

The balancing of rights between platforms that host content and intellectual property owners is an issue older than social media. Several statutory solutions have been implemented in order to allow these platforms to exist while still protecting intellectual property owners. For example, most countries have laws that provide safe harbors for platforms from copyright infringement cases so long as a process exists to remove copyrighted content once a violation has been claimed or established. As a result, every social media platform has a process to either challenge a piece of posted content or request that piece of content be removed from the platform due to an intellectual property violation.

These tools and takedown processes are not enough to fully protect a social media platform that can host billions of violations occurring every day. Social media platforms want their users to be able to post content without getting the platform in trouble. While platforms can use machine-detection and takedown processes to protect all the interested parties, the best way for social media platforms to protect themselves is to shift the burden completely onto the user with certain provisions in the platform's terms and conditions.

All platforms have some statement regarding the content that you are allowed to post on their site within their terms and conditions. For example, at the end of 2014, Twitter's terms and conditions broadly required its users to be responsible "for any Content you post to [Twitter]." Pinterest's terms stated that users "are solely responsible for. . . the User Content you post to Pinterest." Facebook's terms and conditions required that "[y]ou will not post content. . . on Facebook that infringes or violates someone else's rights or otherwise violates the law." These and other similarly-worded terms allow users to post content while taking responsibility for having posted such material.

Between the shifted burden and the safe harbor laws, platforms can avoid significant legal intellectual property exposure concerning posted content. However, shifting the burden also places the individual user into a difficult position of knowing whether they have the right to post such content. While on the one hand there is no issue over completely original content and on the other hand there is no doubt over the legal risks surrounding someone posting content that is blatantly copied from another protected source, there is a plethora of content that may contain a mixture of protected and original content.

For example, one social media trend is the creation of memes: images that are given a series of humorous or thoughtful captions and shared online. Many of these meme images are protected images: a still frame from Lord of the Rings or a professional photograph of a celebrity. The underlying image may be subject to copyright protection or contain a brand's protected trademark even if the caption itself is completely original. Whether the new meme violates the original image's rights is not a simple analysis for courts, let alone a regular social media user. The burden for determining the proper use of this content, however, falls squarely on the shoulders of the user.

2. Other Legal Restrictions on Posted Content

While the largest commercial risk for users revolves around intellectual property, the language around allowed content covers all legal violations.

This could include content that constitutes a legal threat or harassment. It could also include information that violates a court order or another specific legal obligation.

Many of these are hard or impossible for platforms to police. Harassing and abusive content may not need to rise to the level of an actual legal violation for it to be removed and the platform may have its own rules for dealing with or removing such content. Other pieces of content may violate a law of which the platform is unaware or a court order the platform does not possess thus creating a burdensome process to verify the violation. This verification process can be slow and exacerbated by having the content remain on the social media platform and continuing to reach people with the potential to do more harm.

On the other hand, if a platform creates a process to remove reported content until it can be evaluated, that process may be abused by people wishing to censor otherwise acceptable content. Platforms have developed various ways of handling these complaints, from automatic reporting systems that trigger reviews to manual queues of reviewers looking at potential violations. Those systems may carry repercussions for people who make bad faith complaints. Ultimately, the platform will attempt to shift responsibility for those posts to the users who are best situated to evaluate their propriety.

3. Non-Legal Restrictions on Posted Content

Platforms may escape legal culpability for a wide variety of offensive posts. However, culpability may not be a concern if the platform is a breeding ground for offensive content that drives users away. It may be in a platform's best interests to remove certain categories of offensive content that may alienate users or does not build the kind of community the platform is trying to create or foster. While these banned topics can themselves lead to controversy (see Chapter 6, Content, Copyright, and Licenses) this is a decision left up to the platform themselves.

Social media platforms may be vague on what content is allowed or they may expressly forbid certain topics or categories of speech. The Twitter Rules tell users that in addition to content that violates intellectual property law, Twitter will not permit content where a user pretends to be someone else, content that reveals the private information of third parties, or content that is deemed abusive among other categories of forbidden content. Facebook's terms are broader and allows the platform to "remove any content or information you post on Facebook if [Facebook] believes it violates" their terms or policies—and there is no list of what policies it may use in that determination.

B. CONTENT RIGHTS GRANTED TO PLATFORMS

When a social media user posts content, the user not only makes certain representations about having the right to post such content, he or she also gives the platform a specific right to use that content. These one-sided provisions provide fertile grounds for bloggers and journalists to criticize the platforms for over-reaching. In reality, the provisions are far less interesting. Social media platforms need particular rights to allow the platforms to function or to enable revenue-generating activities such as ads or referral links.

1. Rights That Allow the Platform to Operate

Virtually every piece of content posted to a social media platform is protected under intellectual property laws. These laws may cover different subject matter and originate from different countries. The laws will allow different rights or restrictions to be attached to the content. Platforms must deal with all of these potential restrictions and violations for content posted in a manner that they can still function.

Each platform handles content differently in terms of what is displayed and how users can engage with the content. Many platforms allow content to be shared with large groups of people who did not see the original post (Twitter, Facebook, etc.) while others do not (Instagram). Depending on what data the platform hosts and what functionality the platform enables around it, the platform's terms and conditions may reserve a narrow or broad collection of rights.

Consider, for example, an original photograph posted to a social media platform by a photographer. United States copyright law gives certain exclusive rights regarding this photograph: the right to reproduce the photograph, to prepare derivative works of it, to distribute copies of it, and to display it publicly. Depending on what functionality is available on the platform, some or all of these rights may be infringed upon by the platform's operations. Copying the photograph to various servers to display it faster to users, enabling users to add visual annotations to the photograph, letting other platform users download a copy of the photograph, sending the photograph to other users connected to the photographer around the world, or showing the photograph as part of the platform's homepage—all of these are functions that could infringe on one or more of the photographer's rights. The platform must obtain the rights to perform such actions or enable such functions or else risk becoming a giant infringement machine.

Platforms obtain these rights through a wide range of grants. Twitter's terms, for example, require users to grant it the right to "use, copy, reproduce, process, adapt, modify, publish, transmit, display and distribute such Content in any and all media or distribution methods (now known or later developed)." Facebook's terms, in contrast, convey the right to "use any [content that is covered by intellectual property rights] that you post on or in connection with Facebook." Other platforms may fall somewhere in between Twitter's list of specific rights and Facebook's broad reliance on the term "use" but all platforms will have some form of grant from the user to the platform that allows the platform to function.

Social media platforms craft these grants with various concerns in mind. First, the platform wants to have all the rights necessary to operate. Second, the platform may be considering other activities or functions in the future that they would like to cover as well. Third, the platform knows that changing the terms may cause undue attention and inaccurate criticism later on.

2. Rights Concerning Advertising

Operating a social media platform is expensive. The physical hardware necessary to store the copious amounts of posted content, the network bandwidth necessary to distribute and interact with the content, the salaries of the software developers, network engineers, and other professionals required to keep the platform running—social media platforms have incredible scale but they are not without cost.

Even with this overhead, the vast majority of social media platforms are completely free to users. Some platforms have levels of functionality or storage only available with payment but still offer some form of free services. Social media platforms are then put into the position of generating money to cover their expenses and make a profit.

Social media platforms have attempted different activities in order to generate revenue and become successful business ventures. These tactics take one of three forms: paid services (additional storage, additional functionality, etc.), percentages of financial transactions (eBay fees, etc.), and advertising. The platform's revenue for the first two activities is simple to understand and evaluate as they are financial transactions. Advertising is a more indirect route to revenue as it requires selling specially placed content to marketers.

Social media platform advertising can take various forms. One single ad can be formatted multiple ways depending on whether it is displayed on a computer, tablet, or smartphone. Ads can be placed in different locations within a program or website. Most importantly, social media platforms offer marketers the ability to target users through highly specific information available via the platform's data sources.

This targeted advertising is desirable to brands and consumers alike. However, when spelled out to consumers some feel it is intrusive. A social media user who has stated on their profile that they like Star Wars and pajamas would seem to be the ideal customer for a Star Wars pajamas advertisement. But that same user might feel their privacy was violated by allowing the pajama seller to specifically target them.

In the majority of instances this specific information is not given directly to marketers; it is used by the platform to allow advertisers to display customized content to the user. This distinction matters little when the advertisement is shown to the user. But the distinction is important in how the topic is covered in the terms and conditions.

Platforms enable their advertising activity through different terms. Twitter's terms and conditions state that the platform "may include advertisements, which may be targeted to the Content or information on [Twitter], queries made through [Twitter], or other information. . . In consideration for Twitter granting you access to and use of [Twitter], you agree that Twitter and its third party providers and partners may place such advertising on [Twitter] or in connection with the display of Content or information from [Twitter] whether submitted by you or others." This language not only gives Twitter the right to display advertisements in exchange for a user's access to the platform but it also states that Twitter will target those ads based on information (a user's tweets, for example), queries the user has made (searches for products, keywords, or individuals), or other information (anything else they can think of). It is a broad list of targeting behavior that, if specifically thought about, could make a Twitter user uncomfortable—but could result in them seeing relevant advertisements that enables Twitter to continue operating.

3. Rights Around Non-Platform Use

When a user posts content onto a social media platform they have allowed it to be used within the platform. Within the terms there may also be a grant to the platform or others to use that material outside the platform. These grants may be used by a platform to enable advertising on a separate site or for information to be tracked from one site to another. If a user, brand, or organization cares about the widespread dissemination of its posted content they should be sure to check the terms to see whether a platform is granted the right to use the content outside the site itself.

C. RIGHTS THAT ARE NOT GRANTED

An important consideration for content posted on social media sites is that ownership of the content does not transfer. This means that the original author retains all ownership and the only rights granted to the platform are the ones specifically stated in the terms and conditions. Any rights not granted to the platform are retained by the author. And any rights not transferred by the platform cannot be utilized by other users as well.

Even if a platform is granted rights to a user's content, including the ability to transfer those rights to other platform users, the platform may choose not to grant those rights to other users. This can be an important consideration for users of a social media platform when looking at content posted by others.

One of the largest misunderstandings experienced when using social media platforms involves content flagged as Public. While the common sense understanding of the word would appear to allow this content to be seen or used by anyone online this is not necessarily true.

"Public" is used by platforms as a label for content that carries certain rights and restrictions. It could very well mean that anyone online can see the content, copy it, use it, sell it, or any other activity based on the content. This is true for content posted on Facebook. The Facebook terms state

> When you publish content or information using the Public setting, it means that you are allowing everyone, including people off of

Facebook, to access and use that information, and to associate it with you (i.e., your name and profile picture).

Twitter's terms and privacy policy do not clearly state that all tweets may be used by anyone who can view them. However, their terms do state that other companies, organizations, or individuals may partner with Twitter and use your tweets without compensation. What it means to partner with Twitter, and whether that includes something as simple as another individual user of Twitter, remains undefined.

Other platforms allow users to designate their accounts as private. Private accounts do not make their information public by default and may signal to others an attempt to preserve the rights around their content. Failing to set an account to private does not mean their content can be used anywhere. Instead, platform terms can specify their content can be freely shared within the confines of the social media platform but not taken outside the platform.

Users browsing social media platforms for images or videos that are not flagged as private or even explicitly marked Public may mistakenly believe they can download the content and use it elsewhere. However, without an express grant from the author such activity is typically not authorized.

§ 2.03 INDEMNIFICATION

Almost every platform will have an indemnification clause in its terms and conditions.

The only platforms that do not have such a clause are either brand new or without legal representation. Given the nature of social media platforms—encouraging user participation, spreading content across their network, creating a venue for online conversations—the possibilities of users conducting themselves in a way that could result in a lawsuit is practically guaranteed.

Indemnification clauses sometimes come under fire from the mainstream press as a way for platforms to take advantage of users by forcing them to pay for lawsuits. In reality, indemnification clauses are actually important tools to protect the platform from its users' misdeeds. For a social media platform to succeed it cannot perform a rigorous legal review of every piece of content prior to publication. Even if it could review all content, an approved story could later result in a lawsuit impossible to predict at the time of publication. Platforms have neither the financial resources to defend these lawsuits nor the information necessary to defend the merits of the suit. Indemnification not only keeps the platform out of unnecessary cases but also puts the onus on individual users to defend themselves for their actions.

§ 2.04 DISPUTES

Although the choice of law and venue provisions may seem like boilerplate provisions in a platform's terms and conditions, they can actually have a significant impact on users. Social media platforms quickly develop a global user base, the terms may dictate the choice of law and forum if a case ever develops against the platform.

The majority of large social media platforms are located in Silicon Valley. As such, their terms and conditions not only include choice of law provisions selecting California law to govern disputes but also require actions against the platforms to be brought in California courts.

This has not stopped cases from being filed against platforms outside those jurisdictions. In 2012, a student group in France brought a lawsuit against Twitter seeking information belonging to certain accounts sending out anti-Semitic posts. Posting anti-Semitic content is a crime in France, it would take additional elements to be considered a crime in the United States. The student group brought their lawsuit in France under French law despite Twitter's choice of law and venue terms. Twitter did not have an office in France and lost the initial proceeding as well as an appeal of the ruling to turn over the account information. Facing an additional $50 million lawsuit for refusing to turn over the information, Twitter conceded in 2013 and provided the account data.

Besides preventing lawsuits from being filed in other jurisdictions, choice of law and venue language has been ignored by foreign courts in determining whether a lawsuit can continue outside the stated jurisdiction. While the Twitter case above saw Twitter complying with a court order they did not initially contest, Facebook did contest the filing of a lawsuit against their platform by a French user who had several posts removed for containing a well-known painting of a nude woman. The French user brought suit in France and the court decided, after hearing from both sides, that the provision in the Facebook terms requiring lawsuits to proceed in California would not be enforceable against the French user.

While these dispute provisions may not always prove successful in fending off lawsuits, they have been utilized by foreign nationals to take advantage of favorable American legal rules. South Tyneside is the sixth largest conurbation (metropolitan area) in the United Kingdom and, like all cities with politicians, is no stranger to political debate. A series of anonymous Twitter accounts and blogs posted content believed to be libelous by the local authorities. A suit was filed in 2011 against Twitter in California to uncover the identity of several Twitter accounts surrounding the controversy. Twitter turned over the information and thereby established the precedent of having a foreign user sue a platform in its chosen jurisdiction for information (even if the law of their home jurisdiction would not allow such a revelation). Unfortunately for the plaintiff, the information that was turned over was insufficient to reveal the identity of the anonymous author.

§ 2.05 AUTHORIZED USE AND CRIMINAL VIOLATIONS

Terms and conditions will typically contain a provision stating what users are authorized to do on the platform. These statements can be as broad as suggesting that any legal activity can be performed, leaving it up to the user to determine the scope of that limitation, or they can be prescriptive and specific as to the exact actions allowed. While these provisions may seem innocuous, and in most instances are just that, they should also be considered by users, brands, and organizations for the scope of authorized activities. Exceeding that scope may be a criminal act.

One way in which content exceeding the scope could become a more serious matter is by violating the Computer Fraud and Abuse Act (CFAA). The United States passed the CFAA in 1986. The law was created as an amendment to existing computer fraud statutes in order to cover the growing use of computers in government, financial, and other secure work locations. However, its initial scope has been expanded over the years via amendments and applications by the courts.

The CFAA contains numerous restrictions which have been applied to social media platforms and other computer sites. These provisions generally criminalize any attempt to exceed the authority granted by a platform. While some portions of the law require damage to be done to the computer system or a theft of at least $5,000, the most general provision makes it illegal for someone to "intentionally access a computer without authorization or exceeds authorized access and thereby obtains. . . information from any protected computer." Any social media user who exceeds the authority granted by the platform is at risk of criminal and civil prosecution under the CFAA.

A. AUTHORIZED USE OF A SOCIAL MEDIA PLATFORM

The CFAA has been used in a number of cases involving social media with mixed success. In 2012, Craigslist, an online classified ads service that includes housing listings, sued PadMapper and 3Taps, two companies who were accessing Craigslist in order to obtain house listing information (a process known as "scraping" and discussed in greater detail in section 7.03) so that the data could be entered into their own websites. After Craigslist sent notice to the two companies, attempted to block their computers from accessing the service, and changed their terms and conditions to prevent this kind of activity, the lawsuit was filed. Craigslist successfully defeated a motion to dismiss the CFAA claims in 2013.

The Craigslist case is a significant one in light of the court's view of authorization. Most social media platforms require a user to register with the service. Subsequent visits to the platform require the user to log into the site using the credentials created when they first registered. In creating the account, users will be asked to accept the platform's terms and conditions which will include a statement about authorized use. Exceeding that authority can quickly be identified as a potential claim under the CFAA.

However, Craigslist does not require account creation in order to view its listings. The site does not require users to log in with credentials to access the service. While it does require individuals who publish content on the site to accept its terms and conditions, no such requirement exists for a service, such as PadMapper and 3Taps, to simply view the content. For this reason, the Northern District of California held Craigslist's specific notice to the two companies that they were no longer welcome to access Craigslist as a limit on their authorized use. An otherwise public service became limited by providing notice to the breaching party according to the court. Without that notice, and without requiring users to accept terms simply to view content, Craigslist may have faced a different outcome.

B. EMPLOYEE USE OF SOCIAL MEDIA UNDER THE CFAA

The CFAA has also been used in a variety of lawsuits involving former employees. While it has been successfully used against employees who exceeded their authority by stealing proprietary and confidential information contained in an employer's database, such as in *United States v. Nosal*,[1] it was not successfully used against a former employee for accessing Facebook and her email at work.

Wendi Lee was fired from her job in the marketing department at PMSI. Ms. Lee sued PMSI alleging pregnancy discrimination. PMSI countersued against Ms. Lee alleging she had violated the CFAA for excessive Internet use by viewing her Facebook page and checking her email while at work. The

---

1 *United States v. Nosal*, 676 F.3d 854 (9th Cir. 2012).

Middle District of Florida held that Ms. Lee's actions did not violate the CFAA. While noting that PMSI did have an acceptable use policy governing the scope of an employee's authorization to use their provided computers and network access, Ms. Lee's computer access was never turned off prior to her termination—a required distinction for employer authorized use policies governing general computer usage. The court held that the former employer's argument that more than $5,000 in damage had been done due to Ms. Lee's lost productivity was without merit. Under the CFAA, the monetary damage must be to a system or item of value rather than a productivity calculation.

Of importance to social media applications, the federal court also held that there was no loss of information or data belonging to PMSI. The CFAA is intended to protect against the theft or loss of data. When Ms. Lee accessed Facebook or her email, however, she was only accessing her own data.

C. CRITICISMS OF THE CFAA

In recent years the CFAA has come under scrutiny for its use by prosecutors against individuals accused of unauthorized computer access. The most intense debate has taken place over the application of CFAA provisions to Aaron Swartz.

Aaron Swartz was a computer programmer who, among his many accomplishments, helped develop Rich Site Summary (RSS) format (used by the vast majority of Internet news readers as a way to syndicate and distribute blogs and other serial publications) as well as the popular news site Reddit. He was also a noted political and Internet activist who believed in the free exchange of information. Mr. Swartz had publicly written his concerns over digitization of the world's scientific knowledge kept secure by a few private organizations rather than being made available to the world at large.

Mr. Swartz had a history of accessing protected documents he believed should be made public. In 2008 he downloaded and released for free over 2.7 million federal court documents contained in the 500 million document PACER database (access to which was charged at 8 cents per page). In January 2011, Mr. Swartz was arrested by the Massachusetts Institute of Technology police force and the U.S. Secret Service. He was accused of placing a laptop in an unlocked networking closet at MIT, connecting it to the network, and using it to download large amounts of scientific articles and other data from JSTOR, a digital library filled with scientific journals, books, and scanned plant specimens.

Over the next two years, Mr. Swartz was indicted by federal and state grand juries. Although MIT and the JSTOR library did not pursue charges against Mr. Swartz, federal prosecutors continued to pursue the case. Mr. Swartz committed suicide in January 2013. A wave of criticism over use of the CFAA in prosecuting his case took place within the computer and legal realms. An amendment to the CFAA, called Aaron's Law, has been offered in Congress but has not been brought to Congress for a vote. The amendment would remove terms of service violations from the CFAA. This change would not only impact private data stores, as in Mr. Swartz' case, but would also apply to social media websites.

§ 2.06 MODIFICATIONS TO PLATFORM TERMS AND CONDITIONS

Platforms typically reserve the right to modify their terms and conditions. While minor changes may be implements without notice, platforms will often notify users via platform messages or direct emails of significant changes.

Hoax posts will frequently circulate on social media platforms informing users they may unilaterally change their agreement by posting a particular piece of content. They will generally refer to some recent change in a site's terms and conditions that should be negated by posting a message that attempts to put the platform on notice of the user's rights. Such messages, in addition to citing fictional law or conventions, have no legal basis and have no standing to modify the agreement entered into by users when they first register for the platform.

§ 2.07 PLATFORM TERMS AND THE FORMATION OF AN AGREEMENT

Unfortunately, there is a broad and inconsistent spectrum of cases that address the effectiveness of forming a binding and enforceable agreement with a user via terms and conditions presented online. Methods of displaying platform terms for review and acceptance that are held enforceable in one jurisdiction may be held unenforceable in another.

This makes the topic difficult to discuss for both users and platforms alike.

Generally speaking, the greater the ability of a user to review the platform's terms prior to acceptance the more likely a court will hold it to be enforceable. A platform that merely provides a link to its terms provides less access and notice than a platform that requires a new user to read and scroll through the entire agreement prior to signing up for an account. Performing an affirmative action such as checking a box to indicate the user has read and agreed to the terms can be better evidence of acceptance than merely clicking a button. However, no single method has been universally upheld as creating an enforceable contract due in no small part to the fact that virtually none of these agreements allow the user to make modifications or revisions.

The topic of enforceability becomes more problematic when considering a platform that changes their terms for existing users. As shown in the Instagram example, such changes can have little impact in terms of legal rights but a huge impact in terms of community impressions. Platform terms may include provisions that allow the platform to make changes moving forward, but there is also the question of how significant a change needs to be before the platform can do more than just silently update the terms. The balance of enabling a platform to grow while also ensuring that users still understand the terms they are operating under will continue to be an ongoing tension for any platform that makes changes without notifying its users. (For further discussion of this topic, see section 7.02.)

CHAPTER 3
MARKETING AND PROMOTIONS

Marketing regulations, administrative agencies, and case law is a robust field by itself. The overlapping interests of brands and organizations trying to solicit funds, sell products, or run promotions such as sales or sweepstakes on social media has obvious potential conflicts with existing consumer protection regulations that rein in misleading commercial content. While this book does not attempt to explain the entire body of marketing law, there are still significant areas of concern from both the viewpoint of the individual social media user and the brand or organizational perspective when it comes to marketing and promotions on social media.

Professional marketers are paid to get their client's message in front of the public. That message may concern a charity, a product, a service, a new organization, a community event, a political candidate, or any number of potential introductions the marketer wishes to make. As social media platforms exploded into popularity, marketers saw an incredible opportunity to reach millions, then hundreds of millions, then billions of potential consumers. Platforms also saw an opportunity to pay for its operating costs by charging for advertising or specific functionality for marketers. And so the uncomfortable courtship of social media and marketing began.

§ 3.01 GENERAL UNITED STATES MARKETING REGULATION

Every country has its own regulatory system for handling commercial speech. In the United States that power is distributed between states and federal regulatory agencies. The federal overview of commercial content belongs to the Federal Trade Commission (FTC). The FTC Act that gives authority to the agency has two significant sections that provide the body with far-sweeping powers to impact commercial speech.

Section 5 of the FTC Act broadly states in its first subsection that "[u]nfair methods of competition in or affecting commerce, and unfair or deceptive acts or practices in or affecting commerce, are hereby declared unlawful." This broad statement does not define what specific practices are unfair and which ones might be considered deceptive. Rather, it is intentionally broad and undefined. The statement was left broad so as to encompass all potential misleading content and to allow the agency to react to new practices as they emerged.

Section 13 of the FTC Act provided the agency with authority to "enjoin the dissemination or the causing of the dissemination of [false] advertising." False advertising is defined as any unfair or deceptive act that falls under Section 5. This broad authority has allowed the FTC to adapt to changing technologies as it determines what constitutes unfair and deceptive advertising on radio broadcasts, television commercials, and Internet ads. That same authority has now extended to social media as advertisers have turned their attention to it.

Over the decades since its inception, the FTC has pursued numerous actions against brands and organizations who publish false advertisements. It has also issued several guidelines in an attempt to better educate the marketing world about what information or activities constitute a deceptive act. Some of those guides have been as broad as detailing the proper use of the word "free" in advertisements or how to avoid deceptive pricing in an advertisement, while others have been as narrow as to describe the proper ways to market corrective refractive eye surgery. The FTC has also issued policy statements regarding comparative advertisements or how claims can be substantiated.

The FTC has also stepped in to address advertising on social media platforms in recent years. While some of their decisions or statements simply apply existing rules to these new platforms, others are decidedly new to the marketing world.

Although the FTC has the broadest authority and weight in their decisions, they are not alone in contributing to the world of marketing regulations. Several states have their own trade commissions that may also investigate advertisements or marketing activities. Also, the Better Business Bureau has a National Advertising Division (NAD) that is considered influential in this space. Together, these agencies have put forth several rulings and guidelines to help shape the form of social media marketing today.

§ 3.02 REGULATORY GUIDANCE ON SOCIAL MEDIA ADVERTISING

A. EARLY SOCIAL MEDIA ADVERTISING

In the early years of social media platforms, marketers wanted to avail themselves of the hundreds of millions of users browsing social media sites but did not have a sophisticated way of doing so. A brand or organization could establish its own social media profile—a Twitter account, a Facebook page, an Instagram feed—but these accounts were limited to only those consumers connected to its network. Social media platforms were not created for marketers and lacked the tools necessary to design advertising campaigns and reach audiences marketers were expecting.

Instead of putting out social media content that may or may not reach its intended audience, many brands and organizations decided to promote their content via celebrities that already had a significant social media following. Marketers have used celebrity endorsements for decades so this was not a new practice. However, utilizing celebrities also came with the additional benefit of having a direct and measurable audience attached to each celebrity.

While marketers had used celebrity endorsements in traditional print and broadcast campaigns, employing these endorsements in a social media context gave rise to three significant problems.

B. PROBLEMS WITH SOCIAL MEDIA ENDORSEMENTS

The first problem was the technology itself. When a marketer used a celebrity endorsement in print or advertising it was a simple thing to disclose. A brief message at the bottom of the printed advertisement or commercial was sufficient. But disclosing the same message in a celebrity tweet that is limited to 140 characters proved problematic. Figuring out the right disclosure on a YouTube video could be complicated by whether the video appeared on the brand's own channel or if it appeared on other channels. Brands needed to determine the proper disclosure for a paid Facebook status update posted by a celebrity or other endorser. Decades of experience and rulings on the topic for traditional media had questionable applicability to the new social media platforms.

Second, traditional print and broadcast campaigns only reached large, national audiences if there was a significant amount of money behind the campaign. This tended to limit those campaigns to the largest brands and organizations. These large brands and organizations also had the most experience and resources to know about their legal limitations. With the rise of social media platforms and the ability for any content to go viral, suddenly many small brands or organizations were faced with the ability to have content reach an audience previously reserved for only major players. This is a dream come true for many small companies but also creates significant problems for content created without the knowledge of established rules. Large brands and organizations, not pleased with losing consumer attention to smaller companies, also saw an unfair double standard where compliance with the rules depended on the size of the advertiser.

The final problem was trying to figure out who was an endorser and what kind of message made an endorsement. In the traditional marketing world, it is simple to identify an individual paid to make their statement which was then distributed via paid-for broadcast time or print exposure. On social media, distribution is free for the marketers. While it is obvious to classify an A-list movie star who is paid to speak about a product as an endorser, it is difficult to decide if an influential blogger, a company's employees, or anyone with several thousand followers on a particular platform might be considered a celebrity for social media purposes. Determining the line between people that required endorsement disclosures takes on new angles and new concerns.

C. THE FTC REVISES THE ENDORSEMENT GUIDES

In October 2009, the FTC revised their previously issued Endorsement Guides to include specific mentions of social media. Their Guides Concerning the Use of Endorsements and Testimonials in Advertising had previously been issued in 1980 to address the growing use of testimonials (both true and false ones) and endorsements in print and television advertising. The 2010 revision was intended to extend that coverage to social media advertising as well.

The FTC said its issuance of the revised guidance was intended to cover the broadening scope of social media advertising while still applying the three basic rules of the Endorsement Guidelines:

(1) Endorsements must be truthful and not misleading,

(2) Results from a consumer that are not typical must be called out as such, and

(3) If a connection between the endorser and a brand or organization would affect how people evaluate the endorsement then it must be revealed.

While the FTC admitted that the document was intended to cover social media advertising, it also wanted to be explicit that the rules themselves had not changed, just the application into new channels. The revised Endorsement Guidelines did not call out specific rules for social media advertising, choosing instead to incorporate the new technology into existing examples. As a result, of the 36 endorsement examples provided in the revised Guidelines, only four dealt with any kind of social media: three blogging examples and one that involved an online message board. The revised guidelines did not address Facebook, Twitter, or other major social media platform endorsement activities.

In the absence of specific guidance from the FTC on how to disclose relationships, or the entire breadth of relationships that required disclosures, marketers began experimenting with disclosure techniques and best practices. Some resulted in investigations by the FTC, NAD, or other agencies tasked with looking at advertising and new unofficial rules were created.

While US marketers have been given guidance over specific directions, European marketers have been given explicit instructions on what constitutes proper disclosure. For example, the Advertising Standards Authority in the UK required the specific hashtags of #spon (for sponsored), #paid, or #ad to appear in any commercial endorsement. The FTC's guidelines did not give specific examples but instead said the disclosure should be clear and conspicuous.

D. THE FTC ISSUES ITS .COM DISCLOSURES

More than three years after the FTC issued its revised Endorsement Guidelines a new document was released designed to assist advertisers in their social media advertising efforts. Previously, in 2000, the FTC issued guidance on how marketers could properly disclose information on websites rather than traditional advertisements. Because websites and web pages had technical abilities unseen in print or television ads (the ability to pop up additional information, the ability to lead a consumer from one page to another, etc.) the Dot Com Disclosures were issued to help usher marketers into the World Wide Web age.

The revised and renamed .com Disclosures updated the 2000 guidance to 2013 technology by addressing smaller screens and increasing usage of social media. In addition to giving several social media examples including blogs and Twitter feeds, the revised guidelines also expanded on what it meant to provide disclosures that were clear and conspicuous. These disclosures could include limitations or material information about claims as well as apply to the earlier Endorsement Guidelines.

For a disclosure to be clear and conspicuous, a marketer must:

- Place the disclosure as close to the claim as possible;
- Consider different platforms (including their technical limitations) so that placement would not make a claim misleading on a particular device or platform;
- Incorporate the disclosure into the ad whenever possible, but when space-constrained to make the disclosure as soon as possible on a linked page;
- Make hyperlinked disclosures obvious through its style, placement, and destination;
- Try and avoid disclosures that require scrolling to view;
- Stay up to date on research that indicates how consumers view advertisements so as to best place disclosures;
- Display disclosures prior to consumers purchasing the product and display

disclosures several times in lengthy campaigns or websites;

- For products purchased in stores, online ads should still have all relevant disclosures so that a consumer is not surprised after travelling to the purchase destination;
- Prominently display the disclosure (considering font type, size, color, graphics, etc.) and not place the disclosures within terms and conditions of purchase or other contracts;
- Use plain language in making disclosures; and
- Consider the text, graphics, or audio disclosure made depending on the advertisement to ensure the content is delivered to a consumer.

In addition to giving the long list of disclosure elements, the .com Disclosures also gave numerous social media examples of the style and placement of disclosures that help illustrate its requirements.

The FTC's .com Disclosures provided several dozen examples of adequate and improper disclosures. While the majority of its scenarios apply to traditional websites due to the guidelines' origin as a 2000 document, the new examples covering tweets and bloggers provide useful examples of proper disclosures in social media advertising.

One significant note from the .com Disclosures was the FTC's refusal to adopt the growing European standard of using #spon, #paid, or #ad to indicate if a social media message was a commercial endorsement. In one specific example, the FTC indicated that #spon might not be sufficient if a significant proportion of reasonable viewers would not understand that the hashtag indicates a sponsored message. The FTC did not say the hashtag is insufficient but also did not say it would suffice by itself. This lack of concrete guidance makes for a more ambiguous environment in the United States. However, the FTC has provided several example disclosures to assist marketers.

E. TWITTER AND SHORT-FORM SOCIAL MEDIA MARKETING DISCLOSURES

The .com Disclosures recognize that several social media platforms, especially Twitter with its 140-character limitation, provide challenges to marketers in presenting disclosures within a limited length environment. The document provides several examples around these constraints to help illustrate the issues and potential solutions. They all surround a fictional campaign for a weight loss product. The campaign employs a well-known movie star as a paid commercial endorser of the product and shows a number of possible tweets the star may send as part of the campaign.

For these advertisements to make sufficient disclosures in the campaign, the .com Disclosures point out that two elements must be communicated: that the movie star is a paid endorser and that her specific results with the weight loss product may not be typical.

1. Disclosing Paid Endorsements in Short-Form Social Media

One example of a sufficient tweet that discloses both the paid relationship and the typical results is the tweet "Ad: Shooting movie beach scene. Had to lose 30lbs in 6 wks. Thanks Fat-away Pills for making it easy. Typical loss: 1lb/wk." The typical loss portion discusses the movie star's results in comparison to expected results. Starting the tweet with "Ad:" discloses the paid endorsement.

The FTC first introduced the "Ad:" tweet opener during a series of workshops with social media marketing professionals ahead of releasing .com Disclosures. When this technique was first introduced the marketing community was surprised by its inclusion—putting it at the start of a tweet seemed different from other advertisement disclosures that are put at the end of a commercial or bottom of a printed ad. The disclosure also avoided using a hashtag to indicate the tweet was paid for—a practice both embraced in Europe and seemingly expected by social media users.

In the FTC-led workshops when the "Ad:" opener was first discussed, it remained unclear whether this would fulfill a marketers obligation to disclose an endorsement or if, like #spon, it merely might fulfill that obligation. However, when the .com Disclosures guidelines were published this provided example made no such equivocation. The revised guidelines state that the opener signals the paid endorsement without qualification. Marketers wishing to avoid uncertainty around disclosing a paid endorsement have been given at least one option by the FTC.

2. Disclosure Proximity in Short-Form Social Media

Proximity of disclosures can also be a concern for content posted on a social media platform. The .com Disclosures gives an example tweet by the movie star of "Shooting movie beach scene. Had to lose 30lbs in 6 wks. Thanks Fat-away Pills for making it easy." This tweet does not contain any of the required disclosures but the initial tweet is followed by a second post six minutes later: "I am a paid spokesperson for Fat-away Pills. Typical weight loss: 1 lb/wk." While six minutes is not a great length of time, if the typical Twitter user follows several hundred accounts there could be several dozen or more tweets that appear between the movie star's two posts. A typical Twitter user may have to scroll their Twitter screen several times to see both posts or might only see the first post without ever reading the second post containing the required disclosures. Disclosures within short-form social media should be posted within the same space of the claims or with the assistance of third party applications to keep the disclosures within a close proximity to the claims being made.

Using a tweet to provide a link to disclosures has also been criticized if the product is available at a traditional retail store without any other method of disclosing the information to customers in the physical space. Using social media to disclose necessary information is never a substitute for other methods if products are sold through traditional retail establishments because even though social media can be accessed in a variety of locations there is no proximity between the disclosures and the actual sale of products.

3. Disclosing via Links in Short-Form Social Media

The .com Disclosures also consider a variety of tweets that contain a link to additional disclosures for the movie star's advertisement. Although the FTC recognizes that a single tweet of 140 characters may be unable to contain all the necessary disclosures, the guidelines do not provide an approved way to link an external web page with additional information. Instead, the document provides several examples of insufficient links without providing an example of an acceptable way to link this information.

The tweet "Shooting movie beach scene. Had to lose 30lbs in 6 wks. Thanks Fat-away Pills for making it easy. bit.ly/f56" is criticized for its use of a link-shortener like bit.ly. These sites take a lengthy link to a web address and compress the link to a smaller form so it takes less space. Services such as bit.ly typically assign a random name to the link making it impossible for users to see where the link leads to without clicking on it. In this case, the "f56" portion of the link provides no information to the social media user that the link will take them to the product's website for the display of additional disclosure information.

The problem of shortened link names is not solved, however, by giving it a custom address. The .com Disclosures also provides a sample tweet of "Shooting movie beach scene. Had to lose 30lbs in 6 wks. Thanks Fat-away Pills for making it easy. bit.ly/f56/disclose[6]." This tweet's shortened link has additional information that indicates the link leads to some kind of disclosure but this is also insufficient according to the FTC. The link does not do enough to communicate to consumers what kind of information they will find at the link or why they should visit the site.

The FTC also provides another deficient example tweet of "Shooting movie beach scene. Had to lose 30lbs in 6 wks. Thanks Fat-away Pills for making it easy. bit.ly/f56 #Spon." The guidelines previously criticized the #spon hashtag as not being enough to communicate the sponsored nature of the tweet to a consumer. This tweet, however, is further criticized for the placement of the #spon hashtag after the link to website. Placing the hashtag directly after a link, the FTC says, might confuse the consumer and make it even less likely that they would understand the disclosure. It remains unclear whether the increase in confusion is due to putting the hashtag at any point after a link or if only because the hashtag immediately follows the link.

F. BLOGS AND LONG-FORM SOCIAL MEDIA MARKETING DISCLOSURES

The .com Disclosures provide only one example of long-form social media marketing disclosures. The example is of a blogger who maintains a site documenting her and her husband's efforts to fix a house purchased in Pittsburgh. One post on her blog details the changes she made to her home's master bathroom. She discusses painting the walls with a fictional Just One Coat paint from PaintWorld (using the fictional color Canary Sunrise), adding a new shower curtain, and replacing the old sink faucets. Within the blog post she provides a link to the paint she used for the bathroom, the retail store where she bought fabric for the new curtains, and the website where she ordered the new sink fixtures. She indicates the results were all positive and that she is next turning her attention to a gift-wrapping nook in her craft room.

At the end of the blog post she writes "By the way, PaintWorld gave me the paint to try out, but it's so terrific I'll buy it myself this time." The FTC points out that receiving the paint for free must be disclosed but the placement of the disclosure is problematic. The FTC's issues with this example is not solely that the disclosure is at the end. The post itself may face an issue due to having multiple links within the blog post prior to the disclosure. The guidelines indicate that readers could click on the links and visit the external websites without ever returning to the blog post to read the disclosure. These distracting links prevent the disclosure from being clear and conspicuous.

Although not included in the final guidelines, the FTC included two additional examples of the home-fixing blogger during workshops with marketing professionals. One example made the disclosures even less obvious by not even including a mention of the free paint within the blog post. Instead, the blog had a "Disclosures & Disclaimers" link on the side of the blog that, when clicked, would reveal the free paint she had received from PaintWorld. This example was easily identified as insufficient by all workshop attendees.

Another example provided in the workshop, but not included in the final document, was when the blogger revealed earlier in her post that "PaintWorld sent me two gallons to try out, and this paint is amazing." There was a great deal of debate as to whether such a disclosure could be adequate depending on whether it followed any links to an external site. Some workshop attendees felt that the presence of any link prior to a disclosure was enough to keep it from being clear and conspicuous. Others felt that a single link would not be enough to lose readers—that someone reading a blog post will not immediately click on a link as they are reading the blog entry and never return to the original article. The FTC has not resolved this debate, choosing instead to only provide the worst case example of a blog post that puts the disclosure at the very end of a post containing multiple links and describing that as insufficient.

G. APPLYING CAN-SPAM RULES TO SOCIAL MEDIA ADVERTISING

Marketers taking to digital technologies is not a phenomenon first created by social media. As Internet and email usage exploded in the 1990s, marketers began sending unsolicited commercial communications for a fraction of the cost of older direct mail advertisements. In 2003, Congress passed the Controlling the Assault of Non-Solicited Pornography And Marketing Act of 2003 (CAN-SPAM). The law required commercial email messages to comply with a number of requirements pertaining to content (avoid misleading subject lines, correctly labelling adult content, including a physical address of the business sending the message, etc.), transmission activities (no sending emails to addresses harvested by automated programs, no sending emails without content [typically used to test whether an email address is valid], no use of techniques to hide or obscure the sender's origin, etc.), and the requirement to allow recipients to opt out of any future communications.

CAN-SPAM was intended to target emails but its scope has been broadened by courts since the law's passage. In 2011, Facebook successfully fought off a motion to dismiss its case against Max Bounty, an individual responsible for sending millions upon millions of unsolicited commercial emails and social media posts. Facebook accused Max Bounty of using hijacked user credentials and other illicit tactics to send Facebook users unsolicited commercial messages or post advertisements to those user's

Facebook profiles or profiles belonging to the users' friends. The issue of whether Facebook communications fell under CAN-SPAM regulations was decided in Facebook's favor.

The Northern District of California held that even though CAN-SPAM defined an "electronic mail message" as a message sent to a specific email address the law was intended to cover more than email and could be applied on social media platforms. The issue of how social media messages could be compliant with the CAN-SPAM requirements remains open.

Deciding to apply CAN-SPAM to social media posts and messages remains a much-discussed topic beyond the mechanics of compliance. CAN-SPAM dealt with email generally because email is a protocol and network that no single organization controls. Unethical marketers were taking advantage of this open technology to wreak havoc across multiple servers, services, and accounts. Facebook, however, has complete control over how its users interact with each other on Facebook. If Facebook wanted to prevent links to websites from being sent via private message, for example, they could deactivate that functionality—such a decision could not be made for all of email. Questions around both feasibility and necessity of applying CAN-SPAM remains an open issue that must be both considered and watched by social media marketers.

§ 3.03 SOCIAL MEDIA ADVERTISING IN THE REAL WORLD

While the FTC has provided guidance in the form of the revised Endorsement Guidelines and .com Disclosures, it has also taken a step back and allowed marketing professionals to help craft the social media marketing environment through its practices. European regulators have been more prescriptive in required elements or allowed activities; in contrast, the FTC and other U.S. agencies have instead cracked down on certain social media practices as they grow in their influence and deception.

Beyond the documentation, numerous real world examples of marketing practices and decisions illustrate the range of permitted and forbidden actions on social media.

A. ASTROTURFING FORBIDDEN

In 2010, the FTC investigated a small public relations firm, Reverb Communications, over potentially deceptive reviews on the iTunes app store. Apple's iTunes app store has dozens to hundreds of new apps released every day. While there are numerous ways for apps to be discovered by consumers, one way consumers decide what app to purchase is by looking at the app's reviews. Reverb Communications had several clients that produced games for the iTunes app store. The firm would then use its interns to create user accounts on iTunes for the sole purpose of leaving glowing reviews for these new apps.

As a result of these reviews, a consumer browsing the app store may decide to purchase these new apps. The high number of early, positive reviews could also lead the app to be picked up by various third parties that list new apps of interest or even Apple in deciding new apps to feature on high-visibility pages within the app store.

Not only was this practice deemed deceptive but it was also given a name in the marketing world: astroturfing. Astroturf is a plastic grass replacement product used in sports arenas, public spaces, and by some homeowners. The Astroturf name was used to describe these comments since the reviews were creating the illusion of a grassroots movement of positive reviews. Fake grass, fake grass roots, astroturfing. Although the goal of an astroturfing campaign is to create fake support and a disclosure would ruin the impact of such a campaign, the duty to have a disclosure for such activities still applies. Failure to disclose the origin of these reviews is deceptive to the core.

Reverb Communications was ordered to remove the fake reviews. The order further required any additional reviews posted on behalf of their clients to disclose Reverb's business relationship with the app publishers.

Although Reverb Communications was the first official decision on astroturfing, the practice has continued. In 2011, the FTC settled charges against Legacy Learning Systems for its use of a "Review Ad" affiliate program. The sole purpose of the program was to create ads that looked and functioned just like a review and would be posted to websites to appear like reviews. The settlement included a $250,000 payment to the FTC. And in 2013 the New York Attorney General settled charges against more than a dozen companies in an event called Operation Clean Turf. Its targets were companies that posted fake reviews on Yelp, Google, and CitySearch in an effort to improve the status of their clients. Those companies were fined a combined $350,000 for their astroturfing activities.

B. EMPLOYEES AND ENDORSEMENT DISCLOSURES

The Endorsement Guidelines subject an advertiser to liability if they fail to disclose a material connection between the endorser and the brand or organization. While this is a simple rule to apply in the case of a celebrity hired to speak about a commercial product, the connection is not as clear in other relationships. One such complex relationship is that of an employee and the company for which they work.

In 2014, the FTC settled multiple lawsuits against Sony and their advertising agency Deutsch LA over their marketing activities surrounding the launch of the Sony PlayStation Vita (PS Vita). In addition to cracking down on advertisements by Sony for features that did not work, the FTC entered into a specific agreement with the advertising agency over its use of agency employees to promote the PS Vita on social media.

One month before the PS Vita was made available for sale, a senior Deutsch LA executive emailed the entire company telling them about the launch of its client's product. The email encouraged all employees to engage in a pre-sale social media campaign by sending out a tweet or posting with the campaign's hashtag. Numerous employees sent out these messages without disclosing that they work for the ad agency.

The FTC took issue with the employee tweets and posts as they appeared to be the views of an ordinary consumer who had used the product. Tweets like "Got the chance to get my hands on a PS Vita and I'm amazed how great the graphics are" did not reveal that the author had special access due to his being employed by the agency in charge of promoting the new device. Overall, the FTC found two material facts that were lacking in social media posts made by the ad agency employees: that the device was not yet on sale (so the tweets were based on special access or were lying) and that the agency was hired by Sony to promote the device. Both of these facts were material because a consumer who read the tweets might give them a different amount of consideration when making a purchase decision if they had known the material facts about the tweet.

Given the charge by the FTC against Deutsch LA, the question of employee disclosure for a product or service by their employer remains a risky area for social media marketing. On the one hand, employees are also consumers who are free to share their views of products or services. However, the FTC's charges against Deutsch LA focus more on the view of the consumer making a purchase decision—would that consumer consider the author's employer a material fact in evaluating the post? If so then whether the post is based on actual experience appears irrelevant and employees should always disclose their employment status when posting about their employer's products or services.

C. LIKE-GATING AND SOCIAL MEDIA FANS

In 2011, 1-800-Contacts, a national mail order prescription eyewear company, brought an action against a competitor, Coastal Contacts, regarding two marketing activities by Coastal that took place on Facebook. Coastal ran a promotion that would require customers to Like their Facebook page but once that was done the customer could receive a free pair of eyeglasses. After this promotion had expired and Coastal had gained many Likes for its page, Coastal then claimed to have a number of fans equal to the number of page Likes.

1-800-Contacts complained about both of these activities. First, it took issue with the free glasses promotion, saying that customers receiving this offer were only given a limited selection of frames which qualified for the promotion and that this limited selection was not disclosed prior to a customer clicking Like for the Coastal Contacts page. Second, 1-800-Contacts said that equating the number of page Likes received by Coastal Contacts is not the same as having that many fans of the company. Both of these claims were called into question as misleading consumers.

The NAD decided in favor of Coastal on both issues and held that the claims were not misleading. While the NAD did say that Coastal could have disclosed the full terms of the free glasses promotion earlier in the browsing path of a typical consumer, at the time of the promotion there were limited options for disclosing information on a company's Facebook page if the page was not Liked. For a customer to see those terms they would need to click Like, a practice known as Like-gating. The NAD encouraged Coastal to try and include more terms prior to the Like-gate in the future.

The NAD also stated that classifying a Facebook page's number of Likes as the number of their fans was an acceptable practice. It held that social media users understood a variety of social media activities to be described in various ways—including fans, supporters, or just people who have Liked a page. The fact that many people may have first Liked the Coastal page in order to receive the free glasses promotion did not prevent them from being described as fans. One point in favor of Coastal was the high number of customers who completed the free glasses offer (despite the limited selection complained about by 1-800-Contacts).

The Coastal Contacts case provided a helpful first case discussing both Like-gating and describing the community a brand or organization connects with on social media. Now, the practice of Like-gating is drastically different in what Facebook will allow brands and organizations to do in their social media marketing efforts. The idea that customers passing through this Like-gate can still be called fans is a useful tool for modern marketers.

D. WEIGHT LOSS TYPICALITY DISCLOSURES

One of the early lessons to come out of applying the new Endorsement Guidelines was that earlier known disclosure requirements still apply in the social media space. While several platforms made existing disclosure techniques difficult or required modification to disclose the same way as traditional press, disclosure is still required.

In 2012, the NAD looked at a Pinterest board posted by Nutrisystem, a popular weight loss product. The board was called "Real Consumers. Real Success." and contained several pictures of Nutrisystem customers. The photographs also contained captions such as "Christine B. lost 46 lbs on Nutrisystem" and "Michael H. lost 125 lbs on Nutrisystem."

Prior to the Endorsement Guidelines modification to accommodate social media, guidance had long since been established that statements such as these were endorsements and needed a disclosure stating if the results were not typical for a user of the product. These pinned pictures and captions contained no such disclosure.

As soon as the matter was brought to the NAD's attention, Nutrisystem immediately added the disclosures to the photographs and said the lack of disclosure was inadvertent. As a case of first impression for the NAD, no additional action was taken. A clear message was sent: social media would use the traditional advertising rules whenever possible.

E. MATERIAL CONNECTIONS INCLUDE PRIZES OF VARIABLE AMOUNTS

In January 26, 2010, the retail chain Loft invited a number of influential fashion bloggers to a private event. The event allowed these bloggers to have early access to view the store's upcoming summer fashion line. The invitation also promised that all bloggers attending the event would receive a free prize in the form of a Loft gift card. The card would have a value between $10 and $500 and required the blogger to write about the event within 24 hours of attending. Numerous bloggers attended the event and wrote about the upcoming fashions. The FTC decided to investigate some months later.

The gift card given to bloggers was a material connection that needed to be disclosed under the Endorsement Guidelines. The variability of the prize and the fact that the blogger did not know the exact value when writing their blog entry did nothing to change that connection. The blogger was receiving a material benefit in exchange for their coverage of the event without disclosing to their readers that they were writing a blog entry to receive the benefit.

The invitation that Loft sent to bloggers did not require any disclosure of the future gift card in exchange for covering the event. Loft did post a sign at the event asking bloggers to disclose their gift card prizes. Some of the bloggers did in fact disclose this connection—both factors leading to the FTC closing the investigation without taking any action. But another vital element in the FTC deciding not to take any action against Loft was that the brand learned from its mistake. One month after the event took place, Loft adopted a written policy covering this issue. The new policy would communicate to all bloggers their need to disclose the gift card (or any other benefit they received) on their blogs prior to receiving the promised gift.

While the FTC did not comment on the efforts undertaken by Loft in monitoring or enforcing this policy, the existence of the policy itself coupled with the relatively small number of blog posts on the event allowed the FTC to close the investigation without action. It was a warning to the industry.

F. DISCLOSURE MAY BE APPROPRIATE AT THE END OF A SERIES OF PAID-FOR POSTS

In January, 2012, Rio Ferdinand, a famous soccer player in Europe, began sending out a series of strange tweets professing a love for knitting. "Really getting into knitting!!!! Helps me relax after high-pressure world of the Premiership," "Can't wait 2 get home from training and finish that cardigan," "Just popping out 2 get more wool!!!," and "Cardy finished. Now 4 the matching mittens!!!" appeared to his followers. Fans of the athlete were surprised by the admission and responded with various tweets asking if this was a joke or what color he selected for the mittens.

Mr. Ferdinand then followed up the series of tweet with another message: "You're not you when you're hungry @snickersUK #hungry #spon" that revealed the series of tweets to be a promotional campaign for the Snickers candy bar. The tweets capitalized on Snickers' marketing campaign depicting people acting outside their normal behavior when hungry before consuming a Snickers bar returned them to normal. True to form, the final tweet sent by Mr. Ferdinand also included a picture of him eating a Snickers bar. He was not knitting in the picture.

This series of tweets was accompanied by another series of tweets by a well-known European model. Instead of discussing her love for knitting, her tweets discussed various macro-economic theories before ending with a similar final tweet showing her eating a candy bar.

European regulators investigated this campaign because only the final tweets for each celebrity included the proper disclosures. While the FTC in the United States has not issued specific guidance on what is or is not a proper disclosure, in the UK there is a very specific requirement for paid endorsers to use #spon (for sponsored), #paid, or #ad within a tweet to indicate its status. While the final tweet for each celebrity's series did include the required disclosure the earlier tweets did not.

The Advertising Standards Authority (ASA) (the UK administrative agency overseeing advertising) ultimately determined that while the campaign did push the envelope, it did not violate its advertising standards. Even though the initial tweets were part of the campaign and did not contain the required disclosures, they also did nothing to endorse the product or encourage a commercial transaction. It was only the final tweet that revealed the commercial connection and could possibly persuade consumers to purchase the product. That final tweet did contain the required disclosures and the ASA determined that was sufficient for compliance.

This case is significant in that it took place within a jurisdiction with very tight rules: if a tweet is paid for it must contain a disclosing hashtag. And yet even with such ironclad regulations marketers found a way to push the envelope. All of the tweets by the athlete and model were paid for even if they did not contain any marketing content. Only the marketing content tweets were disclosed and that was found to be sufficient—showing that even in the face of absolute rules there can be freedom to innovate without punishment.

G. WELL-KNOWN COMMERCIAL AFFILIATION STILL REQUIRES DISCLOSURE

Two well-known European soccer players each sent out a tweet in January, 2012, which included a professional new year's resolution. Wayne Rooney tweeted "My resolution—to start the year as a champion, and finish it as a champion. . . #makeitcount gonike.me/makeitcount" while a tweet from Jack Wilshere read "In 2012, I will come back for my club—and be ready for my country. #makeitcount gonike.me/makeitcount." Both tweets were paid for by Nike but did not contain the required (in the UK) hashtags of #spon, #paid, or #ad. The UK's Advertising Standards Authority launched an investigation over the tweets' lack of disclosure.

Nike and the athletes responded to an investigation of the tweets by claiming that the links provided in the tweets were sufficient to identify the messages as a commercial endorsement. They also pointed to the well-known affiliation by the two athletes with the Nike brands and to various advertising campaigns in which both players had previously participated. The ASA found neither argument convincing.

The ASA found that including a generic link to a campaign's website was not sufficient to disclose the tweets as being commercial endorsements. It pointed out that the link was propagated throughout social media and Nike encouraged fans to use the link in their own tweets. Just the presence of the link to the campaign's website was not enough to tell the average consumer that the two soccer players had been paid for their tweets.

Equally unconvincing was the argument that the two players had a well-known commercial affiliation with Nike that rendered individual disclosures unnecessary. The ASA ruled that the tweets were misleading and ordered them to be removed from Twitter along with any other tweets in the same campaign.

H. NINA GARCIA AND JC PENNEY SHARES: WHY DISCLOSURE MATTERS

In addition to marketing regulatory action, it is entirely possible for a company to face media backlash or other actions over social media content from a paid endorser if not properly labeled. One example of this took place in the summer of 2012 when Nina Garcia, fashion editor for Marie Claire magazine and well-known judge on the fashion reality television program Project Runway, visited JC Penney headquarters.

JC Penney is a publicly traded chain of retail clothing stores and had recently retained Ms. Garcia as a "resident style voice and fashion collector curator." After her visit, Ms. Garcia sent out a tweet thanking the CEO for a walkthrough of their new concept store and also wrote "Get ready to shop! Its [sic] going to be a game changer!" Ms. Garcia did not disclose that she had a commercial relationship with JC Penney.

The tweet by itself may have gone unnoticed by those not following Ms. Garcia except that shortly after her tweet was posted the stock price of JC Penney began to climb inexplicably. The stock rose approximately 10% before falling a bit, ending the day 5% higher. Business news networks that cover the stock market witnessed this significant move but could not find an explanation for the rise. There was no news about JC Penney, no newly announced deals, no recently released financial results, nothing that could explain the rise in the stock price.

In the absence of any reason for the stock price rise, news outlets settled on Ms. Garcia's tweet as the most likely candidate for the share increase. As word of her tweet causing a run on the stock grew, other news sites covered her commercial relationship with JC Penney.

While stories quickly circulated that Ms. Garcia's tweet caused the stock surge they also quickly died down. Had the story caught the attention of more reporters or regulators then other questions may have been asked around Ms. Garcia's tweet, why her relationship wasn't disclosed, and whether it was designed to increase the stock price or if it was just an unfashionable coincidence. With the proper disclosure of their relationship, those questions could have been avoided.

§ 3.04 SWEEPSTAKES AND CONTESTS

In a consumer driven economy there is nothing more motivating than the opportunity to win free prizes. The psychology behind entering a promotion such as a sweepstakes or contest is a complex and growing field. However, it has been boiled down to its essence by the professional marketer: give a consumer the chance to obtain free goods and they will engage with your brand or organization. The engagement can be fleeting but it is an opportunity to connect with a broader audience in a way that a typical ad cannot provide.

Social media platforms provide marketers the same opportunities via sweepstakes and contests that they provide in the real world. However, social media sweepstakes and contests have the added benefit of drawing on the network of promotion entrants. A consumer visiting a shopping mall may be enticed to enter a sweepstakes for an expensive watch in exchange for their mailing address and contact information. An online user may be enticed to enter the same contest by providing their social media information—and then further enticed with additional entries by alerting five of their Facebook friends of the sweepstakes or tweeting a link to the sweepstakes entry page.

Sweepstakes and contests on social media provide additional benefits to marketers given its expanded audience. But these same promotions come with additional legal risks of that same broad audience, an additional regulatory layer of platform rules, and the risk of entries by non-qualified candidates.

A. REGULATIONS FOR SOCIAL MEDIA SWEEPSTAKES AND PROMOTIONS

1. Sweepstakes, Contests, Lotteries

Understanding the different legal risks that face social media promotions first requires understanding the differences between the types of promotions allowed. Sweepstakes are promotions with two elements: the winner is determined by a random process and the winner receives something of value. All entrants are given an equal chance to win even if individuals can enter multiple times. A bowl of tickets from which a single winning ticket is drawn and given a prize is a simple form of a sweepstakes.

A contest is a promotion with slightly different elements: the winner is determined by skill or some combination of criteria that goes beyond mere luck and the winner receives something of value. A promotion where entrants submit photographs of sunsets to be judged on their color, creativity, and technical skill would be considered a contest rather than a sweepstakes.

A lottery is a special form of sweepstakes that has three elements. The first two are the same as a sweepstakes, random process to determine the winner and a valuable prize, but it also has a third element: consideration for entry. This consideration typically takes a monetary form, such as a purchase, but can also take a non-monetary form in terms of significant time or effort by the entrant in performing some activity that only benefits the promotion sponsor. Purchasing a ticket that has a random chance to win a valuable prize is a lottery.

Classifying a promotion as a lottery is an important legal distinction because, with some small exceptions for non-profit raffles, lotteries are highly regulated activities that can only be run by government agencies.

Several mass market sweepstakes appear to require consideration and yet remain legal. For example, McDonald's regularly runs a promotion where Monopoly game pieces are distributed attached to food items that must be purchased. Once certain sets of game pieces are collected they are exchanged for prizes. This promotion would appear to violate the prohibition against lotteries except that

McDonald's and similar promotions avoid the requirement of consideration to enter the contest. While individuals can purchase items to obtain game pieces, those same game pieces can also be obtained for free by requesting them in a store or writing to a special address to obtain game pieces.

This practice is called an Alternate Method of Entry (AMOE). As long as the AMOE is free, a sweepstakes with other methods of entering that take consideration (such as purchase) will still not be deemed an illegal lottery.

2. Regulations Apply to Social Media Promotions

The same regulations that apply to offline sweepstakes and contests apply to their social media counterparts. This includes the general prohibition against lotteries as well as any state-based regulations on the type of promotion. Federal requirements require prizes over $600 to be reported to the IRS. States have different requirements based on the value of a promotion's prize pool including several states where a bond must be filed for any promotion that awards $5,000 or more.

A promotion's presence on social media does not negate any of these requirements. Hosting a sweepstakes or contest on social media can also mean the promotion reaches audiences that it did not intend to reach, bringing it under the purview of additional, unanticipated regulations. This becomes an especially important risk as a small promotion can easily be shared to other regions, states, or countries than originally intended and might enter a jurisdiction that has harsher penalties or prohibitions. Promotion administrators must carefully guard where their sweepstakes or contest can be viewed and disclose who is eligible to enter in their rules.

3. Platform Regulations for Social Media Promotions

Promotions that take place on social media have the additional burden of complying with a platform's terms and conditions. Just as a sweepstakes that is administered at a booth in a shopping mall must comply with the rules established by the mall itself, promotions run on social media platforms must comply with the rules and regulations set by the platform. Each social media platform can make the choice as to whether to allow promotions or what activities it will prohibit or allow to be connected to promotions. Google Plus, for example, currently does not allow any promotions to take place on their platform. A brand or organization may provide a link to a promotion if that link takes the user to a site not on the Google Plus platform. The sweepstakes or contest itself can not be run on Google Plus.

Facebook has limitations on what activities can be utilized in running sweepstakes or contests. For many years, Facebook required a separate application to be installed to administer any kind of promotion. Brands or organizations that posted a photo with a caption that read "Like this photo to be entered into our sweepstakes" would find the photo removed if Facebook's monitoring team discovered the violation. In 2013, Facebook changed their rules to let promotions use Facebook's core functionality (Liking a picture, commenting on a post, etc.) to enter a sweepstakes or contest. Facebook further clarified the rules to prohibit any activity that would force the spread of promotion content to non-entrants. For example, a user who enters a sweepstakes on Facebook is free to tell their friends about the promotion but the promotion cannot require a user to post to their friends' page in order to enter. Similarly, promotions that require users to post a photo or message to their own profile and tag the brand or organization to enter are also not allowed. Promotion content must be limited to the sponsor's Facebook page to be in compliance.

Similar efforts to reduce the impact of a promotion on a user's social media content can be found on Pinterest. Users of Pinterest create virtual photo boards for items of interest. They may collect, or pin, photographs of dresses, venues, and cakes under a Wedding Ideas board or photos of luxury cars, yachts, and mansions on a When I Win The Lottery board. Several brands ran promotions on Pinterest that required users to create a Pinterest board that would include items belonging to that brand. The user would then be awarded something from their board if they were selected as the winner.

These Pinterest contests were known as Pin It To Win It contests. Pinterest felt that these promotions conflicted with their vision of having users pin photos they were passionate about rather than pinning photos just because they might win something. To avoid this issue, Pinterest changed their rules to prohibit Pin It To Win It contests. Brands could still run promotions on the platform but could no longer require users to only pin from a certain catalog of images or products.

Twitter is generally permissive of promotions but it and other platforms have general prohibitions against any activity that would encourage the creation of fake platform accounts. A contest on Twitter where the winner is determined by who can have their message retweeted the most times could encourage entrants to create fake Twitter accounts to increase their chances to win. The terms and conditions for Twitter and other social media platforms could prohibit this kind of promotion.

Marketers wishing to conduct a sweepstakes or promotion on social media must check the platform's terms and conditions prior to starting its contest. Platforms may adopt new technologies that require changes to a promotion's design or could change its rules to modify the boundaries of allowable promotions. Also, social media's rapid evolution means the rules can change at any time.

B. SOCIAL MEDIA RISKS FOR SWEEPSTAKES AND CONTESTS

In addition to the regulations that apply to all promotions, whether offline or online, there are also special considerations that must be given to sweepstakes and contests that take place on social media. These considerations extend beyond the standard terms set by government agencies and the rules established by social media platforms. Instead, these risks spring from the general risks presented by marketing on social media.

1. Promotions and the Endorsement Guidelines

In the Pin It To Win It promotions described earlier, entrants were given the chance to win a product if they pinned a picture of the product to a board on their Pinterest account. As the FTC established in the Loft decision, having a potential prize in exchange for posting social media content can be considered a material fact that needs to be disclosed. The Loft decision covered gift cards that all had value—the only question was whether the gift card had $5 or $500 or some value in between, it did not consider the case of some bloggers receiving gift cards that had no value. This left open the question on whether contest entries required disclosure if entries were not guaranteed to receive something of value in exchange for the post.

This question was resolved by the FTC when it looked at a Pinterest contest run by Cole Haan, a well-known fashion accessory designer and seller. Cole Haan ran a contest on Pinterest where users were required to post five photos that included Cole Haan shoes and the user's favorite places to wear the shoes. Each photo needed to include the hashtag #WanderingSole and the winning user would receive $1,000. The FTC said that since each user posted the photos to win the contest the required hashtag was not sufficient to disclose the reason for the post.

Friends of the users who may happen to view the shoe photos and hashtag would have no way of telling that the photos were connected to a contest rather than a sincere appreciation for the product.

The FTC closed the investigation saying that "[e]ntry into a contest to receive a significant prize in exchange for endorsing a product through social media constitutes a material connection that would not reasonably be expected by viewers of the endorsement." That material connection requires disclosure under the Endorsement Guidelines. The FTC took no action against Cole Haan by noting that the contest was over and Pinterest had changed its rules to prevent such a contest from taking place in the future. The impact of requiring disclosure for contest entries is an important consideration for any social media promotion in the future regardless of platform.

2. Risks Around User-Generated Content and Action

Of the various methods used for administering a social media promotion the two most popular are a simple sweepstakes and a contest involving user-generated content. Both of these promotions have particular risks in the social media realm that may not be present for their real world counterparts.

a. Sweepstakes and Refer-a-Friend

Sweepstakes are the easiest promotion to administer since selecting a winner at random is simpler than judging entries. However, for a promotion to take advantage of networking abilities a social media sweepstakes will try to have contestants do more than just enter. Social media sweepstakes will attempt to have entrants engage their connections to spread word of the promotion, hoping that their connections will possibly enter the sweepstakes themselves and further spread word of the event. Depending on the method used for a social media sweepstakes to spread awareness of the campaign, such tactics can run afoul of the hosting platform's terms and conditions as discussed above.

Additionally, if a social media sweepstakes also utilizes a "refer-a-friend" tactic it can potentially violate CAN-SPAM requirements. Refer-a-friend mechanics allow a single user to then specifically alert a number of their friends via email, social media post, or private message about the commercial promotion. More than just allowing entrants to discuss the promotion, refer-a-friend typically will send a previously generated commercial email or post to the addresses provided by the entrant. Some may allow the entrant to customize a part of the email or include a brief message but the bulk of the communication is set by the promotion itself.

These messages may need to comply with CAN-SPAM requirements. The FTC's original guides to CAN-SPAM discussed emails that had a button or link to forward the message to a contact. If an incentive is provided to the participant in exchange for sending the message to others, then the message needs to comply with CAN-SPAM. Incentives that bring the message under CAN-SPAM's jurisdiction can include coupons, discounts, awards, or additional entries into the sweepstakes. Social media sweepstakes administrators employing a refer-a-friend mechanism in their promotion should ensure the message is CAN-SPAM compliant if such an incentive is offered.

b. Contests and User-Generated Content

Contests may require more time and effort to administer than a sweepstakes but generally have much greater engagement with individuals entering the contest. This is especially true for contests where entrants must generate some form of creative content. Social media marketers may design a contest to include user-generated content knowing that entrants will be proud of their submission and likely share it with people outside of the contest. Depending on the design of the contest and the submissions, contests with user-generated content can create significant legal risks for the sponsoring brand or organization.

In 2006, the sandwich chain Quiznos held an online contest asking visitors to submit a video that compared their sandwiches to those from the rival Subway chain. Comparison advertising is a field with numerous guidelines and decisions but still generates professional advertisements that toe or cross the line of allowable content. Encouraging non-marketers to make videos that delve into this tricky area of law was bound to create videos that go beyond accepted standards of comparison advertising.

Over a hundred videos were entered in the contest. These submissions were curated by Quiznos and its marketing agency before being posted on a website. After Subway watched the videos it sued Quiznos for deceptive advertising. Quiznos attempted to hide behind the fact that it didn't make the videos. Subway pointed to two factors as to why Quiznos should be held accountable: first, the rules of the contest, which asked participants to make a direct comparison between the two brands; and second, the fact that Quiznos curated the videos prior to publishing them on the official results website for the contest. Subway defeated the summary judgment motion brought by Quiznos. With the case proceeding to trial, Quiznos settled the matter.

Brands and organizations administering contests that require user generated content may face legal exposure based on the content generated. While the Quiznos case dealt with comparative advertising and left the issue open, marketing law is only one area where user generated content could create risks. User generated videos could contain copyrighted music or clips from films, they may be used to spread libelous statements, they might violate a celebrity's right of publicity, or they could be used to knowingly incite violence.

Additionally, depending on the amount of work required, a user-generated content entry could cross the boundary into non-monetary consideration. These entries could put the promotion at risk of being classified as an illegal lottery if there is no alternate method of entry and the winning entry is determined at random.

Another risk concerning user-generated content is ensuring that the organization running the contest secures the proper rights to use the content in the future, if their plan is to do so. A contest participant who submits a video or song or photograph to a contest will be agreeing to the rules of the contest and to have the content judged for purposes of the competition. It is up to the organization running the contest to ensure they have the proper rights to use that content later for marketing purposes.

A contest may utilize a hashtag in designating content for a specific promotion, in which case it may also be beneficial to have the hashtag be specific in what the user is signaling. A contest that has participants tag a photo with #happy may not be as effective as a #BrandHappyGallery hashtag in clearly indicating what the user is agreeing to do—in this case, have a photo appear in the brand's photo gallery.

3. Risks Based on Promotion Design

Beyond the legal risks based on the content and action taken by promotion entrants, the design of a promotion itself can create risk for the administering brand or organization. Chief among these concerns are promotions designed with objective voting and those utilizing a platform during a specific time window.

a. Objective Voting

Picking a sweepstakes winner is a simple matter of pulling a name out of a hat, even if the virtual hat is large enough to contain millions of names. Selecting the winner of a contest requires more work to determine which entry best meets the promotion's criteria. One method marketers have used to simplify this process is to select a winner through objective voting criteria. This includes picking a winner based on the number of times a single tweet was favorited or retweeted, an online poll open to the public, or counting the number of thumbs up votes on YouTube videos. The contest may or may not include a live leaderboard to display the standings of the promotion as voting is underway.

These types of promotions are a frequent target for malicious entrants or users to take advantage of the promotion's design. Malicious entries can take the form of a group of people motivated to skew the results. In 2012, a contest appeared online asking users to submit and vote on names for a new green apple flavor of Mountain Dew. Believing this "Dub The Dew" contest to be official (it was actually run by a pizza restaurant that only sold Mountain Dew and was not administered or run by PepsiCo, the owners of Mountain Dew), a group of online pranksters flooded the site with bogus names and coordinated votes to ensure those names appeared on the leaderboard. Potential winning names included Diabeetus, Sour Granny Slap, and Hitler Did Nothing Wrong.

Other online objective polls have seen singer Pitbull ask which Walmart location he should perform a concert at only to have pranksters flood the site with votes for the most remote Walmart location in the United States: Kodiak, Alaska (he honored the vote and performed a concert there). And Britain's Natural Environment Research Council turned to social media for assistance in naming its new $300 million polar research ship. The winning name was Boaty McBoatface, earning ten times as many votes as the second most popular entry. The Council elected to go with a different name.

While tactics such as those in taking over Dub The Dew, Pitbull's concert, or naming a boat can be simple to identify, other tactics in gaming objective voting promotions are harder to detect. In 2012, Gold Peak Tea ran a "Take the Year Off" contest which had entrants submit a video saying why they should win the grand prize of $100,000 to take the year off from their job. The final videos were submitted to a public vote and the highest voted video belonged to Theodore A. Scott. Mr. Scott was later disqualified after it was discovered he participated in an online forum that existed to trade votes for online contests. In this forum, Mr. Scott agreed to vote for other members' entries in separate contests in exchange for their agreement to vote for his entry in the Gold Peak Tea promotion. This type of activity, known as vote farming, can be harder to detect but just as effective in determining the winner of a contest. While the contest may have generated some good will from the final winner, it generated a host of negative publicity (including articles by the New York Times and other media) about the disqualified entrant.

Social media marketers that employ purely objective methods for determining a contest winner face these technical and public relations risks. These kinds of risks can be avoided by changing judging criteria to include subjective measurements such as creativity or brand integration. While these criteria may take more work to administer fairly, they also avoid some of the most significant risks a social media promotion faces.

b. Platform Usage

Another risk that can be built into a promotion's design is its utilization of a single social media platform. Many users and brands take for granted the broad availability of social media platforms. While a social media platform never intends to experience downtime, it can be an extra risk for a brand or organization relying solely on that platform for a promotion during a specific timeframe.

In 2009, an online trivia contest was held by Alienware, the gaming division of Dell. Questions were posted on Twitter and correct responses were awarded points until the top five point scorers were determined. Those five individuals were then invited to participate in a final round where only the first correct response to a question would receive a point and the first finalist with five points would win a premium gaming system. The finalists were physically located in both the United States and

Europe so a time was set that would work for all finalists.

The final round was scheduled to take place on June 25, 2009, the day that Michael Jackson died. The resulting social media traffic surrounding the pop star's sudden death took Twitter offline for a good portion of the day—it was past midnight in Europe before the service was available again. While Alienware was able to reschedule the final round it is worth noting that a similar contest for a more dated prize (tickets to a concert that evening or a sporting event the next day) could face the same challenges with less chance for resolution.

Social media users and marketers may wish to make alternate plans for their promotions rather than assuming a single platform will always be online and available for the duration of their event.

CHAPTER 4

EMPLOYMENT

Social media is all fun and games until somebody loses a job. The social media explosion hit its first road bumps as random stories emerged of people having job offers rescinded, facing an investigation at work, or even being fired because of something they posted on social media. No other risk seems quite as real to innocent users of social media platforms then the prospect that they might face repercussions on the job.

The risks surrounding employment and social media are a two-sided blade: employees face loss of a potential or actual job and employers must also be careful in how they use or restrict social media use by their employees. Social media risks for both employers and employees come from three different phases of the employment life cycle: getting the job, keeping the job, and losing the job.

§ 4.01 SOCIAL MEDIA AND GETTING THE JOB

A. SOCIAL MEDIA PASSWORDS, PROFILES, AND JOB APPLICANTS

Applying for a job can be a stressful and anxiety-laden process. Although job applicants have some control over the information they submit—resumes, questionnaires, answers to interview questions—there is very little insight into the decision making process that can lead to that job. This leads applicants to worry about any information they provided or any perception they may have created in the eyes of the hiring party. When the public heard that some employers may view social media profiles or even request the applicants' social media passwords that anxiety reached a new level.

Robert Collins joined the Maryland Department of Corrections in July, 2007. In April, 2010, he was a supply officer at a correctional mental health facility. He took an extended leave of absence to take care of a sick family member. Upon his return to work a few months later, he was subjected to a mandatory reapplication process. During that process an investigator demanded Mr. Collins turn over his social media passwords. The investigator requested this information as part of a new process to evaluate whether potential correctional officers had any gang affiliations before putting them in a position of guarding convicted criminals.

Although Mr. Collins provided the password and was cleared to return to his old job, he later quit the job to go back to school. He also took up the matter of his social media passwords with the ACLU and the press. As the story of a potential employer browsing through personal photos, stories, or even barbs and quips with friends on social media became known the anxiety rose to a fever pitch. Soon, several states were hastily passing laws forbidding employers from asking applicants for their social media passwords. Some states went even further to forbid employers from even asking for social media account names, technically making it impossible for an applicant to submit a link to their LinkedIn resume.

After a wave of laws were passed by over a dozen states, the anxiety diminished enough for lawmakers to start asking questions about the implications of these laws. Congress let several national versions die in committee and other states failed to pass their own laws. After pushback from their governor, New Jersey passed a law that included an important exemption—social media profiles and accounts could at least be looked at for business reasons. If, for example, someone applied for a job as a social media community manager, looking at the applicant's social media activity (at least the activity visible to the public) could be highly relevant for evaluating their job skills. New Jersey's law allowed such activity while several earlier versions would not.

Maryland, in the wake of the scandal caused by Mr. Collins' revelation, was one of the first states to pass a law forbidding employers to ask for social media passwords during the job application process. In an ironic twist, Maryland's law was written so that it did not apply to state-controlled agencies such as the Maryland Department of Corrections. The case that sparked the controversy that resulted in the law being passed was not addressed by the law itself.

Another reason for fewer states passing these laws was the realization that employers who were already following their legal obligations in the job hiring process were very rarely using social media information at all. Employers have a legal obligation not to discriminate against job applicants based on several criteria: gender, race, national origin, religion, age, or disability status. Other criteria may also be protected at the state or local level such as sexual orientation, genetic information, or appearance.

Employers aware of their legal obligations are careful not to consider any of those protected categories when making a hiring decision. Some information cannot be prevented from entering the job application process—an interviewer is usually able to ascertain a job applicant's gender, for example. However, the hiring process itself should not allow these protected categories of information to be a factor. If it can at all be avoided, job applicants should not be asked about these protected categories, such as not asking "What religion are you?" during an interview. The more protected information that enters a job application process the more it can expose an employer to a lawsuit alleging that protected information was illegally used in the hiring process.

Looking at a job applicant's social media profile can immediately expose the employer to several protected categories of information beyond the information that may have been readily apparent in a face-to-face interview. The first page of an applicant's Facebook profile might contain posts that reveal the applicant's religion, a disability, or their exact age. Employers may need to look at social media activity in judging an applicant's social media skills but any other social media browsing is a potential minefield of legal exposure. Any employer already aware of their existing legal obligations would have designed a hiring process to avoid extraneous and protected information from entering their consideration—an additional legal requirement to avoid social media profiles was likely unnecessary.

B. SOCIAL MEDIA BACKGROUND CHECKS

One way employers can avoid this issue is to employ a company to perform a social media background check. Like criminal or security background checks, third parties exist to investigate applicants and report back only the relevant findings to the employer.

Social media background checks can also help reduce an employer's risk in the long run. In 2013, a social media editor for Reuters was indicted for his involvement in hacking activities targeting a rival, Associated Press. After the editor was indicted, his questionable social media history came to light: allegations of trolling activities on a variety of websites; his troubling blog posts; and multiple stories of bizarre behavior over rejected relationships appeared with only cursory searching. This information may have influenced Reuters' hiring decision had it been available in a filtered and summarized manner. Social media background checks can provide a safety buffer providing employers, like Reuters, the information they need without the information that might get them in trouble.

C. SOCIAL MEDIA AND JOB OFFERS

Newer entrants to the job market may think that once a job offer is made the job is a done deal. While many companies may treat an offer as such, there is very little legal basis requiring a job offer to be permanent. In the time between a job being offered and a job being accepted, social media can put that job at risk.

In one of the first and most famous instance of someone losing a job as a result of social media, the person had not even started working before she lost the position. A master's student at the University of California at Berkeley completed a job interview with Cisco in early 2009 when she tweeted "Cisco just offered me a job! Now I have to weigh the utility of a fatty paycheck against the daily commute to San Jose and hating the work."

The graduate student was only 22-years-young at the time and despite studying to obtain her master's degree in information management she failed to adequately manage her own opinion about the offered position. Unfortunately for her, Cisco employees were also active on Twitter. One employee quickly responded "Who is the hiring manager? I'm sure they would love to know that you will hate the work. We here at Cisco are versed in the Web."

If the actual tweet was not enough to rescind the job offer, the firestorm that resulted from the tweet going viral was certainly sufficient. Known forever after as the "Cisco Fatty" tweet it serves as a cautionary tale that with the ability to complain to your friends on social media comes the added possibility that you might be griping to your current or potential bosses.

D. SOCIAL MEDIA JOB POSTINGS AND DISCRIMINATION

Job hiring practices can face a challenge of being de jure or de facto discriminatory. De jure discrimination takes place when an employer has an explicit policy to not hire women. De facto discrimination takes place if the same employer has a policy to only hire candidates over 6′2″ knowing that almost no woman will meet the requirement. Although social media platforms have become popular locations for posting and recruiting candidates to positions, employers should be aware of potential de facto discrimination claims depending on the platforms they use.

Social media platforms succeed based on the number of users they have and the activities those users perform. While platforms tend to have broad audiences some can skew towards narrow demographics. Employers posting job openings only on a platform whose user base is 90% male or 95% caucasian could face a de facto discrimination claim. Avoiding this problem can be as simple as posting openings on multiple sites that target a variety of demographics.

§ 4.02 SOCIAL MEDIA AND KEEPING THE JOB

A. SOCIAL MEDIA POLICIES

When social media first rose to popularity many employers attempted to block employee access to social media. While some employers continue to do so today, employers also know that employees will frequently access social media via their personal smartphones or on their home systems after work. As employers realized they could not prevent access they sought to create limitations on its use. Some of these restrictions have been too broad, some have been necessary, but all are found within the confines of an employer's social media policies.

B. THE NLRB AND SOCIAL MEDIA POLICIES

No government agency has had more influence, good or bad, on employer social media policies than the National Labor Relations Board (NLRB). The National Labor Relations Act (NLRA) was passed by Congress in 1935 as a way of protecting worker rights including collective bargaining arrangements, otherwise known as unions. Beyond protecting union rights, the NLRA also established the NLRB as its implementing agency, charging it with not only protecting union rights but also stopping any unfair labor practices.

The NLRB is generally concerned with protected concerted activities in the employment arena. Concerted activities are any action taken by two or more employees that deal with a topic relevant to fellow employees when the action is seeking to initiate, induce, or prepare for a group action. Protected activities are any concerted activity whose purpose is collective bargaining or other mutual aid or protection. A group of janitors banding together to complain about the smell of a cleaning solution is a concerted activity. That same group complaining that the new cleaning solution is toxic and presents a safety concern for any employee handling the substance is a protected activity.

For decades, the NLRB heard cases and settled claims against employers as it related to union agreements, negotiations, or specific hirings and firings. One area the NLRB frequently ruled on were restrictions by employers on certain areas of speech. Employers would use these limitations as justification to fire workers during strikes or fire employees for conduct that could lead to a broader employee action.

As social media exploded into popular use, the NLRB began hearing cases where employees were posting content about their job on social media. Conversations that used to take place around the water cooler were now finding their way onto Facebook and Twitter leading to simpler ways for employees to connect but also creating easier ways for that information to find its way to management and the public. Companies began creating social media policies that ranged from blatant restrictions on rights guaranteed by the NLRA to more innocent policies that could be interpreted to restrict those rights.

1. NLRB on Social Media Before 2010

The early NLRB social media decisions is best summarized by the Sears Holding decision in 2009. In 2008, the International Brotherhood of Electrical Workers began efforts to represent certain employees of Sears and Kmart, retail stores both owned by Sears Holding. While the union sought to define the employees and geographies they wished to represent several websites, email lists, and social media pages on Facebook and MySpace were utilized to educate and recruit employees on the effort.

Seven months after the union efforts began, Sears Holding adopted a policy covering employee use of social and all online media. While the policy forbid a number of online activities the one most frequently discussed by employees was a prohibition on any "[d]isparagement of company's or competitor's products, services, executive leadership, employees, strategy, and business prospects." Employees involved in the union organizing efforts were afraid this prohibition would apply to their organizing activities and be used as an excuse to terminate employees involved in the union program.

A case was filed with the NLRB over this social media policy prohibition in 2009. The NLRB ruled that the policy was acceptable. First, the NLRB noted that employees continued to discuss the union efforts even after the policy was implemented and no evidence was introduced that any employees were terminated or challenged based on the policy. Despite the timing of the policy adoption, the NLRB also found that there was no evidence the social media policy was adopted as a response to the union organizing activities. Furthermore, the NLRB held that the specific prohibition should be read within the context of the entire social media policy and that within the entire document it was not a prohibition against activities protected by the NLRA.

2. NLRB Reversal on Social Media After 2010

As a politically appointed agency, the NLRB had significant membership changes in 2010 that led to a significant change in how the NLRB viewed and decided social media cases. In addition to deciding several significant cases regarding social media policies, the General Counsel for the NLRB issued three reports in 2011 and 2012 discussing social media policies and their application. As NLRB membership can vary between administrations and rulings can be swiftly overcomed, the direction taken by the NLRB since 2010 is informative but could also easily be reversed under a new administration.

a. NLRB Reports on Social Media

The three reports issued by the NLRB documented a new focus on social media policies both for their importance and in how the NLRA would apply to the policies. While the Sears Holding case had analyzed specific social media prohibitions within the context of the broader policy the new cases ignored the context of a broader policy and instead analyzed specific prohibitions. If those prohibitions could be interpreted to restrict an employee's rights under the NLRA then the policy was deemed overbroad. Even a prohibition against posting confidential information, a limitation almost any employer social media policy would include, could be overbroad if confidential information were defined in a way to limit an employee's rights to discuss working conditions (their hourly schedule, for example). Similar social media policy limitations against disparaging, inappropriate, or posts considered disrespectful could be seen to infringe on the rights guaranteed to employees by the NLRA and would be considered unlawfully overbroad.

The second report also specifically discussed the insufficiency of a savings clause in a social media policy. A savings clause was a section of an employer's social media policy that would state the restrictions within the social media policy would not apply to any rights granted to employees under any laws including the NLRA. These savings clauses attempted to impose limitations via the policy while still preserving employee's legal rights but would not list or discuss what rights were being preserved. The NLRB has held that such a clause has too much of a chilling effect on employees—an employee will read the social media policy restriction and not realize where the restriction stops thanks to the NLRA.

The NLRB's third report on social media focuses more on policies than specific cases, discussing where policies were found to be overbroad, where they could be changed to fit the confines of the NLRA, and even endorsing one social media policy as written. Employers seeking to adopt a social media policy that complies with the limits of the NLRB can look to this report while also realizing the NLRB is still evolving its holdings around social media limitations. Directionally, however, from 2010 on there has been a significant move against most social media policy prohibitions. Three cases best exemplify this shift.

b. *Social Media Policies and Union Employees: American Medical Response of Connecticut*

The American Medical Response of Connecticut (AMR) case signalled the reversal in analyzing social media policies as they applied to union workers. In November, 2009, Dawnmarie Souza was an employee for the unionized health care company AMR. After a customer complaint over her performance, Ms. Souza's supervisor asked her to prepare an incident report. Fearing that the report could lead to termination, Ms. Souza requested representation as allowed under the union contract. AMR denied that representation. After being denied representation, Ms. Souza vented on her personal Facebook page by calling her supervisor several negative things. This was done from her personal computer while at home rather than at work.

Ms. Souza was terminated for violating the AMR social media policy. The policy stated that "[e]mployees are prohibited from making disparaging, discriminatory or defamatory comments when discussing the Company or the employee's superiors, co-workers and/or competitors." The NLRB brought an action against AMR one year later alleging that AMR's actions in both denying Ms.

Souza representation and firing her for her social media posts violated the NLRA.

The night before the trial, the NLRB and AMR settled the case. AMR agreed to change their rules so that union members would not be denied representation and also agreed to modify their social media policy to not prevent employees from discussing their wages, hours, or working conditions on social media. This marked the first time that the NLRB questioned an employer's social media policy in how it may impact an employee's ability to exercise their rights under the NLRA and their specific union contract.

c. *Social Media Policies and Non-Union Employees: Hispanics United of Buffalo*

While the AMR case impacted social media policies belonging to employers with union contracts, it was another year before the NLRB would rule that similar limitations applied to non-union employers as well. In Hispanics United of Buffalo (HUB), the NLRB considered the case of five employees who were terminated from their non-union jobs at a local charity.

The case began when an employee at HUB complained to her co-worker, Mariana Cole-Rivera, about the amount of work done by HUB employees and how Ms. Cole-Rivera had handled a particular case. A series of text messages between the two resulted in the employee stating the HUB Executive Director would resolve their differences. Frustrated by the exchange and in preparation for the meeting with the HUB Executive Director, Ms. Cole-Rivera posted on her Facebook profile while at home over the weekend. She posted how the other employee felt the agency didn't help enough people. Ms. Cole-Rivera asked "My fellow coworkers how do [you] feel?" This began a chain of comments from her coworkers expressing frustration over the work they do and how unrecognized they felt for the programs they ran through HUB. Later in the thread, the employee that was being complained about also responded, saying Ms. Cole-Rivera should stop her lies and that the employee would be in the office on Tuesday. Ms. Cole-Rivera expressed surprise at her comments being called a lie but also invited the employee to a social event later that evening. Another worker, after seeing that the employee would be in the office on Tuesday, wrote in Spanish that he would bring popcorn.

On Tuesday morning the HUB Executive Director summoned five of the employees who participated in the Facebook thread and informed them that the employee had suffered a heart attack as a result of the comments. The five employees were terminated for cyber-bullying and harassment on the Facebook thread. A case was brought before the NLRB.

The NLRB found that not only was there no evidence of the employee suffering any harm from the posts (let alone a heart attack) but that the conversation that ensued on Facebook was a textbook case of concerted activity protected under the NLRA. Despite HUB being a non-union organization, the NLRB for the first time ordered the terminated employees to be reinstated with back pay over a social media firing.

d. *Social Media Policies and Individual Posts: Karl Knauz Motors*

One typical distinction held by the NLRB is that a concerted activity must involve multiple employees rather than individual gripes or complaints. Long before social media's rise in popularity, the NLRB held that concerted action can originate with just one person so long as it ultimately involves multiple employees. In Karl Knauz Motors, the NLRB decided that this same distinction applies to social media and that posts by an individual can still be considered concerted activity depending on the context of the posts.

Robert Becker was a car salesman at Knauz BMW, a luxury car dealership owned by Karl Knauz Motors. Mr. Becker had worked as a salesman for Karl Knauz Motors for 12 years. When Knauz BMW held a special event to celebrate the launch of a newly designed BMW 5 series automobile (the best selling BMW model at the dealership). As he learned the details of the event, Mr. Becker had several complaints about whether it portrayed the luxury elements of the brand they sold. The event allowed customers to drive in the new cars (actually driven by professional drivers) but would serve refreshments to customers in the form of cookies and chips bought from a nearby warehouse club and hot dogs served from a rented hot dog stand. Small bottles of water, also purchased from the warehouse, would be available as well.

Mr. Becker had several conversations with his fellow co-workers about their concerns regarding the event. He then proceeded to take pictures when the event took place. Those pictures were then posted along with sarcastic comments onto his Facebook page. Mr. Becker was later terminated for violating the Karl Knauz Motors Employee Handbook which included a provision requiring employees to display a positive attitude about their job.

In the subsequent case before the NLRB it was decided that the posts made by Mr. Becker, despite being made just by him and not involving a discussion with fellow employees on Facebook, could still constitute concerted activity. A concerted activity can take place when an individual is bringing group complaints to the attention of management—the same holds true for social media posts made by one person that communicated the concerns of multiple employees. Mr. Becker's complaints about the event and how it impacted the job for all salespeople were considered concerted activity.

The NLRB noted that Karl Knauz Motors had already rescinded the Employee Handbook sections that conflicted with Mr. Becker's postings but held that those provisions should not be reinstated since they conflicted with the NLRA. Ultimately, they did not order Mr. Becker to be reinstated because of other posts he made on social media making light of a car crash that had occurred at another Karl Knauz Motors dealership. Those posts were not considered concerted activity and were adequate grounds for his termination. The principle that individual social media posts without comments by co-workers can still be considered concerted activity remains an important finding from this case.

C. AVOIDING SOCIAL MEDIA POLICIES

One emerging trend among employers is to avoid having a social media policy altogether. This course of action is due to two factors: first, the NLRB's rulings on social media policies making it difficult to craft enforceable policies that meet an employer's needs, and second, the existence of other policies that likely cover the activities an employer cares about.

If an employer is concerned about employees sharing confidential information on social media they likely already have a policy concerning the disclosure of confidential information. If an employer is concerned about harassing or bullying behavior by employees they likely have a policy prohibiting this kind of activity. These and other risk areas can be addressed in a more direct fashion without resorting to a specific social media provision.

D. SOCIAL MEDIA TRAINING

Many brands and organizations find it useful to offer some form of social media training for its employees. Social media training can not only benefit employees by teaching them how to avoid social media risks, but the brand can also benefit by having a trained workforce that may utilize social media for the organization's benefit. Social media training programs can vary from short instructional videos to detailed series of classes and certifications that can be offered to employees.

Training programs may also differ in its target audiences. Since virtually all employees may use social media on a personal level, some training programs may focus on informing employees about activities to avoid (such as their obligations under the Endorsement Guidelines discussed in the Marketing and Promotions chapter). Detailed training may be made available to employees whose job duties include social media functions. Even more detailed programs may be mandatory for employees who will be considered media spokespeople or individuals authorized to speak on behalf of the brand or organization.

§ 4.03 SOCIAL MEDIA AND LOSING THE JOB

The termination of an employee can raise a number of social media risks in the wake of the employee's departure. These risks belong to both the employee and the employer and should be considered by both as part of the employment life cycle.

A. SOCIAL MEDIA ACCOUNT OWNERSHIP

The issue of who owns a social media account remains a largely unresolved question. Several high-profile cases indicate the risks involved for both employers and employees.

1. Laura Kuenssberg and the Lost BBC Followers

Laura Kuenssberg was a political reporter in the United Kingdom. While working as the chief political correspondent for BBC she created a Twitter account, @BBCLauraK, and grew the account to more than 58,000 followers. In June, 2011, Ms. Kuenssberg changed her Twitter name to @ITVLauraK and tweeted "As you've discovered I will become @ITVLauraK in September!" ITV is a rival network to the BBC in the United Kingdom.

The question of whether the social media account belonged to Ms. Kuenssberg or the BBC network was suddenly thrust into the national spotlight. British press ran headlines such as "BBC loses 60,000 Twitter followers in one day" referring to the switch by Ms. Kuenssberg. Ultimately, the networks took no action and allowed Ms. Kuenssberg to take her account and followers with her to ITV. But the question of whether the BBC had an enforceable right to the account remains unresolved. The BBC may have decided not to take action knowing how often reporters move—Ms. Kuenssberg returned to the BBC in 2013 and changed her Twitter name back to @BBCLauraK.

2. Social Media Account Ownership in the U.S.

In the United States, the issue of social media account ownership also remains largely unresolved. Although one case has been resolved in regards to LinkedIn, the broader issue of branded social media accounts remains unresolved despite one case on point.

PhoneDog, a website that published mobile phone news and reviews, hired a freelance writer, Noah Kravitz, to develop content and build a social media presence for the company. Mr. Kravitz wrote articles, created videos for the website, and grew a Twitter account, @Phonedog_Noah, to more than 17,000 followers. When Mr. Kravitz ended his relationship with PhoneDog he changed the name of the Twitter account to @noahkravitz and changed its password so PhoneDog could not access the account.

PhoneDog sued Mr. Kravitz claiming, among other alleged crimes, that he had misappropriated trade secrets by changing the account's password and that he had stolen the social media account. PhoneDog also said their monetary damages amounted to $2.50 per follower per month and sought over $300,000 from Mr. Kravitz.

The lawsuit survived summary judgment and had other claims revised during its lifetime. It was ultimately settled by the parties without resolving the central issue of account ownership. The question of social media account ownership remains unresolved. Courts and statutes alike have failed to address whether social media accounts should be treated like confidential business records that cannot be taken when an employee leaves (such as customer lists) or if social media accounts should be treated like skills acquired during employment that can be taken when an employee leaves (such as their increased capacity to sell or how to talk with clients).

One case resolved social media account ownership according to the platform's terms and conditions. Dr. Linda Eagle co-founded a company, Edcomm, and started a LinkedIn profile to market the company and list her personal achievements. The company was sold in October, 2010, although all of the co-founders stayed with the company as executives. In June, 2011, Dr. Eagle was terminated.

During her employment at Edcomm, Dr. Eagle had shared her LinkedIn password with some other employees so they could respond to messages she received on the account. After Dr. Eagle was terminated, the company used that password to change Dr. Eagle's LinkedIn password and details of the account. The account was changed to reflect the name and picture of the new Edcomm CEO and retained some of Dr. Eagle's information such as awards and achievements. Dr. Eagle was completely locked out of her account for two weeks.

After regaining control of her LinkedIn account, Dr. Eagle sued Edcomm over the profile hijacking. She won on three state law claims—unauthorized use of name, invasion of privacy, and misappropriation of identity. However, Dr. Eagle was unable to win on any federal claims or prove any damages for the state claims. The court also heavily relied on the LinkedIn user agreement which states that profiles belong to individuals rather than companies even if the company uses their employees' LinkedIn profiles as part of their job. The issue of who owns a social media account for platforms that do not clearly determine ownership or who allow more branded and less personal accounts remains undetermined.

As social media becomes more ingrained in our daily lives, it is possible that treatment of social media accounts may not be simple to classify as customer lists or job skills. Instead, social media accounts may be considered on a spectrum of business or personally owned. This spectrum may include factors such as the timing of establishing the account, the reason for establishing the account, the primary use of the account's content, and the reasonable understanding of who owned the account by its followers.

B. AVOIDING RETALIATION CLAIMS

Social media can often provide an outlet for users' frustrations and annoyances. This is just as true for employers as it is for employees. However, employers should be careful to avoid making statements on social media that can become the basis of a retaliation claim by a former employee.

1. Retaliation via Social Media Posting

In 2011, the owner of the Coyote Ugly Saloon, a chain of bars made popular by the movie "Coyote Ugly," posted a blog entry about her frustrations over being sued. The lawsuit regarded a shared tip pool between bartenders and security personnel. However, the owner, Lilian Lovell, posted on her blog how this upset her because one of the named plaintiffs (suing on behalf of all bartenders) was "someone we terminated for theft." The lawsuit over the tip pool was later amended to include a retaliation claim. The former employee alleged that she was not fired for theft but that this blog post could hinder her ability to gain future employment.

Generally, unlawful retaliation claims require an employee to have engaged in a protected activity, for the employer to have engaged in some activity harmful to the employee, and a connection between the two previous elements. An employee suing over how an entire group was paid can be a protected activity, leaving the difficult analysis of whether the blog post was harmful to the employee. In this particular case, the action survived summary judgment but lost in the end because the former Coyote Ugly Saloon employee was able to find work despite the blog post.

While it may feel good for an employer to vent about terminated employees, doing so may expose the company to further liability and litigation expenses.

2. Retaliation via LinkedIn Recommendations

One often overlooked aspect of LinkedIn is its recommendation system. LinkedIn allows its users to create recommendations for other users—you can receive recommendations from managers, co-workers, or former colleagues. This simple system can create significant risks for employers who have developed policies forbidding recommendations. These no-recommendation policies are typically created as a safeguard against wrongful termination lawsuits. These policies include prohibitions against negative comments regarding former employees, and prevent all recommendations so that negative inferences cannot be made about a former employee (such as when an entire workgroup received recommendations from a former manager except one employee).

These policies may only be communicated by the employer to managers because prior to LinkedIn an employer looking for job-related information would typically only contact a former employee's manager. By communicating these policies to managers, employers would cover the population being asked about former employees. With LinkedIn's system of allowing any member to make a recommendation, employers who have not communicated their no-recommendation policy to individuals outside management roles may find themselves facing the same risks their policies intended to avoid.

CHAPTER 5
LAW OF THE CROWD

While it is fascinating to see how people have found new ways to connect via social media it is even more interesting to see communities form on social media in order to accomplish something. Whether that effort involves writing a new encyclopedia, forming a group to fund a large project, or working together to ensure justice is done, the ability of people around the world to collaborate for the greater good is astounding. With this new form of collaboration comes a host of legal challenges and risks.

§ 5.01 CROWD-SOURCED INFORMATION

Prior to 2000, researching a subject typically included a first investigation with a printed encyclopedia. As Internet usage increased, some of those encyclopedias made the transition to an online site in order to make accessing the content faster without any changes to how content was developed.

In 2001, Wikipedia was launched and fundamentally changed how we view encyclopedias. On paper, most doubted the venture could succeed. It was a website attempting to compete with encyclopedias by allowing anyone to contribute information to articles about any subject. Authors would not be vetted for expertise, the community would research and monitor articles themselves. And they would do it all for free. It seemed destined to fail.

Not only did Wikipedia succeed but it has transformed how encyclopedias are viewed. Since its launch in 2001 more than 23 million users have contributed to its success. As of 2017, there are over 280 editions of Wikipedia. The English edition alone has over 5.3 million articles. More than 800 articles are written each day and the entire site averages more than 10 edits every second.

Although Wikipedia is the most well-known crowd-sourced information site, the notion of turning to social media users in order to compile information goes well beyond an encyclopedia. Other sites turn to the crowd to develop solutions to problems or generate ideas to improve a business. In 2007, Dell became one of the first companies to launch a site, called IdeaStorm, that asked users to submit ideas for improving the company's products and services. Users could submit ideas and vote on ideas submitted by others. Dell then implemented ideas receiving the most community support. This site inspired other companies such as Starbucks to launch their own business-improvement sites utilizing the wisdom of the crowd.

A. ACCURACY

One of the largest criticisms to face crowd-sourced information is whether the resulting submissions are accurate. Inaccurate information in any publication arena can carry a number of risks for individuals making the inaccurate statements, for people who rely on the information, and for platforms that provide that information to others. The concept of having a website where anyone is free to edit published content seems fraught with the potential for information vandalism.

In 2005, *Nature* magazine attempted the first serious inquiry into the accuracy of Wikipedia articles. The magazine selected 42 scientific articles from both Wikipedia and the Encyclopedia Britannica, sent the articles to anonymous academic reviewers, and then tallied the number of minor and major mistakes identified in each article. The reviewers found an average of 4 errors for each Wikipedia article while Encyclopedia Britannica articles averaged 3 errors. A total of 4 serious errors was discovered across the entire article population for both Wikipedia and Encyclopedia Britannica. This led the magazine to conclude that Wikipedia comes close to Encyclopedia Britannica in terms of accuracy for its science articles. Other studies have attempted similar reviews in different areas and have found substantially the same.

Wikipedia has an active community of contributors and editors that strive to keep their articles accurate. However, every crowd-sourced information platform may have their own method for ensuring its accuracy or may abandon quality control altogether. While the concern over information accuracy is a valid one, it is worth noting that there are methods and platforms that have dealt effectively with the issue.

B. EDIT WARS

It has been said that history is written by the victors. It could also be said that Wikipedia articles are written by the last edit. While there does exist a thriving community of contributors and editors at Wikipedia, the democratic nature of crowd-sourced information can also lead to spirited debates over content, tone, and presentation on diverse topics. This can lead to edit wars, a series of back-and-forth changes to an article or topic where both sides attempt to gain control of an article.

Unlike mere vandalism of a crowd-sourced information article, which is usually fleeting and easily identified, edit wars are typically indications of a deeper disagreement over the topic at hand. Platforms, such as Wikipedia, may develop their own process for resolving the debate but it is an issue worth considering for those offering crowd-sourced platforms or relying on information from such platforms.

§ 5.02 CROWDFUNDING

One of social media's key strengths is its ability to align connections and their networks of connections around a single conversation. When that conversation turns to "Can you give me some money?" then hobbies can rise to a professional level, new products can be brought to market, companies can be launched, and charitable causes can be funded in minutes.

An estimated $2.7 billion was contributed on United States crowdfunding platforms in 2012. In 2013 that number rose to $5.1 billion. By 2015 over $17.2 billion had been collected via crowdfunding when including loans. Globally, in 2015 over $34 billion has been collected via crowdfunding sites with regions seeing as low as 50% annual growth or as high as 200% growth. Some of the largest crowdfunded projects to date include: a space simulation video game ($144 million); a cooler that includes an integrated blender, a recharger for portable electronics, and other features ($13.3 million); the Pebble smartwatch ($10.3 million for the first generation, $20.3 million for the second); a political action committee focused on changing campaign finance laws ($6 million); and a motion picture based on a fan-favorite TV mystery series ($5.7 million).

The rise of crowdfunding platforms not only demonstrates a powerful expression of social media's potential but it also increases the risk areas that should be considered by users of these platforms—both those attempting to raise funds and those contributing funds to the causes.

There are three types of crowdfunded ventures: perk-based crowdfunded ventures, equity-based crowdfunded businesses, and crowdfunded charitable causes.

A. PERK-BASED CROWDFUNDED VENTURES

Perk-based crowdfunded ventures have received the most attention thanks to platforms like Kickstarter and Indiegogo. Projects posted on these platforms can have a wide variety of purposes: funding an independent film, letting a band record an album, bringing a new kitchen gadget to the market, publishing a graphic novel, or creating a fashion line.

While the purposes behind each of these projects can vary widely, the common element among all perk-based crowdfunded ventures is that an individual who pledges money towards the project does so in exchange for some perk or reward. The project may specify that a pledge of $20 will result in a t-shirt, a $50 pledge may bring a poster, and a $100 pledge might bring a special collectible toy. Different levels of pledges may promise perks from physical objects to acknowledgements to a hug from the creator. Whatever the promised perk, this is what the individual shall receive if the project is fully funded.

Contributing to a perk-based crowdfunded venture is similar to placing an online order for the perk itself. Some users of crowdfunding platforms, however, can confuse contributing towards a perk-based project as granting them some ownership in the underlying company. When Oculus Rift, a virtual reality headset, appeared on Kickstarter it raised over $2.4 million. Less than two years later, the company was sold to Facebook for approximately $2 billion. Some contributors to the Kickstarter campaign falsely believed they were entitled to a portion of that amount.

B. EQUITY-BASED CROWDFUNDED BUSINESSES

Equity-based crowdfunded businesses do not exchange individual items for the money pledged by contributors. Instead, individuals who contribute funds will be given an ownership stake in the business. That ownership stake can differ depending on the project—from ownership of voting rights (similar to a stock purchase) to profit participation to full partnership including debt obligations.

The risks, and regulations, around equity-based crowdfunded businesses are enormous. Contributors to a perk-based crowdfunded project may mistakenly believe they are entitled to a piece of the project's success, contributors to an equity-based crowdfunded business may find themselves facing significant burdens of owning a business that finds itself in debt or legal trouble. While a business may pitch itself as a sure-fire success in the short term, the business could cease to exist in a matter of months leaving investors without recourse.

In 2012, Congress passed the Jumpstart Our Business Startups (JOBS) Act in an effort to relax current regulations around business fund raising. The law recognized that prior to social media, new businesses had few options in obtaining money: large financial institutions, wealth investors, and selling shares of the company. Banks and wealthy investors could give a new business millions of dollars, selling shares was the easiest way to involve a large number of people who could contribute less. However, selling shares in a business is a highly regulated affair for both the business and people who purchase shares on an open market.

The JOBS Act, specifically Section III of the Act, was designed to relax those standards so that companies could use crowdfunding to raise funds. Crowdfunding was seen as a way for a new company to engage a large audience—something that selling shares could do previously but generally needed an established business record to be done. The Securities and Exchange Commission (SEC), the government agency tasked with regulating sales of business shares and its markets, was tasked with developing new rules to allow common investors to invest in new companies via crowdfunding platforms. Those rules were finalized and posted in 2016.

Starting in May, 2016, companies are allowed to raise equity-backed funds via crowdfunding efforts. As should be expected, investing in a company this way comes with limitations on how much a company can raise and how much an individual can contribute based on their net worth and total investment portfolio. The SEC website and several platforms based around equity crowdfunding can provide more detail around this rapidly evolving space.

C. CROWDFUNDED CHARITABLE CAUSES

Charitable causes seeking to obtain money via crowdfunding can be broad, ongoing efforts to collect funds for multinational charity organizations or narrow attempts to raise funds for an individual's funeral expenses.

Risks around crowdfunded charity causes are similar to risks around off line charities. Charities face the risk of ensuring its money is used for charitable purposes if it is a registered, tax-exempt charity. Individuals may wish to investigate the charity of their choice to ensure it does what the individual believes it to do and that it is a legitimate charitable organization. Individuals should also be cautious of charity scams which may be easier to execute online than in person.

D. CROWDFUNDING MECHANICS AND RISKS

Different models exist for various crowdfunding efforts making it important for individuals and organizations attempting to raise funds to carefully check the terms for each platform before launching their campaign. Some platforms also offer multiple funding models making the sites more flexible but also potentially confusing for users.

1. Goal-Based Funding Mechanics

The most common crowdfunded effort involves a campaign that sets an overall financial goal within a given timeframe, typically two to four weeks. Individuals will pledge funds towards that goal and a tally is publicly posted. At the end of the posted time if the campaign has exceeded its goal then the money is collected from the pledges and distributed to the creator. However, if the goal is not met then no money will be collected from individual pledges.

The full amount of the moneys pledged are not passed on to the project creator. Platforms will deduct fees after the money is collected and prior to distributing the funds to the creator. Fees can range from 3% for registered non-profits to 9% or higher. Such fees taken by the platform will not include payment processing fees for individuals who contributed to the project using credit cards or certain online payment options such as Paypal. Those additional fees can take 2%–5% from those payments as well. Platforms can also charge fees for distributing the funds via wire transfer or other methods. Projects placed on crowdfunding platforms should take all fees into account when calculating the required amount to successfully complete the project.

One additional risk that some goal-based projects may not initially consider is the time it will take to process the perks promised to backers. Kickstarter and other platforms have learned to assist project creators in establishing limits for perks to help projects from getting out of control. Other platforms may lack this limiting ability or projects may continue to add perks as the project continues. Groups that are not used to fulfilling order requests may soon find themselves overwhelmed with ordering, handling, processing, and shipping the promised perks to their backers. Fulfilling those orders can take time or hiring a third party to handle the work can take more money out of the project's funds.

Goal-based funding not only provides a method of collecting enough money to complete a project prior to starting work, it also provides valuable market research to see if the project is viable in the long run. Traditional businesses began to pick up on this benefit with the Kickstarter campaign to fund a Veronica Mars movie. The movie was based on the TV show that had a passionate fan base but had struggled with TV ratings (the average ranking over its three year run was 143 out of 151 shows). The creator of the series, Rob Thomas, worked with the studio who owned the rights to the series and characters to launch the Kickstarter as both a way of funding the movie and testing its marketability. With a goal of $2 million set on the project, the Kickstarter was launched on March 13, 2013.

The project reached its goal in ten hours. By the end of the campaign over 90,000 fans had provided more than $5.7 million to fund the movie. With funding in hand and a still-passionate fan base, the movie was shot and released one year later.

a. When Projects Fail Post-Funding

There are many reasons why a project may fail after being funded for innocent reasons. Kickstarter and other crowdfunding platforms attract individuals who may lack experience in the area of their project, the project creator may fail to correctly appreciate the task they set out to accomplish or to deal with the obstacles they may face.

One Kickstarter project sought $25,000 to complete a video game called Haunts: The Manse Macabre. After collecting more than $28,000, the project worked towards completion. Then the project lost both of its programmers to other jobs and it was unable to find additional programmers. This was compounded by the work taking longer than expected after the exit of the first two programmers, leaving an unfinished game and no money left. The project creator communicated the bad news and refunded its backers. It still left many without their promised returns due to the project's failure.

In 2011, a Kickstarter project sought $15,000 to bring a new iPhone bumper-style case to market. The project collected over $85,000 by the time it was finished. When the cases started to ship backers realized that the case was interfering with their phone's signals. The company conducted multiple tests and confirmed the problem for some users but was unable to solve the problem for the current case. They explained to their backers that this can happen with young companies and went on to develop a new case for the next version of the iPhone.

b. Potentially Fraudulent Projects

Beyond the various reasons why a project could fail after receiving its funds there are also projects that were never intended to be completed. Several Kickstarter and other projects have been accused of being fraudulent scams to collect money and then disappear.

In 2011, a project appeared on Kickstarter called the Tech-Sync Power System. It promised a new technology that would allow customers to control their house's lights via mobile devices connected over WiFi. The initial units were priced at $20 and the project sought $2,000 to be fully funded. It quickly received that amount and the numbers continued to grow.

The project caught the attention of another Kickstarter user who had recently attempted to build a similar unit. He questioned the project's claims and pricing levels and others followed suit. As pledges to the project continued to grow, the creator of the project gave evasive answers and then posted that the project would be taken over by another individual. The creator then posted that he had been hacked and the project was not being transferred. The resulting drama proved too much for Kickstarter and the project was cancelled. Since it was cancelled, pledges were never collected and the project's backers were never charged.

Backers of the Tech-Sync Power System had an easier time than those that backed the Asylum card deck. The project sought $15,000 to print a customized deck of playing cards featuring blood spattered cards and crazed characters. The project received over $25,000 in pledges and was fully funded. Backers waited to receive their cards and other promised perks to no avail. Then the creator of the project stopped posting updates. Backers reported the project to Kickstarter. However, since the money had already been collected and distributed, there was nothing Kickstarter could do.

Eighteen months after the project was funded, the Attorney General of Washington filed the first consumer protection lawsuit based on a crowdfunded project in the United States. The lawsuit sought to collect over $25,000 collected by the project's creator from its 810 backers, at least 31 of which were Washington residents. Lawsuits like this, where a state agency takes over the legal actions, are the best case scenario for victims of these alleged fraudulent projects. As crowdfunding platforms excuse themselves of liability for all projects, the only legal recourse is for backers to go after the creator of the project—a difficult task when the backer and creator live in different states; and a difficult financial decision when the promised perk has a value of $25 and a lawsuit will cost much more.

Crowdfunding platforms do employ systems to identify potentially fraudulent projects, but it can be difficult to do so. Some may be easy to detect—such as when an individual copies all of the images, video, and text from a successful project on one platform and posts it on another as their own. Others are harder to detect when they promise technology or products previously unseen on the market. Are they scams or revolutionary inventions? The distinction may be impossible to tell during the time the project is seeking funds.

2. Ongoing Contributions

Several platforms or payment technologies allow an individual or organization to collect money on an ongoing basis. These long-term projects can take the form of a simple donate button on a website or using a crowdfunding platform to launch a constant campaign to raise funds.

This crowdfunding mechanism creates a simple way for projects to receive ongoing funding. They may lack the drive or call to action present with a goal-based project or a time-driven timeline, but for organizations that are constantly working toward goals that their community will support this can provide the greatest benefit over time.

3. Flexible-Goal Funding

A hybrid between goal-based funding and ongoing contributions, flexible-goal funding is initially set up like a goal-based project. It will have a stated goal and timeframe within which it intends to raise the money. However, unlike a traditional goal-based venture, if a flexible-goal project does not reach its goal the money will still be collected and distributed to the project creator. Such projects may incur higher fees from the crowdfunding platform but the creator does not face an all-or-nothing outcome from the venture.

Flexible-goal projects can create an even greater set of risks if perks have been promised. Perks may be calculated by the creator based on an overall successful project rather than partial funding. Creators with a flexible funding project may receive the pledged funds even if the overall goal was not met but they may be at a disadvantage due to perks that must be distributed.

4. Special Concerns for Microloans

One area of crowdfunding that has special concerns surrounds the popular use of crowdfunded charitable microloans. The most well known platform supporting these programs is Kiva, a platform that specializes in providing funds to organizations around the world who offer microloans—small amount loan—in countries where banking might not be easily accessible or to individuals who may not qualify for loans through traditional banks in their region. These loans may be used to launch a business, buy inventory for a local store, or help a farmer expand the land he can plant with money for seeds and tools.

Capital contributions for these loans are gathered by Kiva and distributed to partner organizations in the field. The partner organizations are then responsible for gathering repayments; interest from the loans goes back to the partner organization and the initial funds go back to Kiva users which can then be withdrawn from the platform or reinvested in another microloan. Kiva itself operates on grants and additional contributions made by members.

Kiva was launched in 2005 after a Bay Area couple was inspired by the work of Nobel peace prize winner Muhammad Yunus in the area of microcredit loans. The platform gained a national audience after being mentioned in former President Bill Clinton's book *Giving*, in 2007. As individuals flocked to the platform, they not only contributed to these loans but also formed groups that could communicate and coordinate their charitable efforts. Groups were created for contributors from specific cities, with common interests, or who all shared the same religion.

Early in Kiva's history, the platform had one specific microloan posted on the site for a carrot farmer. The loan came from a non-English speaking country so Kiva, as is its practice, relied on the local partner lender to provide the details of the loan and the individual receiving the loan. After posting the loan it was fully funded and the money distributed.

Unfortunately, the translation for the loan was lacking in accuracy. Rather than being a carrot farmer the loan recipient raised and slaughtered pigs for meat. This difference in crops may not have mattered to most contributors but a large portion of the loan had been funded by a Muslim religious group, a religion that forbids the consumption of pork. Kiva reached out to the group and worked through the issue but this loan showed that there are potential risks around accurately describing crowdfunded efforts even when the underlying purpose is charitable.

Kiva also faced controversy in 2008, when it was discovered that one of their partner organizations was offering a loan to a businesswoman in Peru. Sara Alva Vasquez Rodriguez sought $3,000 to purchase a freezer for her cockfighting business. Cockfighting, while illegal in the United States, is a legitimate business in Peru. The loan was funded in three days but the controversy began soon after that as individuals, some of whom had already contributed, then discovered the purpose of the loan.

In the face of the controversy, Kiva had a difficult decision to make. Although individuals providing the capital for the loans were located in the United States, the recipients were in other countries with their own legal and social norms. Cockfighting, banned in the US, is an accepted and established practice in Peru. Was it acceptable to allow loans for businesses that would not be allowed in the US but were fine in the host nation? If a loan for cockfighting was allowed, what about one for a dog fighting arena in a country where that was legal? What about the funds to start a drug-producing laboratory in a country where the drug was legal even if it was not in the US?

Kiva's response to the controversy was not to develop a bright-line test about what loans would or would not be acceptable to post on their site. But it now had an additional factor to consider internally as part of their screening process. The only concrete development to come out of the controversy was the start of a new Kiva group—Kivans Against Cockfighting Loans. As of the start of 2015, the group has participated in over 1,000 loans that do not involve animal fighting businesses.

§ 5.03 JUSTICE AND THE CROWD

Whenever a group is formed and a misdeed is denounced there will ultimately be calls for justice. The development of a justice system within any society is a rich area of history and study. Social media, being both a reflection of its members and a new community itself, has found itself in the center of many issues concerning existing justice systems and new forms of justice.

A. WHEN CROWDS GO WRONG

Communities that have formed via social media have been able to tackle significant problems. Groups have raised money for charity, reunited people separated by decades and thousands of miles, or solved significant computer programming challenges by all working together. There are many problems that are well suited for a large group of people throwing their collective efforts together to develop a solution. Finding bombing suspects is not one of those problems.

On April 15, 2013, two bombs exploded near the finish line of the Boston Marathon. Three people were killed and 264 others injured. The nation watched in horror at the terror that developed over the day and as details of the attacks became known.

Some online groups took it upon themselves to scour photos and videos in the area and find the bomber or bombers. Since the bombings took place at a sporting event finish line, thousands of photos taken by eager fans and supporters of runners were already online. The groups also found publicly viewed feeds from security cameras in local businesses and on the streets surrounding the marathon finish line.

The groups aligned on several individuals that they felt were suspicious. Some of these people were seen in one picture to have a bag only to be found in a later picture without a bag. To these groups, looking for a suspect, the absence of a bag signalled potentially leaving an explosive device. In reality, seeing people at a sporting event with a bag in one photo and not having a bag in another photo might instead indicate that they had simply placed their bag in a secure space (perhaps a bag with running gear, being a marathon).

Several of these groups aligned on two specific young men. They found photos of the young men with bags before the bombing and photos of the young men without bags after the bombing. Less than detailed analysis of the photos with the bags—analysis that consisted of drawing circles and arrows on the photo with a simple application—indicated that the bag could have been holding a bomb. Many captions on the photographs pointed out that the young men had brown skin. In fact, the majority of suspects identified by these amateur and completely unqualified groups had dark skin.

While critics pointed out the lack of forensic skill and less than subtle racism of the accusations, the cybersleuthing was picked up by mainstream media. The New York Post published one of the photos of these two young men on their front page the next day. One of the individuals turned himself in to Boston police—not because he had been involved in the bombing but because he feared being turned on by the public. This individual, it turned out, was a high school student who had run the marathon.

The two bombing suspects later identified by law enforcement agencies were not identified in any of the pictures posted by these online groups. A large collection of social media users, it turns out, are not a replacement for trained detectives.

B. WHEN CROWDS CAN HELP

Although crowds may not be helpful in replacing skilled investigators, social media can be used effectively in criminal investigations in two significant ways: collection of evidence and collaboration among trained professionals.

On June 14, 1994, the Vancouver Canucks lost the Stanley Cup finals to the New York Rangers. An estimated 70,000 people took part in a large riot following the loss. The riots resulted in over 200 injuries and $1 million in property damage.

Local police took advantage of the increasing use of security cameras to collect over 100 hours of video footage. They viewed the videos in an attempt to locate suspects. Watching and processing the 100 hours of footage took over four months to complete. Approximately 100 people were charged with crimes from the riot.

Fast forward to June 15, 2011, and another hockey-induced riot broke out in Vancouver. This time the Canucks had just lost the Stanley Cup finals to the Boston Bruins and the resulting riot was significantly larger than its 1994 counterpart. Over 150,000 people joined in the riots that caused over $5 million in damage.

Due to the explosion in social media usage, local authorities discovered that rioters had actually posted photos of themselves participating in the riots. They also knew that thousands of others had photos or videos of the events. The Vancouver police asked the public to send in any materials they had of the riots and residents responded in force: more than a million photographs and more than 1,200 hours of video were sent to authorities. This combined with footage the police were able to obtain from nearby security cameras for a total video collection of over 5,000 hours. Vancouver needed a better way to review all the materials than what they had employed in 1994. It would take them over 15 years to review the material at its previous pace. Social media had a way to help.

Vancouver authorities worked with the Law Enforcement and Emergency Services Video Association to develop a plan to review all the material. They ultimately formed a task force with more than 50 professionals across three countries to review and tag the material. The group was able to review more than a million photographs and 5,000 hours of footage in two weeks. During that time they tagged more than 15,000 criminal acts. Each act was included in a police database with video or photographic evidence and then attempts were made to match the acts to individuals.

As a result of social media's assistance in gathering evidence and professional collaboration in reviewing the evidence, more than 300 people were charged with crimes from the riots.

C. WHEN CROWDS CREATE NEW FORMS OF JUSTICE

Social media communities are not limited in their interplay with existing forms of justice. They can also create their own forms of justice when the current system leaves them without recourse. While the ethics of such action may be debated, the application of such novel justice is a phenomenon worth watching. One such example is the case of Jonathan Coulton.

Mr. Coulton is a musician who gained an Internet fan base with his one year project to record and release one new song a week between September, 2005 and 2006. During the 52-song project, he recorded only one cover song—a mandolin-and-banjo themed remake of the 1993 Sir Mix-a-Lot hit "Baby Got Back." All 52 of Mr. Coulton's songs were sold on CD and as digital downloads.

In January, 2013, Fox aired an episode of their musical drama Glee. The episode included a college group singing a mandolin-and-banjo themed remake of "Baby Got Back." The arrangement sounded eerily familiar to Mr. Coulton's fans and one such fan downloaded both Glee and Mr. Coulton's remake to compare them. This fan discovered that the two songs were musically identical—every note was the same. Even a sound effect of a duck quacking that Mr. Coulton had introduced remained in the Glee version. Glee had downloaded Mr. Coulton's version of the song and simply sung over it.

Unfortunately, Mr. Coulton was without a legal recourse for Glee's actions. Artists who record cover versions of previously recorded music have two options: seek a license from the original artist to create a derivative work or obtain a compulsory license under copyright law. While a derivative work license allows the new artist greater freedom in creating an original work that can later be protected, this path also comes with a significant limitation: the original author can say no. Compulsory licenses are provided by law and cannot be denied but they also leave the new artist with no protectible interest in the work.

Mr. Coulton had elected to obtain a compulsory license for his "Baby Got Back" and had no legal basis for challenging Glee's actions. Instead, he re-released his song digitally under the name "Baby Got Back (In the Style of Glee)" so that anyone searching for the Glee song will likely discover his version as well.

While Mr. Coulton may have lacked legal recourse, his fans took it upon themselves to hand out a new form of justice. Upon learning that Fox and Glee had not technically violated the law, Mr. Coulton's fans decided that Fox and Glee had still done something wrong. They decided to mete out their own form of social media justice by reviewing both songs online. In the days following Mr. Coulton's re-release, thousands of interested individuals reviewed both versions of the remake. The Glee song ended with a 1.5 star (out of 5) rating on the largest digital music store, iTunes. Mr. Coulton's version was rated 5 out of 5 stars. The comments on both versions also made clear what Mr. Coulton's fans thought of the situation. Social media allowed a new form of justice to take place when the legal system was lacking, an intriguing phenomenon to watch.

§ 5.04 VIRTUAL CURRENCY

The last few years have seen the creation and rise in popularity of virtual currencies such as bitcoin. These currencies differ from traditional currencies in that they are not backed by a government or bank and they are not technically currencies.

A. WHY VIRTUAL CURRENCIES WERE CREATED AND HOW THEY WORK

Transactions in an online world require an intermediary: some group that connects the buyer and the seller and promises both that a transaction has taken place. The most commonly used intermediary are credit card companies such as American Express or Visa. These companies were well-suited to adapt their earlier business model of being a transaction intermediary when the buyer and seller were in the same location to the newer model of governing a transaction when the parties are not together (a practice they had already begun when handling phone and mail transactions).

Handling these transactions does not come for free. Processing the different transactions carries risks of non-payment, risks of lost goods, and risks surrounding identity theft. To cover these expenses, credit card companies will typically charge 2.5% to 3% of the total transaction to the seller. Software developers thought there should be a way to utilize the power of the crowd to develop a solution that was more efficient.

The solution to this problem was first popularized by Bitcoin. The Bitcoin developers created a platform to verify transfers of currency via public broadcast on the Internet. Developers of this solution decided to use the confusing name of Bitcoin, with a capital B, to the underlying technology and network, while the currency itself is named bitcoin, with a lowercase b. Holders of bitcoins could utilize the Bitcoin solution to transfer the virtual currency from one party to another.

The chief benefit to users would be the price—Bitcoin was theorized to be operable while only deducting 1% of the transaction rather than 2.5% to 3%. If all online transactions in 2013 had utilized this new method that only charged 1%, it is estimated that nearly $12 billion in transaction fees could have been saved.

The Bitcoin network relies on two major components: individuals that use the network to transfer bitcoins and processors that verify the transfer of those bitcoins. Individuals would use software (called Wallets) to publicly declare that a specific bitcoin (or fraction of a bitcoin) was being transferred from the buyer to the seller. Computers participating in the process to verify the global list of bitcoin transactions (known as the Block Chain) would then attempt to verify the transfer by performing a complex series of calculations designed to create a unique verification result for groups of transactions. Such a system would bypass the existing credit card processors and also have the additional benefit of tracking every move made by every unit of currency.

Computers that process the Block Chain are rewarded for their verification efforts by receiving bitcoins in exchange for their work. These new bitcoins awarded to the processing systems serve not only as a financial incentive but also as a form of virtual mints controlling the introduction of new currency into the market. By keeping the introduction of new currency to a minimum the system attempted to limit the amount of currency and prevent inflation.

B. LEGAL RISKS AROUND VIRTUAL CURRENCIES

While a new form of online payment that could save buyers and sellers billions of dollars seems compelling in theory, in reality there are a number of risks around using this emerging technology. Some of these risks are unique to a virtual currency while others are a result of being a new type of currency lacking in sponsorship and experience to handle problems that nations and banks have learned to prevent.

1. Lack of Stability

The price for a single bitcoin has fluctuated wildly from its inception. For example, the price in November, 2013 for one bitcoin was just under $1,000, less than a month later the price was down to $640 and a few weeks after that it was up to $880. While this roller coaster of pricing can lead to windfalls and losses by bitcoin holders, it is difficult to establish a currency on such wild swings. Currencies require some form of stability—once they become unstable then its users will resort to other methods of payment. This is especially true for a virtual currency where nobody is required to use it and there are always other options available.

2. Lack of Protection

Yes, credit card companies charge a higher amount than the Bitcoin network does. With that extra amount comes extra features including protection. Credit card companies have sophisticated methods of detecting and preventing fraudulent use, something Bitcoin is completely lacking. Laws exist to protect consumers from fraudulent credit card charges, capping an individual's loss at $50 for lost or stolen cards. Bitcoin has no cap on individual loss. While Bitcoin does have superior tracking ability—if a bitcoin is stolen from you, you can find out exactly where it went—it has no ability to regain control of that bitcoin and return it to the rightful owner.

3. Commodities, Not Currency

Another risk involving the use of virtual currency is that most countries do not treat it as currency. Instead, the United States and several other countries treat bitcoin or other virtual currency as commodities. This lumps bitcoin into the same category as stocks and bonds. While that may be considered important for an investment portfolio, it may be unattractive as a method of payment for most transactions.

Consider a bitcoin purchased by a user for $200. A month later the price of bitcoin has risen to $500 so the user decides to buy a new computer for that amount. He buys the computer, paying with the bitcoin in his possession. Under U.S. law he has now realized a $300 gain on a commodity and will be taxed for the difference in value. This is an issue that consumers are not accustomed to facing when paying for a good with actual currency.

4. The 51% Attack

Processing transactions that will be added to the Block Chain is an intense computational problem that has multiple parties racing to complete the task to obtain the reward. In order to verify that the work is complete, other computers working on the Bitcoin network will check that the work is accurate before awarding the payment for the processing work.

This leaves the Bitcoin network vulnerable to the 51% attack. If any one person or group were able to control 51% of the computers working on the Block Chain they could effectively rewrite the rules for how Bitcoin works. The changes could be as subtle as to give a preference to processing work done by their own computers or as blatant as instantly transferring every bitcoin in existence to their own wallet. This kind of risk is unknown in the traditional currency world and could present a significant obstacle to adoption of either virtual currency or Bitcoin-like processing networks for actual currency unless it can be addressed.

CHAPTER 6

CONTENT, COPYRIGHT, LICENSE

Social media may be defined as online conversations but the only way to have a conversation online is through the ability to interact with content. With all of the content and conversations that the social media explosion has enabled, numerous legal concerns have arisen around the creation, posting, and sharing of content. These concerns have come under the treatment of content as speech as well as the application of copyright law to social media content.

§ 6.01 SPEECH AND SOCIAL MEDIA

A. FREEDOM OF SPEECH AND SOCIAL MEDIA ENGAGEMENT

The majority of social media content consists of content, original or otherwise, that can easily be understood as speech. The question of whether engagement with social media constitutes speech can be a complicated matter. Submitting a comment on a social media post is easier to classify as speech, but the issue of whether a simple interaction, such as a Like on Facebook, could be considered speech was an open question in the early days of social media.

The first case to call into question whether Liking a page constitutes speech was *Bland v. Roberts*.[1] Bobby Bland and five other former employees of the

---

[1] *Bland v. Roberts*, 730 F. 3d 368 (4th Cir. 2013).

Hampton, Virginia Sheriff's Department sued the Sheriff, B.J. Roberts for retaliation. One group of employees argued that the retaliation was based on an illegal attack on their free speech rights because they had all Liked the Sheriff's opponent's campaign Facebook page. At the summary judgment phase of the case, the Eastern District of Virginia held that merely Liking the Facebook page of the re-elected Sheriff's rival was not enough to constitute speech and dismissed the claim.

On appeal, the Fourth Circuit reversed the holding of the district court and found that Liking a Facebook page did constitute speech. Liking a page, it said, not only connected a Facebook user to the page itself but also sent a direct and indirect message to other Facebook users. Directly, a message could appear on other users' Facebook pages informing them that the original user had Liked the page in question. Indirectly, the user who Liked the page can now have their name and profile picture appear on the page as one of the individuals who had Liked the page.

Both of these communications, the court said, can communicate a message within the context of a political campaign. The fact that the messages could be conveyed with a single click by the user rather than having the user type out a longer, custom message, was of no constitutional significance. While the context can certainly matter, the court's definition of speech as applied to the most basic form of engagement establishes that any form of engagement should be considered speech for legal purposes.

B. RESTRICTIONS ON SPEECH IN SOCIAL MEDIA

Restrictions on social media speech can come from a variety of sources. If you are a publicly traded company, that restriction can even come from the SEC under the guise of advocating information accessible to everyone.

This issue first presented itself in June, 2012, when Reed Hastings, the CEO for Netflix, publicly posted on his Facebook page that his company had streamed more than 1 billion hours of content in a month for the first time. The posting was available to several hundred thousands of users following Mr. Hastings and the story appeared on technology news sites in minutes.

However, the manner by which Mr. Hastings posted the information drew concern from the SEC over its potential violations of Regulation FD. This regulation was ratified by the SEC in 2000 as a way of ensuring that everyone who trades stock would be on a level playing field when it came to material information. Prior to Regulation FD's adoption, stock brokerage firms or investment banks could receive information from publicly traded companies (typically in the form of an investment call or meeting that only certain traders were invited to attend) that private individuals would not receive until much later. This created an unequal playing field in a market where individuals were increasingly trading stocks on their own due to the rise in Internet-based stock trading.

Regulation FD attempted to level the field by requiring all material information to be disclosed to everyone at the same time. If the information was to be disclosed during a call, that call had to be open to everyone. If the information was to be disclosed online, it needed to be disclosed on the company's website or via press release. Unfortunately, the regulation could not predict the rise of social media and the fact that more people (including tech reporters) were following Mr. Hastings than were reading any corporate announcements on the Netflix website. Despite this information actually reaching the public so quickly, the SEC informed Netflix they were investigating the post.

In April, 2013, the SEC closed the investigation into the Netflix post without taking any action against Netflix. Although the SEC announced no formal rule changes, they did release a Report of the Investigation that included guidance for social media posts by publicly traded companies. That guidance suggested publicly traded companies could use social media channels to distribute material information but only after disclosing which social media channels they might use to disseminate the content. Publicly traded companies with active executives, or a presence on various social media platforms, should heed this advice and identify which channels investors should monitor for material content if they do not release the information via traditional means.

C. RIGHTS OF PUBLICITY RESTRICTIONS IN SOCIAL MEDIA

Rights of publicity are a set of state-granted rights that allow individuals to protect their name, image, and likeness in commercial endeavors. Generally considered a set of rights belonging to celebrities, due to their ability to charge for behaviors that others merely do for free, these rights can impact the social media activities of corporations or other organizations.

1. Rights of Publicity in General

Although there is no single federal law that grants rights of publicity, the dozens of states that have enacted laws protecting these rights all follow the same basic tenets of measuring a violation. The states can vary on what exactly is protected under these statutes, but at a minimum they all protect an individual's name, image, and likeness from commercial use that violates a three prong test.

First, to violate an individual's rights of publicity there must be material that is published or distributed. Second, a reasonable person must be able to view the material and believe the material represents the individual. Third, the material must either contain a representation made for commercial gain or the material must interfere with the individual's commercial use of their rights. For example, a celebrity that charges money to endorse products would have a claim against a rogue brand that ran an advertising campaign including a photograph of the celebrity along with text that states the celebrity endorses the product.

2. Social Media and Rights of Publicity

Social media has given brands and organizations the same abilities to engage or share content on their platforms but actions taken by brands and organizations can be interpreted very differently than the same action taken by an individual. If an individual publishes a letter to their favorite hip-hop star asking them to change their rap moniker, most people would interpret the letter as an amusing fan letter. If a major brand such as Taco Bell sends a letter to major newspapers where they ask rapper 50 Cent to change his name to 99 Cent in order to celebrate the restaurant chain's new value menu, people may think that the two parties were working together.

When Taco Bell sent this letter in 2008 it was quickly brought to 50 Cent's attention by friends who wondered why he was doing a promotion with Taco Bell. 50 Cent wondered the same and then sued Taco Bell for violating his rights of publicity. Taco Bell settled the claim for an undisclosed sum.

Brands and organizations must be careful involving celebrities in their commercial efforts even if indirectly. While Taco Bell may have felt they could make a public inquiry to a celebrity without prior approval, rights of publicity are violated in the eye of the third party beholder. If the public sees this kind of inquiry as proof of the two sides working together a lawsuit may result. Just as Taco Bell faced legal risk over their published letter, the same could hold true for a brand or organization that posts social media content involving celebrities without that celebrity's approval.

Given the ease with which material can be shared and the ability for celebrities to tie their personal brands with commercial brands for profit, there is a wide range of activities that could be alleged to infringe upon an individual's right of publicity. When Katherine Heigl was photographed leaving a Duane Reed pharmacy the photograph appeared on a number of celebrity news sites without incident. However, when Duane Reed itself sent the photograph from its Twitter account, Ms. Heigl demanded the photograph be removed because that particular dissemination made it appear as though she had a commercial relationship with the store chain. Merely changing the source of the communication can change the perceived relationship, an issue with celebrities that brands should be aware of on social media.

3. Truth Is Not a Defense

One interesting note to rights of publicity that applies to social media is that truth is not a defense to rights of publicity claims. In 2002, Tony Trujillo was named Thrasher magazine's Skater of the Year. The award was presented to him at a lavish party in Las Vegas hosted by the publication and Vans, a shoe and clothing company popular among skateboarders. Nikki Sixx, co-founder and bass player of Motley

Crüe, was hired to attend the ceremony and present Mr. Trujillo with his award.

Vans took a photo during the event of Mr. Sixx presenting Mr. Trujillo his award and turned it into an advertisement. The ad was put in Thrasher magazine and turned into a poster for in-store displays at Vans retail locations. Although the ad did not mention Mr. Sixx by name, he was easily identified in the photograph. The advertisement was for a line of Vans shoes and the content of the ad congratulated Mr. Trujillo for his award while encouraging readers to check out Mr. Trujillo's line of Vans shoes (Vans was a sponsor of and partner with Mr. Trujillo).

At the time the ad was published, Mr. Sixx had his own line of clothing that he believed competed with Vans. Upset over his inclusion in an ad for a competitive product, Mr. Sixx sued Thrasher and Vans for violating his rights of publicity. A jury awarded him $600,000 plus attorney's fees. The fact that the photograph in the ad was an unmodified, truthful depiction of an event Mr. Sixx attended was irrelevant to the rights of publicity violation.

It may be very tempting for a brand or organization to see social media content that includes a celebrity using their product or at an event for their organization and want to share that content like other social media users. Doing so from a corporate account, however, carries the risk of making the content look like an advertisement which might violate the celebrity's rights of publicity.

§ 6.02 COPYRIGHT

Copyright law in the United States has its origin in the Constitution. Article I, Section 8, Clause 8 of the founding document grants Congress the right "To promote the Progress of Science and useful Arts, by securing for limited Times to Authors and Inventors the exclusive Right to their respective Writings and Discoveries." This lofty goal and powerful ability has been applied to increasingly complex forms of content over the centuries.

The foundation of all social media platforms is content. While functionality for the posting, sharing, and engaging with content is necessary for a site to exist, the true measure of its success will be based on how users post and create content on the site. The application of copyright law to this body of work can be a simple matter of applying old rules or formulating new applications of established laws to new technologies.

A. APPLICATION TO SOCIAL MEDIA

Copyright law concerns itself with the restriction of rights surrounding creative works. Because social media is a technology that facilitates conversations the results of its application is a wealth of content. Social media users post text messages, photographs, videos, drawings, posters, animations, and a host of other forms of content. All of this content can be creative and, therefore, covered by copyright law to various degrees.

The question of whether original content posted to social media may be covered by copyright depends entirely on the content itself. Copyright law concerns itself with original creative expressions that are fixed in a tangible medium. Entering content into a computer, whether posting on a website or typing into a computer, can fix the content for the purposes of copyright so long as that information is stored. Since social media platforms store content for display or distribution, social media content is considered fixed for purposes of copyright law.

The question of originality and creativity can be harder to ascertain for social media content. A photograph or movie made by an individual will likely be both original and creative—its publication on social media versus display in a gallery or theater does not matter. Text posted to social media, however, can also be protected by copyright although the application may be more complicated. Length may be a primary concern. A lengthy text posting along the lines of an essay or short story is easier to identify as containing creative expression and worthy of copyright protection. Facebook, as of 2014, allows users to post text updates up to 63,206 characters—more than enough to contain the length of several famous short stories.

Twitter, however, allows only 140 characters to be posted at a time. While it is entirely possible to post original, creative content within that space—an urban legend says that Ernest Hemingway famously drafted a six word short story that contained only 33 characters—it is also possible that a short text post may contain content that copyright law will not protect.

B. FACTORS IN DETERMINING COPYRIGHT APPLICATION

The law stops short of setting a firm line on what is or is not creative content. Over centuries of application, however, a number of factors have emerged that courts may use in determining whether content should be considered original and creative and therefore worthy of copyright protections.

1. Expressions Are Protected, Ideas Are Not

One of the most fundamental tenets of copyright law is that an expression will be protected while a basic idea will not. An author that writes a novel about a man shipwrecked on a deserted tropical island will be able to assert copyright protection for the creative aspects of his works but not the core idea of it. Another author is free to write their own book about a man shipwrecked on a deserted tropical island. The second author is not, however, free to merely copy the work of the first author simply because the core idea is not protected.

What constitutes expressive elements of a copyrighted work can be difficult to pin down. The entirety of a work is almost certainly a protectable expression. However, the expressive elements could also extend beneath the entire work—the selection of creative elements could also be a creative expression depending on their selection and presentation.

A man shipwrecked on a deserted tropical island will likely concern himself with establishing a shelter, a source of water, and food so that he may survive. Books about deserted tropical island dwellers that begin with these pursuits are unlikely to infringe on another's creative elements. These are ideas rather than expressions. However, if Book A contains a series of several dozen specific events around these pursuits and then Book B copies every one of these events, Book B may be liable for copying the expressions of Book A. This would be true even if Book B used different words to describe the same events. The distinction of idea versus expression is a wide spectrum of content that may be difficult to accurately place content upon.

Social media posts, like any form of content, may contain ideas and expressions. An individual sending a tweet "This Starbucks has a really long line." is unlikely to have created something original or creative worthy of copyright protection. The Twitter user standing behind him who tweets "The sleep-deprived snake, groggily seeking caffeine, creeps slowly towards its coffee prey" may have something more likely to be protected by copyright.

2. Facts Not Protected

Copyright law does not protect the publication of facts. Social media posts that merely contain facts will unlikely gain the protection of copyright law. However, the longer the collection of facts the more likely that a thin protection of copyright may apply to the organization or presentation of those facts.

Further, other creative elements may enter the compilation that are worthy of protection.

For example, while individual recipes cannot be copyrights as they are a process rather than a creative expression, a cookbook could still be copied as to its selection, arrangement, and presentation of those recipes. These limited creative expressions tend to only present themselves in longer compilations of unprotected elements. As a result, it is possible for a lengthy social media post consisting entirely of facts to gain some protection.

3. Length May Not Be a Factor but Indicative of Others

There is no length requirement for an original, creative work. The shorter the work the harder it may be to prove it is original, creative, or even an expression of some sort. An essay may be copyrighted, the individual letters composing the essay may not. Somewhere in between is enough expression and creativity to be protected.

While this element has long been considered in copyright law, social media platform limitations provide a true test of the factor's importance. As of 2014, 200 billion tweets are sent every year. While many are lacking in creativity or originality, it is also possible that within the 200 billion tweets are some original creative works worth of copyright protection.

The U.S. Copyright Office has long explained that names, titles, and short phrases cannot be copyrighted. However, the difference between a short phrase and a copyrightable statement has never been defined with certainty. Instead, two potential applications to short-form social media posts may provide a legal theory of copyright application.

a. Short-Form Social Media Posts as Protected Epigrams

Ashleigh Brilliant has made a career of publishing short creative works. Although he has stated that he limits himself to 17 words for his creative expressions, he has been known to extend himself to the rare 18 or 19 word phrasing. In the 1970s, while Mr. Brilliant sold his works in various formats, a company copied several of his phrases and sold them on t-shirts. In the resulting lawsuit, Mr. Brilliant succeeded in asserting a copyright claim on his short phrases as the courts held that his works were epigrams rather than short phrases. As epigrams, the works could therefore be protected by copyright law and the t-shirt company could not continue to copy Mr. Brilliant's works.

An epigram is defined as a pithy saying that expresses an idea in a clever and amusing way. Although the court did not spell out ways of distinguishing between a short phrase and an epigram, the possibility exists for courts to take this route in granting protection to short-form social media posts.

b. Short-Form Social Media Posts as Protected Jokes

Another type of short-form content that could be readily compared to tweets are jokes. In 1995, comedian Jeff Foxworthy successfully obtained a preliminary injunction against a t-shirt company for selling shirts that contained versions of his "You might be a redneck if. . ." jokes. Although the majority of the lawsuit focused on Mr. Foxworthy's trademark claims, the copyright protection of the individual jokes was an issue addressed by the Northern District of Georgia. They held that the particular wording and structure were enough to prove that the individual jokes were not just the comedian's idea but also his expression and worthy of copyright protection. Such a ruling could have applicability in the social media space where jokes are posted on a regular basis.

C. SOCIAL MEDIA ACCOUNTS AS COMPILATIONS

Regardless of whether any individual post made by a user on a social media platform could be protected by copyright there is also a tenable theory that the entirety of an individual's social media account on any given platform could be protected by copyright law as a compilation. Even if the individual only posted facts they found interesting or links to articles they Liked, the selection and presentation of such a list could result in some degree of protection as a copyrighted work.

D. OWNERSHIP OF COPYRIGHT

Social media platforms make it clear that they do not own content posted to their sites. They do so for two primary reasons: to not scare off potential users concerned about content ownership and to escape any liability that comes with owning posted content. To the extent that any content posted to social media is protected by copyright law, those protections belong exclusively to the individual user who posted the content. This can create tension, however, in that social media platforms have the ability to remove (and possibly destroy) original creative works protected by copyright that have been posted onto its platform.

This relationship between platforms and users creates a complicated and undefined relationship between the two parties. The user retains all rights to the work while the platform has physical possession of the work. While users are not typically limited in their ability to post the content to other sites or keep copies for themselves, sites have invited users to post original creative works which may have value. Does this invitation create a special relationship between the platform and the user beyond the platform's terms and conditions? Two potential theories may apply to this relationship that could serve to expand the relationship between social media platforms and their users, an expansion that could be important to consider within the context of a platform's ability to remove or destroy content.

1. Social Media Platforms as Agents

Agency relationships are generally created when a principal entrusts an agent with certain rights belonging to the principal. The agent then acts on the principal's behalf. Although this relationship is not explicitly created through the acceptance of most social media platform terms of use or service, agency law does not require an explicit discussion of the relationship for an agent relationship to form.

Social media platforms are granted specific rights by their users and entrusted to use those rights within the boundaries of the platform. At the same time, the platform is careful to not own any of the content or rights, they merely take a license for certain purposes. Although untested, this may create an agent-principal relationship between platform and user for the purposes of social media content.

Agents owe their principals both specific duties around authorized activities and also general fiduciary duties. Could those fiduciary duties confer additional limitations on a social media platform? If a user has chosen to type a screenplay into their Facebook status and not save a copy anywhere else, does Facebook have a special relationship to ensure that content is not destroyed or deleted? Although this potential theory is untested, the reservation of rights by social media platforms could create unintended consequences for the platforms in the future.

2. Social Media Content as Graffiti

Another potential theory in analyzing the relationship between platforms and users is to consider posted content as graffiti. Graffiti, like content posted to social media, may be original and creative and deemed protected by copyright. Also, it could be content that copyright law will not protect for a variety of reasons. To the extent that content is protected there is still the question of control and ownership.

While the treatment of graffiti under copyright law has a mixed history, owing in no small part to the questionable legality of several pieces' creation, there is an intriguing comparison with social media posts. At one point, Facebook even called their user profiles Walls. Facebook allowed users to write on each other's Walls even though Facebook ultimately controlled all those Walls and could destroy them at a moment's notice. Are social media platforms merely large collections of walls that have invited the public to paint all they want but they can still destroy, move, or sell those walls as they wish?

With the rise of popular street artists such as Banksy, the question remains open and intriguing. Banksy has painted several murals on walls belonging to private owners. The owners have then sold the walls as works of art or painted over the walls. Whether the owners have infringed on Banksy's rights or Banksy has retained the rights to his works contained on another's property remains an untested issue. Other lawsuits have emerged over the protection and copyrightability of graffiti in recent years but have not yet established a clear standard. Social media posts may well follow or build upon this theory.

E. DIGITAL ESTATES

Since individuals own their social media posts and the overall account which houses them, the collection of social media activity could reasonably be construed to be part of that individual's estate at the end of their life. Just as a poet's body of work becomes part of their estate after their death, so too could the social media accounts belonging to any individual user. Does this impose a special set of restrictions upon a social media platform to handle content differently if it belongs to a deceased user?

Several social media platforms already have processes in place to handle a user's account after death. Platforms may freeze the account so no additional activity may take place, it may put the account into a special memorialized status to enable their friends to post messages but otherwise not have the account remain active, or it may disable the account completely.

While a handful of states have passed legislation that allow certain fiduciaries to access the digital accounts of deceased individuals, the vast majority of states have not passed any laws on the subject. The National Conference of Commissioners on Uniform State Laws has worked on a Fiduciary Access to Digital Assets Act which may be adopted by states looking to protect these interests. For now, the question of whether a deceased individual's digital account may be accessed depends on the decedent's state of residence and any existing policies of the social media platforms. Additionally, social media platforms such as Facebook have begun to include functionality that allows users to designate what happens to their account when they pass away. But even those tools carve out areas of content that can only be addressed by the legal system.

F. COPYRIGHT LIABILITY OF SOCIAL MEDIA PROVIDERS

As broad platforms that allow users to post content, social media providers can become the host of various pieces of content that infringe copyrights. Users may upload original sound files, photographs, or videos but they can easily exceed their authority and share a song by the Beatles, a photograph by Ansel Adams, or the movie Star Wars. Providers must therefore be careful to avail themselves of statutory safe harbors to prevent the platform from becoming the potential subject of a copyright infringement lawsuit thousands, if not millions, of times a day.

In the United States the Digital Millennium Copyright Act (DMCA) provides a safe harbor from copyright infringement lawsuits to any online service provider if certain requirements are met.

1. Requirements for DMCA Safe Harbor

There are two main requirements for a provider to fall within the DMCA safe harbor: first, it must adopt a process that allows the content to be removed and terminate accounts of repeat offenders; and second, it must not interfere with copyright owners' abilities to monitor protected works.

a. Copyright Infringement Policies

Section 512 of the U.S. Copyright Act lays out the requirements for a provider's copyright infringement policy if it wishes to fall within the safe harbor provision.

There are no specific requirements for two categories of mostly automatic network activity. The first category is the transmission, routing, and providing connections that transmits information through the provider's network that is intermediate and transitory. If User A is transmitting information to User G and part of that transmission involves the information temporarily being routed through Providers B, C, D, E, and F, there is no need for those five providers to adopt any special process to fall within the safe harbor for infringing information.

The second category of automatic safe harbor protection covers the caching of information. Caching is a computer network process where often-requested content is copied and distributed to multiple locations in order to transmit the content to individual users in a faster and more efficient manner. If that information happens to violate copyright protections then the act of caching it will not give rise to multiple acts of infringement.

The third safe harbor category is the one most social media providers attempt to utilize. It covers any service where a user can store information. Any post on a social media platform is stored on the platform's servers making this the most relevant safe harbor category. For a social media provider to fall within this safe harbor it must:

- Not actually know the material is infringing;
- Not be aware of information which makes it apparent that the content is infringing;
- Once informed that the content infringes copyright protection, the provider must act expeditiously to remove the material;
- While possessing the right and ability to control the material, the provider must not receive financial benefits directly attributable to the infringement content; and
- Comply with the DMCA notice and takedown provisions.

The DMCA notice and takedown provisions require the platform to establish a process that allows copyright owners to request the takedown of infringing material.

A platform complying with these steps and implementing a takedown process cannot be held liable for monetary damages relating to the infringing material. This provides a powerful incentive for platform providers to err on the side of taking down any content flagged as infringing or for which it receives a takedown request. Platforms that automatically take down all such content are protected from expensive copyright infringement actions even if the process is abused—since platforms are not required to post content sent by its users there is only tenuous damage scenarios that exist for a platform taking down content that does not infringe copyright.

An often overlooked aspect of the takedown process is the statutory requirement for repeat violators to be noted and their accounts disabled. It is not enough for social media platforms to simply respond to takedown requests—they must also track the user that posted the content and, if the user continues to post infringing material, the provider must have a way of adjudicating or removing the user from its service. Failing to track repeat offenders or deal with them accordingly can render the rest of the platform's process ineffective at gaining safe harbor protections.

b. Non-Interference with Copyright Owners' Monitoring

Copyright owners may avail themselves of technology to digitally mark a file in order to indicate their ownership or origin. These marks, often called watermarks, may be undetectable to individual users but can be easily seen by computers. In audio files, small changes to the audio file that cannot be detected by human ears can allow for information to be encoded to show ownership. On pictures or movies, information can be hidden within frames or even in the data between frames to identify the owner. Watermarks can also be visible or detectable by the end user in the form of visually displayed information or spoken audio cues.

For a social media provider to avail itself of the DMCA safe harbor they must not adopt or enable technologies that strip out this watermarking information.

G. COPYRIGHT LIABILITY OF SOCIAL MEDIA USERS

Social media users post billions of pieces of content every day. From text messages to photos to videos to sound files, the content floods the Internet on a constant basis. While much of that content may be original and some of it may also be protectable under copyright laws, some of that content may already be protected under copyright laws and owned by someone else. Social media users may unwittingly share protected material by spreading stories, articles, photographs, or videos that belong to someone else.

Social media platforms generally require users to only post content that they are authorized to post. While the terms may explain this requirement in detail, many times the terms do not provide clarifying language to inform users that the content must either be original or the user must have the authority to post the content. If a user posts material that is owned by someone else the user puts themselves at risk of a copyright infringement lawsuit and possibly indemnifying the platform for any legal action it may face as well.

1. Defenses

A social media user could be liable for copyright infringement whether filed directly or through indemnification of the host platform. Should an infringement action begin, a social media user may avail themselves of several defenses to the claim.

a. Fair Use

By far the most widely known, yet less widely understood defense, to copyright infringement is Fair Use. Fair Use is a valid copyright infringement defense but it can be difficult and costly to ascertain whether the defense applies to any individual infringement. Moreover, the Ninth Circuit has clarified that while Fair Use has traditionally been treated as a defense to copyright infringement, it is, in fact, an action that precludes infringement from taking place. Rather than assuming a copyright violation has taken place and then applying the Fair Use test, instead Fair Use should be looked at prior to making a determination of copyright infringement. Given the complexity in applying the Fair Use test, the practical impact of when the test is applied is unclear. However, content platforms, such as YouTube, have been encouraged to have complainants consider whether an alleged infringement is Fair Use before letting the platform know if a violation has occurred.

b. The Four Factors of Fair Use

i. Purpose and Character

The first factor in determining a Fair Use defense is the purpose and character of the infringing use. The more transformative the use, the greater the likelihood that this factor will point towards a Fair Use determination. The more derivative the use, the less likely a Fair Use determination will be made.

Generally speaking, a use may be considered transformative if it advances the arts or somehow contributes to an artistic endeavour in a way the original material does not—a difficult determination for artists to make let alone a court. Many courts have looked at the purpose and character of the use to see if it merely replaces the original objects in commerce to help profit the infringer rather than providing new artistic content.

ii. Parody Versus Satire

Although not one of the four fair use factors, one frequent subject of transformative use is parody. While parody is considered one of the transformations Fair Use protects, determining what is parody can be complicated. The distinction between parody and satire, however, is often missed by content creators. Parodies will transform the original work to ridicule or criticize the original work while satire will modify original work to ridicule or criticize a different topic. The distinction is crucial as parody may obtain Fair Use protection while satire will not.

For example, the Supreme Court evaluated whether the 2 Live Crew song "Pretty Woman" could be considered a parody of Roy Orbison's "Oh, Pretty Woman" and found that it could. While the 2 Live Crew version was an infringement of the original's copyright, the subsequent version also ridiculed the lecherous nature of the original singer by creating even stronger sexual lyrics. The infringing work in this case was directly addressing the original work, an element that could render the infringing work a defensible parody.

By contrast, the Ninth Circuit found that the book "The Cat NOT in the Hat! A Parody by Dr. Juice" was not a parody despite the title's suggestion. The book was a comic retelling of the O.J. Simpson murder trial told in the style of Dr. Seuss's The Cat in the Hat. The infringing elements in this case, taking the style, tone, and meter from the beloved childrens book, were not used to ridicule or criticize Dr. Seuss or The Cat in the Hat. Rather, the sole target of the humor was the infamous murder trial, rendering the book a satire rather than a defensible parody.

iii. Nature of the Copyrighted Work

The second factor in a Fair Use determination focuses on the nature of the original protected work. The closer the original work is to the core of protected material, the more work that the infringing material will need to do to somehow transform the new material into Fair Use. Modifying a motion picture or song, for example, will involve more effort than modifying something protected by copyright as a mere compilation of facts or less creative work such as a bare news broadcast.

iv. Amount and Substantiality

The third factor looks at the amount and substantiality of the original work taken by the infringing work. Although this factor is certainly important for transformations involving criticism or reporting, it can be less important in other transformations such as parodies where using the heart of the original work may be required in order for the new work to exist.

v. Effect upon Potential Market

The final factor in a Fair Use determination is what effect the infringing work may have upon the potential market for the original work. An infringing movie sequel, for instance, could certainly be transformative compared to the original but would also have a direct impact upon the potential market for the original to license the rights necessary for someone to make an authorized sequel. While copyright law is concerned with advancing the arts, it is also concerned with protecting the value of the original author. The conflict between the two in a content-driven economy can make for a difficult collision in the Fair Use test.

c. The Lack of a Clear Fair Use Test

The four factors used in determining Fair Use are not given equal weight. In fact, no specific weight is given to any of the factors. A court cannot simply tally which factors fall on the side of the original creator and which ones benefit the infringer. The factors are meant to be a detailed look at how the new work advances the arts and impacts the original. As a result, the application of the Fair Use test is difficult and complicated.

This makes the practical application of Fair Use to social media content problematic. While an infringer may truly believe they fall within the Fair Use doctrine, there is no simple way for determining this outside of a copyright infringement lawsuit. Social media platforms are under additional restraints as safe harbor defenses encourage platforms to take down any alleged infringed content without doing any substantive analysis of the infringing work. Even if a platform had the resources to perform such analysis, it is less inclined to do so for fear of falsely finding the alleged work is a Fair Use.

Social media users, however, face multiple erroneous sources claiming that infringing works will be considered Fair Use if it copies only a certain amount of the original work. Some sources will claim that users are free to copy 150 words from a novel, for example, or that they can safely copy 30 seconds of video from a protected film. No such bright line limits exist and, in fact, directly contradict what many courts have found to be important in determining the nature and substantiality factor. However, the misperception that an objective amount of copyrighted material may be freely copied is rampant among social media users.

2. De Minimis

Another potential defense to copyright infringement is if the copying was de minimis, or so trivial that a court will not find the copying to be an infringement. Unfortunately for social media users and platforms, there is no clear standard on what constitutes de minimis copying. Courts have found a computer program where less than 30 lines of code out of half a million lines of code was not insubstantial, or that the inclusion of a recognizable art poster for less than 30 seconds of a television program was also not de minimis copying. While the potential exists for a trivial copying of protected material, it is a difficult defense to establish along the lines of Fair Use.

3. Waiver

One potential copyright infringement defense that has seen less success in social media applications is the idea that content creators have waived their copyright protections by publicly posting their materials onto social media. Although content creators have the right to waive their copyright protections, and many may choose to do so by adopting certain versions of a Creative Commons License, the mere act of posting content on a social media platform does not waive any statutory or common law copyrights.

CHAPTER 7

PRIVACY

§ 7.01 INTRODUCTION

As individuals place more and more information about themselves online, there is increasing concern about safeguarding user content from social media providers and outside third parties. This chapter will explore the privacy protections currently available to those who use social media. This discussion will occur in two parts.

Section 7.02 explores the various privacy protections that work to limit how social media providers access and use information from their users. This section will start with an analysis of several statutes that protect user information from social media providers. This will be followed by a discussion of the privacy policies of social media providers. The section concludes with an examination of the major privacy litigation brought by both the Federal Trade Commission (FTC) and private individuals against social media providers for violating user privacy.

Section 7.03, which examines privacy safeguards directed at third parties, is divided into two sections. The first part of Section 7.03 will look at non-state actors; however, employers will not be covered as they are discussed in depth in Chapter 6. The focus here will be on relevant case law and recently enacted statutes like the Privacy Rights for California Minors in the Digital World.

The second part of Section 7.03 will examine state actors and the constitutional issues that arise when governmental entities or officials violate a social media user's privacy. This part will be limited to issues that arise in the civil arena. For a discussion about the constitutional issues that arise in the criminal context, see Chapter 9.

§ 7.02 SAFEGUARDING CONTENT FROM SOCIAL MEDIA PROVIDERS

A. STATUTES

The user's first layer of privacy protection against social media providers are federal and state laws. At present, there are no federal laws specifically dedicated to the protection of privacy rights on social media. However, there is an irregular patchwork of federal laws that safeguard specific types of personal information in any context to include social media. One such statute that was created prior to the tremendous growth in social media but has nonetheless proved successful in protecting the privacy of young social media users is the Children's Online Privacy Protection Act (COPPA).[1]

The impetus for COPPA, first passed in 1998, was to give parents some control of the information that their children under the age of 13 shared online. To accomplish this goal, COPPA requires companies that operate websites and online services, including social media providers, to notify parents directly and

---

[1] 15 U.S.C. § 6502(b)(1)(A)(1).

obtain their approval before they collect, use, or disclose a child's personal information. The type of personal information collected about children that triggers COPPA includes:

first or last name of the child

physical or email address of the child

telephone number of the child

social security number of the child

geolocation information about the child

photos or videos containing the child's image

audio files with a child's voice

screen or user names of the child

persistent identifiers of the child

COPPA also requires social media providers to post a clear, understandable privacy policy; maintain the confidentiality and security of the information collected; keep information only for a limited purpose; and give parents the ability to prevent the social media provider from collecting additional information.

In order for COPPA to apply, the social media platform must either be directed towards children under 13 or the platform must have knowledge that it is collecting personal information from children under 13. In certain instances, a social media provider may also find itself subject to COPPA requirements through the actions of a third party e.g., a plug-in or ad network on the social media platform collects personal information from children under 13.

United States v. Godwin illustrates how COPPA has been enforced against social media providers.[2] Here, the FTC charged Jones Godwin, who operated Skid-e-Kids, with violating COPPA by collecting personal information from children without first obtaining parental consent. The FTC also claimed that Godwin made deceptive claims in Skid-e-Kids' privacy policy.

According to the FTC Complaint against Skid-e-Kids, the company, which billed itself as "Facebook and Myspace for kids," permitted children under 13 to register their birth date, gender, username, password, and email without requesting a parent's email address. Once registered, children were able to create an online profile and share photos, videos, and make friends. The actions taken by the children were in direct contrast to the privacy policy on the Skid-e-Kids' website, which indicated that parents would be contacted prior to activation of their child's account.

Due to the nature of Skid-e-Kids' COPPA violations, the FTC imposed a $100,000 penalty on Godwin in his individual capacity rather than on Skid-e-Kids. Fortunately for Godwin, all but $1,000 of the penalty could be suspended if he provided truthful information about his financial condition and complied with the oversight provisions in the FTC's Consent Decree which included either

---

[2] *United States v. Godwin*, Case No. 11–CV–03846–JOF, FTC File No. 1123033 (N.D. Ga. Nov. 8, 2011).

retaining an online privacy professional or joining an FTC-approved safe harbor program. Skid-e-Kids was also prohibited from any future violations of COPPA and misrepresenting how information about children is collected and used.

In ensuring compliance with COPPA, social media providers must also be cognizant of the activities of third parties who use their site. While the FTC has yet to take action against a social media provider for the activities of third parties, it has gone after other types of websites. *United States v. Retro Dreamer* illustrates how a website provider may violate COPPA through the actions of a third party.[3] In this case, the defendant, Retro Dreamer, offered a number of mobile apps for download to include Ice Cream Jump, Happy Pudding Jump, Ice Cream Drop, Sneezies, Wash the Dishes, Cat Basket and Tappy Pop. These apps, which send and receive information over the Internet, were directed towards children. Some of the defendant's apps were free to download, while others cost money. The defendant generated revenue through the sale of certain apps, in-app advertising, and in-app purchases.

Problems arose for the defendant when it allowed third-party advertising networks to collect personal information in the form of "persistent identifiers" from users of the apps some of whom were under the age of 13. The FTC defines "persistent identifiers" as "pieces of data that are tied to a particular user or device." The defendant apparently allowed collection

---

[3] *United States v. Retro Dreamer*, Case No. 5:15–cv–2569 (Dec. 17, 2015).

of information to occur without first providing notice or obtaining parental consent from the app users many of whom were under the age of 13. In the Complaint, the FTC noted that defendant was actually forewarned about a possible COPPA violation by one advertising network which informed the defendant that some of their apps appeared to target children under 13. Ultimately, the defendant received a $300,000 civil penalty and was told to delete any information collected from children under 13.

Many social media providers attempt to comply with COPPA by restricting access to those under 13. This age restriction is often found in the terms of use employed by the social media provider. Some providers even go so far as to require users to verify that they are 13 and older. Nonetheless, these restrictions have not stopped a large number of children under the age of 13 from accessing certain social media sites.

Other preventive measures taken by social media providers to avoid running afoul of COPPA is participation in a safe harbor program. Those in an approved COPPA safe harbor program are first subject to the disciplinary procedures of the program rather than FTC enforcement, which, generally speaking, involves more severe penalties. Finally, some social media providers execute agreements with their ad networks and other third parties affirming that information covered by COPPA is not being collected by third parties.

B. PRIVACY POLICIES

The second layer of protection for users comes from the privacy policy of the social media platform itself. Privacy policies may be distinguished from terms of use in that the latter generally set forth more broadly the rules for a user's interaction with the social media provider's site. Also, contract law is generally applied to terms of use but not necessarily to privacy policies. It should be noted, however, that some social media providers incorporate their privacy policy in their terms of use. For a more in depth discussion on terms of use see Chapter 2.

While privacy policies vary among platforms, they do share many similarities. For example, most policies include the following:

Type of information the site is collecting both voluntarily (such as a form submission or post) and involuntarily (e.g., through cookies, IP addresses, or GPS)

How the information is collected

How the provider will use the information (e.g., customizing web presence, providing information and advertisements to users)

How the provider will disclose the information (e.g., to subsidiaries and affiliates, in connection with a legal obligation, to advertisers)

How the provider protects the information from others

Description of rights of review to correct information

How long the policy is in effect

How changes are made to the policy

How to safeguard or adjust personal privacy settings

State specific rules or regulations

Contact information for the social media provider.

Except for COPPA, there are no federal laws that specifically address the privacy policies of social media providers. However, there has been legislative action by states in this area. The most active state has been California which passed the Online Privacy Protection Act in 2003.[4] This California law, which applies to social media providers, requires website operators that collect "personally identifiable information" about California residents to conspicuously post privacy policies that:

Identify the categories of consumer personally identifiable information that the operator collects and the categories of the third-party persons or entities with whom the operator may share that information

Identify whether a process exists to review and request changes to any personally identifiable information and provide a description of that process

---

4 California Business and Professional Code § 22575(b)(1)–(7).

Describe the process of notifying users of material changes to the privacy policy

Identify the effective date

Disclose how the operator responds to web browser "do not track" signals

Disclose whether other parties may collect personally identifiable information about an individual consumer's online activities.

Other states with laws specifically targeting privacy policies include Nebraska and Pennsylvania, both of which have amended current statutes to prohibit misleading statements in a privacy policy.[5] Finally, Delaware recently enacted the Delaware Online Privacy and Protection Act (DOPPA) which, among other things, requires operators of websites and apps to conspicuously post a compliant privacy policy.[6]

Generally speaking, social media providers are free to modify their privacy policies. In doing so, the social media provider must provide the user notice and the opportunity to opt out. The one big caveat here concerns instances where the social media provider does not obtain user consent e.g., the user neither agrees to the new terms nor returns to the site. In those scenarios, it is unclear whether the social media provider can impose the new terms on old content left on the site of the social media provider.

---

[5] Nebraska Revised Statute § 87–302(14) and 18 Pennsylvania Constitutional Statute § 4107(a)(10).

[6] 80 Delaware Laws, c. 148 § 1.

C. LITIGATION

1. FTC

The user's third layer of privacy protection against the social media provider is litigation. To date, cases have been brought by the individual user, the state attorneys-general, and the FTC. The FTC, pursuant to its authority to police unfair and deceptive trade practices, has brought actions against social media providers for a variety of matters to include failing to adhere to their own privacy policies. These FTC actions rarely lead to an actual judicial decision. This is because most companies reach a settlement agreement with the FTC, which, in turn, allows the company to avoid litigation and any admission of wrongdoing.

In re Facebook provides an example of a typical FTC action in this area.[7] Here, Facebook employed a Privacy Wizard to help users set new privacy settings. However, the Privacy Wizard never told the users that they could no longer limit the visibility of certain parts of their profile to others. The FTC found this practice by Facebook to be deceptive to users. Rather than proceed to litigation the parties settled with Facebook agreeing to provide notice to users and obtain affirmative consent from them when making changes that materially affect its privacy policy. Facebook was also required to get third-party compliance assessments. In addition, the FTC

---

7 *In re Facebook, Inc.*, FTC File No. 092–3184 (Nov. 29, 2011).

prohibited Facebook from misrepresenting its privacy and security statements.

2. Users

Besides relying on the FTC, users have brought their own claims against social media providers. To date, these claims have been met with mixed success. Most claims do not make it past the motion to dismiss stage. Those that do are generally quickly settled. The main hurdle for users is standing—a requirement for a lawsuit to proceed to the next stage. In order to have standing, plaintiffs, generally speaking, must establish that: (1) they will suffer an imminent injury to a legal right; (2) the injury was caused by the defendant's conduct or omission; and (3) a favorable decision by the court will redress the injury.

Cohen v. Facebook illustrates the standing challenges facing social media users.[8] In *Cohen*, the plaintiffs brought a class action suit against Facebook for misappropriation of their name and likeness based on "Friend Finder," an online tool that searches a user's email accounts to identify acquaintances that the user has not yet friended. Plaintiffs claimed that these searches caused them emotional distress. The issue here is did Facebook misappropriate user information to promote "Friend Finder"? To this question, the court said "no."

---

[8] *Cohen v. Facebook, Inc.*, 798 F. Supp. 2d 1090 (N.D. Cal. 2011) ("Cohen I"); *Cohen v. Facebook, Inc.*, No. 10–cv–05282–RS, 2011 WL 5117164 (N.D. Cal. Dec. 27, 2011) ("Cohen II").

According to the *Cohen* court, this is not a situation where the defendant allegedly publicized the name or likeness of the plaintiffs to any audience. Rather, the court found that the publicized names or likenesses were done in a context in which they already appeared. Plaintiffs were "friends" with the individuals who saw the display. Thus, no facts existed to support cognizable harm.

Rather than dismiss the suit outright, the court in *Cohen* allowed the plaintiffs to amend their complaint. In the Amended Complaint, plaintiffs tried a different approach. Now plaintiffs claimed that their names and likenesses had economic value to Facebook. The issue here was whether the use of names and likenesses of non-celebrity private individuals without compensation or consent caused injury sufficient to support standing where the plaintiffs cannot allege that their names and likenesses have any general commercial value. Again, the court found the argument put forward by the plaintiffs unpersuasive and the case was dismissed. According to the court, plaintiffs do not have "an obvious economic interest in [their] likenesses and cannot allege that their names and likeness have any general commercial value."

In contrast to *Cohen* is *Fraley v. Facebook*.[9] In *Fraley*, plaintiffs claimed that Facebook through its "Sponsored Stories" used their "names, photographs, likenesses and identities to sell advertisements for products, services, or brands without obtaining

[9] *Fraley v. Facebook, Inc.*, No. 11–cv–001726–LHK, 2011 WL 6303898 (N.D. Cal. Dec. 16, 2011).

consent." Sponsored Stories, which was automatically activated by default, was a form of paid advertising that appeared on a user's Facebook "news feed," displaying a friend's name and photo next to the advertiser's logo and stating that the friend Liked the advertiser or its product. For example, if a user went to Rosetta Stone's Facebook page, where the user is required to click the "Like" button before seeing a software demonstration of the product, the user's picture would subsequently appear on the news feed of Facebook friends alongside Rosetta Stone's logo. With the Sponsored Story program, Facebook could turn a user's Likes into advertising revenue.

Plaintiffs claimed that it was improper for Facebook to disclose plaintiffs' names on Facebook to plaintiffs' friends asserting that they Liked a particular advertiser or its product. Specifically, plaintiffs alleged that by "misappropriating their names and likenesses for commercial endorsements without their consent," Facebook violated their rights of publicity under California Civil Code Section 3344 and California's Unfair Competition Law, Business and Professions Code Section 17200. In response to the claims raised by the plaintiffs, Facebook filed a motion to dismiss arguing that plaintiffs "fail[ed] to state a claim for misappropriation under California Civil Code because they [did not] allege[ ] any actionable injury, they consented to the use of their names and likeness, and the republished content is newsworthy under § 3344(d)."

Unlike the plaintiffs in *Cohen*, the judge in *Fraley* found that the plaintiffs had stated a theory of economic injury. The trial judge found that users were "likely to be deceived into believing [they] had full control to prevent [their] appearances in Sponsored Story advertisements while otherwise engaging with Facebook's various features, such as clicking on a 'Like' button, when in fact members lack such control." The court also found that the umbrella protection afforded by Section 3344(d) was removed because Facebook used plaintiffs' content for commercial purposes. Finally, the judge determined that the issue of consent was a "disputed question of fact." Once the court denied the motion to dismiss, the case was settled for twenty million dollars. For more on Rights of Publicity in the context of social media, see Chapter 6.

§ 7.03 SAFEGUARDING CONTENT FROM THIRD PARTIES

A. STATUTES

In addition to the statutes that protect user information from social media providers, there are laws both on the federal and state level that limit third party access to user information. Although the federal laws were not initially created specifically to safeguard the privacy of social media users, they have nonetheless proved effective in that regard. The first federal statute to be examined is the Fair Credit Reporting Act (FCRA) which protects information in an individual's credit file to include credit and employment history. *Robins v. Spokeo* illustrates how users have invoked the FCRA in the context of social media.[10]

In *Robins*, the plaintiff filed a putative class action suit alleging that Spokeo, which bills itself as a "people search engine," violated his rights under the FCRA by disclosing inaccurate information about him that harmed his employment prospects. Specifically, plaintiff claimed that his Spokeo profile contained numerous inaccuracies e.g., marital status, age, current employer, and educational background. Plaintiff further claimed that Spokeo was a consumer reporting agency that marketed to human resource professionals, law enforcement, and those in need of background checks.

In response to Robins' Complaint, Spokeo moved to dismiss the lawsuit claiming that the plaintiff did not suffer any "injury-in-fact." The trial court agreed with Spokeo and dismissed the lawsuit. However, on appeal to the Ninth Circuit Court of Appeals, the trial court was reversed. The Ninth Circuit found that a violation of a statutory right, in this case the FCRA, is usually sufficient injury to confer standing. The case then went to the United States Supreme Court. The high court remanded the case back to the Ninth Circuit Court of Appeals so that it could consider both aspects of the injury in fact requirements—an injury in fact must be both concrete and particularized. Apparently, the Ninth Circuit focused only on particularization.

---

[10] *Robins v. Spokeo*, Case No. 2:10–cv–05306–ODW (C.D. Cal. Sept. 19, 2011).

Other federal laws relied upon by social media users to safeguard their privacy from third parties include the Gramm-Leach-Bliley Act which covers privacy rights and obligations related to personal financial information.[11] This law requires financial institutions to provide consumers notice of privacy policies and the opportunity to opt out of having information shared with others. There is also the well-known Health Insurance Portability and Accountability Act (HIPAA) which protects "all individually identifiable health information held or transmitted by a covered entity or its business associate, in any form or media, whether electronic, paper or oral."[12] In addition, there is the Family Educational Rights and Privacy Act (FERPA) which protects student educational records.[13] Finally, there is the Controlling the Assault of Non-Solicited Pornography and Marketing (CAN-SPAM) Act which was previously discussed in Chapter 4.

On the state level, California has led the way with respect to social media privacy laws. The Privacy Rights for California Minors in the Digital World also known as the Online Eraser Law is arguably the most sweeping legislation in this area.[14] This law, which applies to websites, online services or apps, protects California minors on the Internet in two ways. First, the law limits the ability of website operators to market certain products and services to

---

[11] 15 U.S.C. §§ 6801–09.

[12] 45 C.F.R. § 160.103.

[13] 20 U.S.C. § 1232g.

[14] California Business and Professions Code § 22581.

minors e.g., cigarettes, alcohol, firearms and other items that are illegal for minors to purchase. Second, the law allows minors using a particular website to request removal of content that the minor posted on the website. Many feel that the second provision, which allows minors to remove content, was written specifically for social media.

In order for the Online Eraser Law to apply to a social media provider several requirements have to be met. First, the site has to be directed towards minors or the operators of the site must have actual knowledge that a minor is using the site. Second, the content must have been posted by the minor not a third party. Third, the minor cannot have received compensation for the content. Fourth, the content must in some manner identify the minor. Put differently, anonymous content need not be removed. Also, if the content is required by federal or state law it need not be removed.

The Online Eraser Law also imposes several notice requirements on social media providers to include notifying the minor of the right of removal. In addition, the social media provider must provide users clear instructions on the removal process. Finally, the social media provider has to alert the minor that removal "does not ensure complete or comprehensive removal of the content information."

Since the Online Eraser Law has only been in effect since 2015, there are numerous uncertainties and questions surrounding the law. First, it is unclear when a person can request removal of material. For example, must that person be under 18 at the time of the removal request or can the request be made at anytime during the individual's lifespan so long as the information to be removed was posted while that person was under 18? Other questions arise about the constitutionality of the law and whether it violates the Dormant Commerce Clause or the First Amendment. Finally, there have been concerns about whether the new law is preempted by the Communications Decency Act, a statute discussed in detail in Chapter 8.

B. LITIGATION

1. Non-State Actors

In addition to statutes, user information can be safeguarded against third parties through litigation. This litigation is brought by both the user and the social media provider and normally arises when the third party attempts to improperly access user information from the site of the social media provider e.g., scraping, which is a form of data extraction.

Currently, many social media providers prohibit third parties from scraping information from their site whether conducted manually or by automation. Those sites that allow scraping generally require that it be done through their own Application Programming Interface (API) in order to control the content accessed. The following case illustrates the legal challenges that arise when third parties improperly conduct data scraping.

In *Facebook v. Power Ventures,* the defendants, Power Ventures, created a website to aggregate a user's social media accounts.[15] In essence, this site would allow a user to see friend lists, messages, posts, profile pages, etc. all at one website. To encourage users to join Power Ventures, the company offered Power.com users the chance to win $100 if they successfully invited and signed up new Power.com users. As part of this promotion, Power Ventures provided participants with a list of their Facebook friends and asked them to select who should receive a Power invitation. The invitations sent to those friends purported to come from "Facebook" and used a "@facebookmail.com" address, not a Power.com address. However, the text of the message included information about Power.com. Finally, Power Ventures allowed Power.com users to access their Facebook profiles through Power.com.

While Facebook allows third parties to use applications to interact with Facebook users, those third parties must adhere to the site's terms of use. In this case, Power Ventures, at least initially, attempted to adhere to Facebook's terms of use and scrape information through Facebook's Connect program. However, that process was soon abandoned and Power Ventures began accessing and gathering information from Facebook on its own without adhering to Facebook's terms of use.

Eventually, Facebook filed a lawsuit against Power Ventures alleging that they violated the CAN-SPAM Act, the CFAA, and California Penal Code 502. Initially, the court found Power Ventures liable

---

[15] *Facebook, Inc. v. Power Ventures, Inc.*, Case No. 08–cv–05780–JF (N.D. Cal. Oct. 22, 2009).

on all counts. With respect to the CAN-SPAM Act, Facebook claimed that Power Ventures accessed its social media site in an unauthorized manner and then sent unsolicited and misleading commercial emails to Facebook users. Power Ventures argued that it was Facebook not them who actually sent the emails because "the emails were authorized by Facebook users and sent from Facebook's own servers." The court found Power Venture's argument unpersuasive noting that while "Facebook servers did automatically send the emails at the instruction of the Launch Program, it is clear that Defendants' actions—in creating the Launch Promotion" served to "originate the emails as required by the [CAN-SPAM] Act."

The court also found that Power Ventures violated the CFAA because its use of Facebook exceeded Facebook's terms of use which prohibited unauthorized scraping. As for California Penal Code 502, this related to efforts by Power Ventures to access Facebook despite knowing that Facebook did not want them on its site. Apparently, Power Ventures kept trying to get around security measures created by Facebook to prevent access to its site. Here, the court found that "in light of the undisputed evidence that Defendants anticipated attempts to block their access by Plaintiff, and utilized multiple IP addresses to effectively circumvent these barriers. . . Defendants violated Section 502 by accessing Plaintiff's network without permission."

On appeal, the defendants found partial success with the Ninth Circuit Court of Appeals which determined that the defendants had not violated the CAN-SPAM Act.[16] In the eyes of the appellate court, the methods used by Power Ventures complied with the CAN-SPAM Act because users on Facebook affirmatively agreed to allow Power Ventures to share promotions through event invitations. However, the appellate court did uphold the trial court's finding that the defendants violated the CFAA because they continued to access Facebook even after receiving a cease-and-desist letter from them. Ultimately, the appellate court sent the case back to the trial court to reassess damages.

2. State Actors

Similar to private businesses, state actors have also improperly accessed user content on social media. *R.S. ex rel. S.S. v. Minnewaska Area School Dist. No. 2149* illustrates the problems that can arise when a state actor (a school official) compels another individual to reveal her social media password in order to access that individual's social media account.[17]

In this case, a 12-year old female student in the confines of her own home posted the following on Facebook.

> *[I hate] a Kathy person at school because [Kathy] was mean to me.*

---

[16] *Facebook v. Power Ventures and Steven Vachani*, No. 13–17102 (9th Cir. 2016).

[17] *R.S. ex rel. S.S. v. Minnewaska Area School Dist. No. 2149*, 894 F. Supp. 2d 1128, 290 Ed. Law Rep. 711 (D. Minn. 2012).

The post was meant only for her friends. However, one of R.S.'s friends alerted school administrators about the post. The principal viewed the post and found it to constitute bullying. As a result, he punished R.S. This led R.S. to write a subsequent post which read as follows;

I want to know who the f%$# told on me[.]

R.S. was again punished for her post only this time more severely.

Later, school officials received a complaint from a parent that R.S. was communicating with another student online about sexual topics. R.S. was called out of class to discuss her online conversations with two school administrators and a deputy sheriff who was assigned to the school. The three adults interrogated R.S. about her online conversations and then demanded her Facebook password and username. Once in possession of this information, the school officials searched R.S.'s Facebook account.

R.S. subsequently sued the school officials alleging intentional infliction of emotional distress, invasion of privacy, and violations of her First and Fourth Amendment rights. With respect to her Fourth Amendment rights, defendants challenged whether R.S. had a reasonable expectation of privacy in the information she posted on Facebook and the private communications that she made with other students via Facebook.

On a Motion to Dismiss brought by the defendants, the court drew a distinction among the various methods of communicating on Facebook. The first category included communications that were generally accessible by the friends of a Facebook user e.g., wall posts. The second category included communications that operated more like email between two people. The court noted that the communications in this second category "are not open to perusal by one's friends or by the general public."

With respect to this second category of communications, the court analogized them to a private letter that was only available to R.S. and R.S.'s correspondent. The court went on to say that "based on established Fourth Amendment precedent, that R.S. had a reasonable expectation of privacy to her private Facebook information and messages." This finding led the court to deny the defendants' Motion to Dismiss with respect to the Fourth Amendment claim.

This case never went to trial as the parties ultimately settled the matter. The school district agreed to not only change its policies to strengthen student privacy, but also to pay a $70,000 settlement to be divided between the plaintiff and the ACLU.

As illustrated by *Minnewaska Area School Dist. No. 2149*, some school officials may go too far in their efforts to monitor student conduct on social media. This has led some states to pass laws restricting access to student social media accounts. At present, 11 states (AR, CA, DE, IL, LA, MD, MI, NJ, NM, OR and RI) have statutes in place regulating who may access a student's social media account.

In addition, California has recently enacted a law to regulate the method by which schools monitor the publicly available information on a student's social media account.[18] Pursuant to California Assembly Bill 1442, which became law in 2015, school districts and charter schools who want to monitor the social media accounts of students must adhere to the following:

Provide notice to students and parents about the adoption of any such program

Provide opportunity for public comment about the program

Allow students to see any information collected about them

Provide students the opportunity to correct information

Destroy any information collected after the student turns 18 or is no longer enrolled

Monitor and collect information relevant only to school or pupil safety.

Other examples of state actors invading the privacy of social media users outside of the educational setting include the case of *Sondra Arquiett v. United States*.[19]

Arquiett initially came to the attention of law enforcement during their investigation of a drug ring.

---

[18] California Education Code § 49073.6.

[19] *Sondra Arquiett v. United States*, 7:13–cv–007552 (N.D.N.Y. 2015).

Upon her arrest, Arquiett turned over her phone to the police and consented to it being searched. Charges were filed against Arquiett and she ultimately pled guilty to distribution of illegal narcotics. The trial judge handling the case determined that Arquiett was a minor player and sentenced her to six months of weekend incarceration, six months of home detention, and probation. While Arquiett was awaiting sentencing, the Drug Enforcement Agency (DEA) set up a bogus Facebook page under her name with photos obtained from her phone. Arquiett only became aware of the Facebook page after her friends contacted her about some of the more risque photos being posted on the page.

Initially, the government asserted that there was nothing improper with the Facebook page which contained photos of not only Arquiett, but also her young son and niece. In at least one of the photos, Arquiett was wearing either a bathing suit or a bra and underwear. The government initially argued that when Arquiett was first arrested she consented to the search of her phone and said she wanted to help. Thus, she implicitly agreed to the creation of the Facebook page.

Arquiett sued the DEA for violating her constitutional rights and the Federal Tort Claims Act. Once the mainstream media became aware of the lawsuit and the DEA's undercover social media operations, the government changed its position and decided to settle the case for $134,000. The DOJ also announced that *this settlement demonstrates that the government is mindful of its obligation to ensure the rights of third parties are not infringed upon in the course of its efforts to bring those who commit federal crimes to justice. It also takes into account emerging personal privacy concerns in the age of social media, and represents a fair resolution of plaintiff's claims.*

CHAPTER 8

TORTS

§ 8.01 INTRODUCTION

This chapter highlights the various ways social media impacts the law of torts. The goal of this chapter is not to examine every possible tort that arises from social media. Instead, this chapter will focus on the areas of tort law that have been most influenced by social media.

The first part of the chapter will look at the liability of social media providers for the actions of their users. Generally speaking, Section 230(c) of the Communications Decency Act (CDA) gives providers of an "interactive computer service," including social media, immunity for the acts of its users.[1] This part of the chapter also examines third party liability to include discussing whether parents can be held liable for the tortious social media acts of their children or employers for the conduct of their employees.

Next, the chapter looks at the methods individuals and entities rely on to limit criticism that occurs on social media. With commentary on social media influencing consumer choices, businesses have grown increasingly concerned about receiving any type of negative or unfavorable online reviews. This in turn has led some businesses to take steps, some legal some not, to restrict online criticism.

---

[1] Title 47 of the United States Code (47 U.S.C. § 230).

The penultimate section of the chapter discusses social media and defamation. The chapter concludes with a brief discussion of the step-by-step procedures for removing an unfavorable social media post.

§ 8.02 LIABILITY FOR SOCIAL MEDIA PROVIDERS

A. SECTION 230

In 1996, Congress passed the Telecommunications Act, the first major overhaul of telecommunications law in more than sixty years.[2] One of the main goals of this legislation was to prevent minors from gaining access to indecent and pornographic online material. To help ensure that operators of Internet sites would assist in this policing effort, Section 230(c) of the CDA was added to the Telecommunications Act.

Generally speaking, Section 230(c) gives providers and users of an "interactive computer service" civil immunity for the online content posted by others. The phrase "interactive computer service," which includes social media providers, is defined as "any information service, system, or access software provider that provides or enables computer access by multiple users to a computer server, including specifically a service or system that provides access to the Internet and such systems operated or services offered by libraries or educational institutions."

At the time of Section 230(c)'s passage, Congress believed that providers of interactive computer

[2] Public Law 104–104, 110 Stat. 56 (1996).

services would be more inclined to regulate and edit the online content of others if given immunity. Prior to the passage of Section 230(c), providers and users of interactive computer services could be held liable, especially if they exercised editorial control, for the online content posted by those who used their services, see *Stratton Oakmont, Inc. v. Prodigy Services*.[3] A secondary goal of the CDA was to encourage the growth and development of online businesses.

While most of the CDA was struck down in 1997 by the Supreme Court in *Reno v. ACLU*,[4] Section 230(c) remained intact and reads as follows:

> (1) *Treatment of publisher or speaker*
>
> *No provider or user of an interactive computer service shall be treated as the publisher or speaker of any information provided by another information content provider.*
>
> (2) *Civil Liability*
>
> *No provider or user of an interactive computer service shall be held liable on account of—*
>
> *(A). any action voluntarily taken in good faith to restrict access to or availability of material that the provider or user considers to be obscene, lewd, lascivious,*

---

[3] *Stratton Oakmont, Inc. v. Prodigy Services*, 1995 WL 323710 (N.Y. Sup. Ct. 1995).

[4] *Reno v. American Civil Liberties Union*, 521 U.S. 844 (1997).

> *filthy, excessively violent, harassing, or otherwise objectionable, whether or not such material is constitutionally protected; or*
>
> *(B). any action taken to enable or make available to information content providers or others the technical means to restrict access to material described in paragraph (1).*

The first clause of Section 230(c) states a "provider" or "user" of an interactive computer service will not be deemed the publisher or speaker of content created by others. This clause protects a user or provider from liability for content created by third parties. Exceptions to this rule of immunity include intellectual property claims, federal criminal prosecutions, and violations of the Electronic Communications Privacy Act (ECPA) and related state laws.

The second clause of Section 230(c), which has two parts, concerns activities related to online filtering. Section 230(c)(2)(A) immunizes a provider or user who voluntarily and in good faith restricts access or availability of objectionable third party content. Section 230(c)(2)(B) immunizes a provider or user for providing instructions on how to restrict access to objectionable content. Similar to the aforementioned first clause of Section 230(c), the second clause is subject to the same three statutory exclusions: intellectual property claims, federal criminal prosecutions, and violations of the ECPA and related state laws.

To date, most Section 230(c) litigation has involved the first clause of the subsection statute. However, with the growing use of online filtering, there has been an increased interest in the second clause. With respect to the first clause, courts have taken a very expansive view of Section 230(c) granting social media providers immunity for a variety of torts committed by their users including defamation, invasion of privacy, negligence and negligent misrepresentation.

Section 230(c) immunity has also been extended to claims of equitable relief. For example, plaintiffs can't force social media providers to remove content by obtaining an injunction or some other form of equitable remedy.

In *Reit v. Yelp*, the court, relying on Section 230, denied a request by the plaintiff for a preliminary injunction against Yelp.[5] Here, the plaintiff, a dentist, attempted to force Yelp to remove specific anonymous comments posted on Yelp about the dentist's practice and office. The plaintiff claimed that these comments which described his office as "small," "old," and "smelly" and his equipment as "old and dirty" led to a dramatic drop in the number of daily appointments.

In determining whether to grant Section 230(c) immunity courts have sometimes applied the "Material Contribution Test" to determine whether the social media service provider materially contributed to the improper conduct complained of.

---

[5] *Reit v. Yelp*, 907 N.Y.S. 2d 411 (N.Y. Sup. Ct. Sept. 2, 2010).

Jones v. Dirty World Entertainment illustrates the application of the Material Contribution Test.[6] In this case, Sarah Jones, a high school teacher and NFL cheerleader, sued Nik Richie the owner and operator of thedirty.com, a gossip website. In her suit, Jones alleged defamation, libel *per se,* false light, and intentional infliction of emotional distress. Jones' claims stemmed from two posts made on thedirty.com in which anonymous posters questioned plaintiff's chastity and accused her of having a sexually transmitted disease.

As the operator of thedirty.com, Richie added his own online comments about Jones and encouraged others to comment as well. Unlike the anonymous comments, Richie claimed that his comments were not defamatory. As a result, Richie argued that he was immune from suit based on Section 230(c). In rejecting Richie's claim of Section 230(c) immunity, the trial judge determined that:

(1) the Name of the site (thedirty.com) encourages material which is potentially defamatory or an invasion of privacy;

(2) Richie acts as editor and only selects a small percentage of submissions to be posted;

(3) Richie reviews the postings but does not verify their accuracy; and

(4) Richie adds his own comments.

---

[6] *Jones v. Dirty World Entertainment Recordings, LLC*, 755 F.3d 398 (6th Cir. June 16, 2014).

The case then proceeded to trial where a jury found in favor of Jones.

On appeal to the 6th Circuit Court of Appeals, a three-judge panel found that Section 230(c) did apply to Richie and dismissed the lawsuit. According to the 6th Circuit, the trial judge applied the wrong standard (Encouragement Test) to determine whether an interactive computer service creates or develops content. The panel then went on to adopt the Material Contribution Test to determine whether an interactive computer service develops or creates content.

In applying the Material Contribution Test, the panel found that Richie did not *materially contribute to the illegality* of the defamatory third party posts. Thus, Richie should be granted immunity. The panel found that simply selecting posts for publication was not material contribution nor was providing commentary. This is because the comments by Richie were not themselves defamatory and they occurred after the defamatory posts by third parties were already made.

The 6th Circuit's ruling in *Jones* was in line with prior decisions around the country which have found that Section 230(c) immunity applies even when the social media provider encourages or edits the content in question. A few notable exceptions to this general trend of granting immunity can be found in the 9th Circuit Court of Appeals.

One of the first cases to reject Section 230(c) immunity for a provider of an interactive computer service was *Fair Housing Council of San Fernando Valley v. Roommates.com.*[7] Here, the 9th Circuit Court of Appeals found that Roommates.com was not entitled to Section 230(c) immunity because it required users of its website to include information that was illegal under the Fair Housing Act (FHA). For example, users of Roommates.com were required to create a profile and answer a series of questions from a drop box menu that covered such topics as gender, family-status, and sexual-orientation. Roommates.com then made roommate matches based on this information. According to the 9th Circuit Court of Appeals,

> *[b]y requiring subscribers to provide the information as a condition of accessing its service, and by providing a limited set of pre-populated answers, Roommate becomes much more than a passive transmitter of information provided by others; it becomes the developer, at least in part, of the information. And section 230 provides immunity only if the interactive computer service does not 'creat[e] or develop[ ]' the information 'in whole or in part.'*

Another case from the 9th Circuit that rejected Section 230(c) immunity for a social media provider was *Jane Doe No. 14 v. Internet Brands, Inc.*[8] Here, the appellate court refused to apply Section 230(c) immunity to plaintiff's claim that Internet Brands,

---

[7] *Fair Housing Council of San Fernando Valley v. Roommates.com, LLC*, 521 F.3d 1157 (9th Cir. 2008).

[8] *Jane Doe No. 14 v. Internet Brands, Inc., DBA Modelmayhem.com*, 767 F.3d 894 (9th Cir. Sept. 17, 2014).

which owned modelmayhem.com, had failed to warn about a known rape scheme. In *Internet Brands, Inc.*, the plaintiff alleged that in February 2011 Emerson Callum and Lavont Flanders used the website modelmayhem.com to lure her to a fake audition where she was drugged and raped all of which was then recorded for a pornographic video. Plaintiff claimed that defendants had knowledge of prior criminal investigations involving Lavont Flanders but failed to disclose that information to users of modelmayhem.com.

Initially, the district court dismissed plaintiff's claim based on Section 230(c) immunity. However, the 9th Circuit reversed and remanded. The appellate court distinguished between plaintiff's failure to warn claim and Section 230(c) immunity. According to the 9th Circuit, the plaintiff's failure to warn claim did not attempt to hold the defendant liable as the "publisher or speaker" of online content posted by another. Here, the court emphasized the fact that the rapists did not post any content on modelmayem.com but instead merely used the website to contact the victim who had uploaded her profile to the site.

Questions remain as to whether the holding of *Internet Brands, Inc.* can be reconciled with similar Section 230(c) cases like *Doe v. Myspace.*[9] In *Doe*, the 5th Circuit Court of Appeals affirmed a lower court decision finding that Myspace was immune from civil liability resulting from a sexual assault pursuant to

---

[9] *Doe v. MySpace*, 528 F.3d 413 (5th Cir. 2008).

Section 230(c). According to the federal district court that heard *Doe v. Myspace*,

> *[i]t is quite obvious the underlying basis for Plaintiffs' claim is that through posting on MySpace, Pete Solis and Julie Doe met and exchanged personal information which eventually led to an in-person meeting and sexual assault. . . If MySpace had not published communications between Doe and Solis. . . they never would have met and the sexual assault never would have occurred. No matter how artfully Plaintiffs seek to plead their claims, the court views Plaintiffs' claims as directed toward MySpace in its publishing, editorial, and/or screening capacities.*

It appears that the key take-away from *Internet Brands, Inc.* is that Section 230(c) immunity may not protect social media providers from failing to warn individuals about known dangers at least in the 9th Circuit Court of Appeals.

B. CRITIQUES OF SECTION 230(c)

There have been numerous critiques of Section 230(c). These criticisms tend to grow each year as more and more people learn about the immunity granted to social media providers. One major complaint with Section 230(c) is that victims, at times, are left without a remedy. This is because victims often cannot seek redress from the social media provider pursuant to Section 230(c) and the original poster of the harmful content is either unknown or judgment proof. The challenges associated with unmasking the anonymous social media poster will be examined in greater detail in section 8.05.

Another criticism is that the law no longer fulfills its original congressional purpose. Here, opponents claim that Section 230(c) was created to protect minors; however, it is now having the opposite effect. Rather than encouraging social media providers to police their websites, Section 230(c) allows them to ignore problems. By limiting liability for social media providers, Section 230(c) has removed any legal incentive for social media providers to regulate users or their content. However, it should be noted that Section 230(c) continues to fulfill one of its other main purposes. The law has greatly aided in the growth and development of social media platforms.

Finally, Section 230(c) creates a double standard between online and offline providers of information. Traditional media outlets such as newspapers and magazines are not provided immunity for the content of their users. There is no offline equivalent to Section 230(c). This results in a rather strange dichotomy in which a media outlet that publishes a story both online and offline might be sued for defamation for the offline version of the story but not the online version because of Section 230(c).

§ 8.03 LIABILITY FOR THIRD PARTIES

As discussed previously, social media providers generally cannot be held liable for the content posted by its users pursuant to Section 230 of the CDA. However, this has not stopped plaintiffs from trying to hold individuals and companies liable for the social media content posted by others if a special relationship exists such as parent-child or employer-employee. *Boston v. Athearn* serves as an example of how parents might be liable for the social media content of their children.[10]

In *Boston*, a young boy, Dustin, created a bogus Facebook page of a fellow female classmate, Alexandria. While pretending to be Alexandria, Dustin posted both sexist and racist comments. Alexandria and school officials eventually became aware of the page. Dustin was questioned about the page and admitted to creating it with another girl from his school. Dustin's parents were notified about the Facebook page and the school subsequently punished Dustin with an in-school suspension. This, however, did not lead to the removal of the page. In fact, the page remained active and continued to accept and extend friend requests for 11 more months. The page was eventually deactivated two weeks after Alexandria, through her parents, sued Dustin and his parents for libel and infliction of emotional distress.

At the trial stage, Dustin's motion for summary judgment was granted. Alexandria appealed arguing that questions of material fact existed with respect to whether the parents breached a duty to supervise Dustin's use of a computer and an Internet account. Alexandria also claimed that a material question existed as to whether Dustin's parents, as

[10] *Boston v. Athearn*, 764 S.E. 2d 582 (Ga. Ct. App. Oct. 10, 2014).

landowners, breached a duty to remove defamatory content existing on their property.

As to the first claim, the appellate court agreed with Alexandria writing that

> *a reasonable jury could find that, after learning on May 10, 2011, of Dustin's recent misconduct in the use of the computer and Internet account, the Athearns failed to exercise due care in supervising and controlling such activity going forward. Given that false and offensive statements remained on display, and continued to reach readers, for an additional eleven months, we conclude that a jury could find that the Athearns' negligence proximately caused some part of the injury to Alex sustained from Dustin's actions (and inactions).*[11]

It remains to be seen if other courts will follow the lead of *Athearn* and find parents liable when their children create bogus social media accounts. In many ways Athearn can be limited to its facts. Here, the parents knew about the account but failed to take steps to shut it down until the lawsuit was filed. Generally speaking, negligent supervision claims arise when a parent is aware of a child's proclivity for tortious mischief or the child is entrusted with a dangerous instrument.

Other examples of third party liability involve employers and their employees. The challenge here for employers is that they face the proverbial Catch-

---

[11] *Boston v. Athearn*, 764 S.E. 2d 582 (Ga. Ct. App. Oct. 10, 2014).

22. As discussed in Chapter 6, many states have passed laws prohibiting employers from monitoring or accessing the non-public content of their employees' social media accounts. Furthermore, employers may face both civil and criminal penalties if they require an employee to reveal information from a private social media account. Employers may also be subject to legal action by the employee if the employee is disciplined for certain online conduct. Yet, even with all of these constraints placed on employers, they may nonetheless still face liability for their employee's social media conduct, especially if it relates directly to their employment or occurs at the workplace. This last point is illustrated in *Howard v. Hertz.*[12]

In *Howard*, several employees of Hertz had a discussion about a customer on Facebook. This discussion included racially charged statements and comments about the customer's declined credit card. Upon learning about the Facebook discussion, the customer sued Hertz alleging negligent supervision, negligent retention, and negligent training by the employer. The plaintiff also brought claims against the individual employees who posted comments.

Hertz moved to dismiss the case arguing that the customer failed to allege any basis to hold it responsible for its employees' online statements. The court denied the motion to dismiss finding that the social media content referenced in plaintiff's complaint was posted on a computer owned by Hertz

---

[12] *Howard v. Hertz Corp.*, 2016 WL 316781 (D. Hawaii Oct. 23, 2014).

during work hours. Furthermore, the trial court determined that Employee A had a propensity for posting "hostile statements and information." The court noted that Hertz either knew or should have known about Employee A's propensity for harassment, hostility, and violent speech.

Ultimately, the court granted the defendant's summary judgment motion finding, among other things, that the plaintiff failed to show that "Hertz foresaw or should have foreseen the danger posed by. . . [Employee A] and should have been more closely supervising his Facebook use earlier or should have fired him earlier." While Hertz was not found liable, this case illustrates how employers in the future may not be as fortunate, especially if they are aware or on notice of the employee's improper conduct.

§ 8.04 LIMITING CRITICISM ON SOCIAL MEDIA

With social media, consumers from around the world share their experiences both good and bad with each other online. As a result, online comments now play a very large role in shaping consumer choices. Not surprisingly, companies and others who offer online services have grown increasingly concerned about receiving any type of negative reviews regardless of whether it is done by an irate consumer or some competitor trying to limit competition.

This section will examine two methods by which businesses attempt to prevent individuals from posting negative information about them or their products on social media. The first measure to be examined is the Strategic Lawsuit Against Public Participation (SLAPP). SLAPP is a legal complaint or counterclaim brought against individuals and organizations with the intent to intimidate and discourage them from engaging in public criticism. The second measure to be discussed is the anti-disparagement clause.

A. SLAPPs

The term "SLAPP" was first coined by Professors George Pring and Penelope Canan as they studied how some lawsuits were used to chill speech through unnecessary litigation.[13] SLAPPs are often framed as claims involving defamation, libel, slander, malicious prosecution, and/or abuse of process. The goal of a SLAPP is not necessarily to win the particular lawsuit but rather to harass, delay, or escalate litigation costs to such an extent that the other party abandons their criticism or opposition.

To combat the growing number of SLAPPs and protect First Amendment rights, states across the country have enacted anti-SLAPP statutes, which allow for the early dismissal of cases that may chill the exercise of free speech. While there is no federal anti-SLAPP statute at present, 30 jurisdictions have passed some version of an anti-SLAPP law. Typical features of an effective anti-SLAPP statute include: (1) an expedited motion to dismiss (to avoid costly

---

[13] Penelope Canan & George W. Pring, *Studying Strategic Lawsuits Against Public Participation: Mixing Quantitative and Qualitative Approaches*, 22 Law & Soc'y Rev. 385 (1988).

discovery); (2) interlocutory appeal; and (3) the recovery of legal fees.

Under most anti-SLAPP statutes, the person being sued files a motion to dismiss because their conduct involves speech or a petition on a matter of concern. The individual bringing the SLAPP must then demonstrate a probability of success. If this burden cannot be met, the court will normally dismiss the case and possibly award attorney's fees to the defendant.

Bently Reserve vs. Papaliolios illustrates the unsuccessful use of an anti-SLAPP statute in the context of social media.[14] This case arose from a less than flattering online Yelp review made by the tenant about the landlord. The review by the tenant reads as follows:

> *Sadly, the Building is (newly) owned and occupied by a sociopathic narcissist—who celebrates making the lives of tenants hell. Of the 16 mostly-long-term tenants who lived in the Building when the new owners moved in, the new owners' noise, intrusions, and other abhorrent behaviors (likely) contributed to the death of three tenants (Pat, Mary, & John), and the departure of eight more (units 1001, 902, 802, 801, 702, 701, 602, 502) in very short order. Notice how they cleared-out all the upper-floor units, so they could charge higher rents?*

---

14 *Bently Reserve LP v. Papaliolios*, 218 Cal. App. 4th 418, 428 (2013).

> *They have sought evictions of 6 of those long-term tenants, even though rent was paid-in-full, and those tenants bothered nobody. And what they did to evict the occupants of unit #902, who put many of tens of thousands of dollars into their unit, was horrific and shameful.*
>
> *This is my own first-hand experience with this building, and its owners. I know this situation well, as I had the misfortune of being in a relationship with one of the Building's residents at the time, have spent many days and nights over many years in the Building, and have personally witnessed the abhorrent behavior of the owners of the Building.*
>
> *"There is NO RENT that is low enough to make residency here worthwhile."*

The review was repeatedly published on Yelp. After each publication plaintiffs asked Yelp to remove it, which Yelp did. However, this did not stop plaintiffs from eventually suing the defendant, Andreas Papaliolios for libel.

Approximately two months after plaintiffs filed suit, the defendant attempted to invoke California's anti-SLAPP statute and have the suit dismissed. According to the defendant, the libel action brought against him "was aimed at suppressing his right to speak in an open forum about an issue of public interest." The defendant also claimed that "plaintiffs would be unable to show a probability of prevailing under their libel claims because the statements in the review were mere opinions and thus not provably false."

In examining the defendant's motion to strike, pursuant to California's anti-SLAPP statute, the court applied a two-part test. In Part one, the court examined whether the challenged cause of action arose from a protected activity within the meaning of the statute. In Part two, the court looked at whether plaintiffs established a probability of prevailing on the merits.

In focusing on the second prong, the court in *Bently Reserve* determined that despite some hyperbolic statements ("sociopathic narcissist," "celebrates making the lives of tenants hell," and "other abhorrent behaviors") the Yelp review included purported facts about the building which could either be proved or disproved at trial. For example, in the Yelp review, the defendant stated that plaintiffs sought to evict six tenants and evicted tenants after they "put . . . tens of thousands of dollars into their unit." This is a factual matter that could be proven or disproven at trial. Thus, the trial court denied the defendant's use of the anti-SLAPP statute's motion to strike.

Another important aspect of *Bently Reserve* is that the court addressed the issue of whether courts should treat online content differently from offline content with respect to defamation. Put differently, should a more relaxed defamation standard apply to online content due to the nature of social media and the Internet? According to the court in *Bently Reserve*,

> *while* [prior judicial decisions] *allow courts to dispense quickly with defamation claims arising from true rants and raves, they do not preclude the courts from taking serious Internet speech seriously. Internet posts where the 'tone and content is serious,' where the poster represents himself as 'unbiased' and 'having specialized knowledge,' or where the poster claims his posts are 'Research Reports' or 'bulletins' or 'alerts,' may indeed be reasonably perceived as containing actionable assertions of fact.*

An example of an anti-SLAPP motion that was at least partially successful can be found in *Wong* v. *Jing*.[15] In this case, the plaintiff, a dentist sued the father (Tai Jing) and mother (Jia Ma) of a former patient alleging (1) libel per se and (2) intentional and negligent infliction of emotional distress. Wong claimed that defendants made the following comments about her practice on Yelp.

> *"1 star rating .... [¶] Let me first say I wish there is [sic] '0' star in Yelp rating. Avoid her like a disease! [¶] My son went there for two years. She treated two cavities plus the usual cleaning. She was fast, I mean really fast. I won't necessarily say that is a bad thing, but my son was light headed for several hours after the filling. So we decided to try another dentist after half a year. [¶] I wish I had gone there earlier. First the new dentist discovered seven cavities. All right all of those appeared during the last*

---

[15] *Wong v. Jing*, 189 Cal. App. 4th 1354 (Nov. 9, 2010).

> *half a year. Second, he would never use the laughing gas on kids, which was the cause for my son's dizziness. To apply laughing gas is the easiest to the dentist. There is no waiting, no needles. But it is general anesthetic, not local. And general anesthetic harms a kid's nerve system. Heck, it harms mine too. Third, the filling Yvonne Wong used is metallic silver color. The new dentist would only use the newer, white color filling. Why does the color matter? Here is the part that made me really, really angry. The color tells the material being used. The metallic filing, called silver amalgams [sic], has a small trace of mercury in it. The newer composite filling, while costing the dentist more, does not. In addition, it uses a newer technology to embed fluoride to clean the teeth for you. [¶] I regret ever going to her office. [¶] P.S. Just want to add one more thing. Dr. Chui, who shares the same office with Yvonne Wong is actually decent.*

Defendants responded to plaintiff's lawsuit with an anti-SLAPP motion under California Code of Civil Procedure Section 425.16. Defendants claimed that the Yelp review which related to the practices of the dental office was protected free speech. Defendants also pointed to the fact that Yelp is a public forum and the review itself would be of interest to others. While the trial court did find that the action arose from protected speech i.e., "a writing made in a place open to the public or a public forum in connection with an issue of public interest," the trial court also found that the plaintiff had established a "probability of success on the merits." Thus, the trial court denied the defendants' anti-SLAPP motion.

On appeal, the issue before the court was whether the plaintiff had established a probability of prevailing on the merits of all three of her claims. As for the claim of libel, the appellate court determined that the lower court properly denied the anti-SLAPP motion because the plaintiff "made a prima facie showing of probable success." However, the appellate court determined that the lower court erred in denying the anti-SLAPP motion for the last two claims because plaintiff "failed to make a prima facie showing of probable success on her cause of action for intentional or negligent infliction of emotional distress." Specifically, the appellate court found that the plaintiff's "showing does not reflect the sort of serious emotional distress with which a reasonable, normally constituted person would be unable to cope." As a result of the defendants' partial success on their anti-SLAPP motion, they received a total of $80,741.15 in legal fees. The award of legal fees is a key component to anti-SLAPP statutes.

B. ANTI-DISPARAGEMENT CLAUSE

The second method used by businesses to prevent the appearance of negative online comments is incorporating anti-disparagement clauses into online agreements. With these clauses, businesses attempt to get customers to waive their right to publicly discuss the services or products that they received. At present, the agreements take one of two forms. In the first format, the customer agrees to a contract that prohibits her from making or posting any negative remarks, criticisms, or comments about a business, its goods or services. These clauses are normally inserted in the terms and conditions that online companies require consumers to agree to prior to conducting business. A few companies forego the anti-disparagement clause at the front end and instead only require it when the consumer attempts to obtain a refund on products and services.

The second form of the anti-disparagement clause involves transferring copyright ownership of any online review from the customer to the respective business. This transfer of ownership is important because it then gives the business the power to demand the removal of any negative online post. This demand for removal can be directed to the consumer or third parties by invoking the Digital Millennium Copyright Act (DMCA).[16]

A few businesses have attempted to extend the anti-disparagement clause to third parties who have not necessarily agreed to the original contract terms. For example, a hotel in New York, which handled a number of weddings, required soon to be married couples who use their facility to sign a contract preventing them or anyone affiliated with them from posting a negative online review about the hotel. In theory, the anti-disparagement clause for this hotel applied to everyone in the wedding party. However, it is highly questionable whether the soon-to-be bride and groom could sign away the rights of others.

---

[16] 17 U.S.C. § 512.

Not surprisingly, many have questioned whether either form of the anti-disparagement clause is legally enforceable, see *Robert Lee v. Stacey Makhnevich*.[17] Those in favor of anti-disparagement clauses argue that the American legal system has upheld contracts of silence in areas such as protection of trade secrets and intellectual property, confidentiality of employer-employee and fiduciary relationships, and preservation of individual privacy. Furthermore, proponents claim that the courts have traditionally recognized the principles of freedom of contract, duty to read a contract before agreeing to its terms, and deference to written agreements.

Opponents of anti-disparagement clauses argue that these agreements run contrary to public policy and violate consumer protection laws. As for arguments grounded in contract law, opponents claim that anti-disparagement clauses lack proper consideration, privity of parties and are unconscionable.

There are numerous risks for businesses both legal and commercial with using an anti-disparagement clause. *Palmer v. Kleargear.com* serves as an illustrative example of what can go wrong when companies attempt to enforce an anti-disparagement clause against a customer.[18] In *Kleargear.com* the defendant, imposed a $3,500 fine against the plaintiff, a former customer, who had attempted to

---

[17] *Lee v. Makhnevich,* (Case No. 1:11–cv–08665, 2013 WL 1234829 (S.D.N.Y. March 27, 2013).

[18] *Palmer v. Kleargear.com*, no. 13–cv–00175 (D. Utah, filed Dec. 18, 2013).

purchase a desk ornament and key chain both of which cost less than $20. The fine arose because the customer's wife made less than flattering comments ("horrible customer service practices") about Kleargear.com on Ripoff Reports. Kleargear.com alleged that this fine, which was imposed three years after the initial purchase, was due to the customer's violation of the anti-disparagement clause that was included in the terms of use on its website. The clause read as follows:

> ***Non-Disparagement Clause***
>
> *In an effort to ensure fair and honest public feedback, and to prevent the publishing of libelous content in any form, your acceptance of this sales contract prohibits you from taking any action that negatively impacts KlearGear.com, its reputation, products, services, management or employees.*
>
> *Should you violate this clause, as determined by KlearGear.com in its sole discretion, you will be provided a seventy-two (72) hour opportunity to retract the content in question. If the content remains, in whole or in part, you will be immediately billed $3,500.00 USD for legal fees and court costs until such complete costs are determined in litigation. Should these charges remain unpaid for 30 calendar days from the billing date, your unpaid invoice will be forwarded to our third party collection firm and will be reported to consumer credit reporting agencies until paid.*

The customer never paid the fine but did attempt, without success, to get Ripoff Reports to remove the post. Ultimately, Kleargear.com reported the fine as a debt to the credit bureau. The customer then sued Kleargear.com claiming Fair Credit Reporting Act violations, defamation, and other torts. The federal judge who heard the case invalidated Kleargear.com's anti-disparagement clause and granted the customer a default judgment along with $306,750 in damages. The court also made the following findings:

> *The "non-disparagement clause" is void as procedurally and substantively unconscionable*;
>
> *The "non-disparagement clause" is unenforceable under the First Amendment because the appearance of such a term in a contract of adhesion is not a voluntary, knowing and intelligent waiver of a constitutional right, and any attempt to enforce such a term in court would invoke the power of the state so as to constitute state action.*

In light of the conduct of Kleargear.com and other companies, some states like California have passed legislation to prohibit anti-disparagement clauses. The California law can be found in Chapter 308, Section 1670.8 of the Civil Code and reads as follows.

> *(a) (1) A contract or proposed contract for the sale or lease of consumer goods or services may not include a provision waiving the consumer's right to make any statement regarding the seller*

or lessor or its employees or agents, or concerning the goods or services.

(2) It shall be unlawful to threaten or to seek to enforce a provision made unlawful under this section, or to otherwise penalize a consumer for making any statement protected under this section.

(b) Any waiver of the provisions of this section is contrary to public policy, and is void and unenforceable.

(c) Any person who violates this section shall be subject to a civil penalty not to exceed two thousand five hundred dollars ($2,500) for the first violation, and five thousand dollars ($5,000) for the second and for each subsequent violation, to be assessed and collected in a civil action brought by the consumer, by the Attorney General, or by the district attorney or city attorney of the county or city in which the violation occurred. When collected, the civil penalty shall be payable, as appropriate, to the consumer or to the general fund of whichever governmental entity brought the action to assess the civil penalty.

(d) In addition, for a willful, intentional, or reckless violation of this section, a consumer or public prosecutor may recover a civil penalty not to exceed ten thousand dollars ($10,000).

(e) The penalty provided by this section is not an exclusive remedy, and does not affect any other relief or remedy provided by law. This

section shall not be construed to prohibit or limit a person or business that hosts online consumer reviews or comments from removing a statement that is otherwise lawful to remove.

On the federal level there is the recently enacted Consumer Review Fairness Act (CRFA).[19] The CRFA, modeled after California's law, prohibits contract clauses that require the consumer to waive her right to make any negative statements regarding the goods or services involved in a contract. The CRFA would not preempt any state law addressing anti-disparagement clauses such as the one currently in place in California.

Some believe that the CRFA is superior to the California law because it addresses the use of copyright and trademark rights in non-disparagement clauses. Furthermore, this bill excludes from its protections employer-employee or independent contractor relationships. In addition, the bill does not invalidate contracts that prohibit disclosure of trade secrets, proprietary commercial or financial information, human resources and medical files, or law enforcement records.

§ 8.05 DEFAMATION

Over the past thirty years, the number of trials for libel, privacy and related claims involving print and broadcast media has steadily fallen from 266 in the 1980s to 192 in the 1990s to 124 in 2000s. However, this is not to say that the tort of defamation is on the

[19] Consumer Review Freedom Act of 2016.

decline or no longer raised in the Digital Age. Rather, it appears that defamation now encompasses a wider assortment of defendants. Today, claims of defamation that were previously brought against traditional media outlets are now being directed towards individual bloggers and those who post directly to social media platforms.

Historically, defamation has been defined as a false and unprivileged statement of fact harmful to someone's reputation, and published "with fault," meaning as a result of negligence or malice. Since defamation is a creature of state law, the precise requirements to raise a successful claim vary by jurisdiction. However, generally speaking, the following elements are required to prove defamation:

(1) False statement of fact;

(2) published to another;

(3) that is understood as;

   (a) being of and concerning the plaintiff; and

   (b) tending to harm the reputation of the plaintiff.

Written and published defamatory statements are "libel," while spoken statements constitute "slander." At common law, slanderous statements required plaintiff to prove economic harm. Also, if the person defamed is a public figure, the plaintiff must prove actual malice, which means that the defendant knew the information was false or had reckless disregard for the truth. In contrast, private information about nonpublic individuals could be defamatory if negligently published.

To date, defamation claims have arisen from a number of different social media platforms. The first ever Twitter defamation trial involved the singer Courtney Love. She was sued by her former lawyer for allegedly sending defamatory tweets about the lawyer's performance and ethical conduct to her 300,000 followers. Among the tweets in dispute was the following:

> *I was f!@#$%^& devestated [sic] when Rhonda J. Holmes esq. was bought off @FairNewsSpears perhaps you can get a quote.*[20]

Love sent the tweets after her attorney declined to bring a claim of fraud against the individuals managing the estate of her late husband, Kurt Kobain.

Love had initially argued that "the Tweet was on the Internet and qualifies as an opinion because of common hyperbole and exaggeration in the Internet context." The trial judge found this argument unpersuasive and the case proceeded to trial. Fortunately for Love, a jury sided with her and she was not found liable for her actions.

Love's success could be partially attributed to a prior ruling by the trial judge which found that Love was a limited public figure; therefore, the plaintiff had to prove that Love either knew the statement

---

[20] *Gordon & Holmes v. Love*, No. BC462438, 2011 WL 2062323 (Cal. Super. Ct. May 26, 2011).

was false or made with a reckless disregard of the truth.

Like in the offline world, separating fact from opinion is not always easy on social media. Making the distinction, however, is necessary because defamation claims must be based on a false fact not a false opinion. In *Milkovich v. Lorain Journal Co*, the U.S. Supreme Court established a two-part test to assist in distinguishing between fact and opinion.[21] First, the statement must be provable as false. Second, the statement must be capable of being reasonably interpreted as stating actual facts.

The following case illustrates how some courts attempt to make the distinction when dealing with social media related content. In *Feld v. Conway,* the plaintiff, Mary Feld, bought a thoroughbred horse and arranged for it to be shipped to a horse farm.[22] Unfortunately, the horse in question ended up being sent to a slaughterhouse in Canada instead. This turn of events led to an intense online discussion in the horse thoroughbred community. At some point during the discussion, Crystal Conway, who worked in the thoroughbred industry but had no prior relationship with Feld, tweeted the following:

> *Mary Feld aka Gina Holt—you are f!@#$%^ crazy!*

---

[21] *Milkovich v. Lorain Journal Co.*, 497 U.S. 1 (1990).

[22] *Feld v. Conway*, 16 F. Supp. 3d 1 (D. Mass. Apr. 14, 2013).

This tweet by Conway led Feld to sue her for defamation. Feld's suit, however, was dismissed by the court which described the tweet as follows:

> *[It] was made as part of a heated Internet debate about plaintiff's responsibility for the disappearance of her horse. Furthermore, it cannot be read literally without regard to the way in which a reasonable person would interpret it. The phrase "Mary Feld . . . is f!@#$%^& crazy," when viewed in that context, cannot reasonably be understood to state actual facts about plaintiff's mental state. It was obviously intended as criticism—that is, as opinion—not as a statement of fact.*

Other issues that arise with distinguishing facts from opinions on social media concern the use of hyperlinks. While hyperlinks cannot stop a claim of defamation from going forward, they can greatly reduce the likelihood that the claim will be successful. Supporting facts with hyperlinks allow readers to draw their own conclusions. As a result, those facts may be deemed only an opinion. Without supporting hyperlinks, readers must rely solely on the content provided. This point is illustrated in *Adelson v. Harris*.[23]

In *Adelson*, the plaintiff, Sheldon Adelson, owned casinos and resorts around the world. In 2012, he sued the National Jewish Defense Counsel (NJDC),

---

[23] *Adelson v. Harris*, 973 F. Supp. 2d 467 (S.D.N.Y. Sept. 30, 2013).

among others, for defamation for publishing the following statement on its website:

> *this week, reports surfaced that in addition to his anti-union and allegedly corrupt business practices, Adelson 'personally approved' of prostitution in his Macau casinos*

The statement was accompanied by a hyperlink to an AP story in which a former employee of a company run by Adelson claimed that Adelson had approved a "prostitution strategy" for the company's Macau properties.

In *Adelson*, the court found that the hyperlink to the AP story was sufficient to defeat Adelson's defamation claim against NJDC. The court went on to explain that:

> *[t]he hyperlink is the twenty-first century equivalent of the footnote for purposes of attribution in defamation law, because it has become a well-recognized means for an author or the Internet to attribute a source. . . . [Hyperlinking to sources] fosters the facile dissemination of knowledge on the Internet.*

The *Adelson* court also stated that "protecting defendants who hyperlink to their sources is good public policy."

Some states provide additional privileges and defenses to journalists who are accused of defamation. This has raised the issue of whether a blogger should be deemed a journalist for the purposes of receiving additional defenses for defamation claims. To this question, the 9th Circuit answered in the affirmative.

The issue arose in *Obsidian Finance Group v. Cox*.[24] Here, the defendant, an active blogger, was held liable, after a jury trial, for a defamatory post she made about the plaintiff. The defendant subsequently appealed and argued among other things that the trial court erred by not requiring the plaintiff to prove actual malice, which applies to media outlets who are sued for defamation in the state of Oregon. The trial court had refused to treat the defendant as a media outlet finding that she did not hold a degree in journalism, was not affiliated with traditional media outlets, and did not adhere to certain journalistic standards.

On appeal, a unanimous three-judge panel affirmed in part and reversed in part the district court's ruling. On the issue of whether bloggers should be treated similarly to traditional media with respect to claims of defamation, the 9th Circuit Court of Appeals stated that:

> *[t]he protections of the First Amendment do not turn on whether the defendant was a trained journalist, formally affiliated with traditional news entities, engaged in conflict-of-interest disclosure, went beyond just assembling others' writings, or tried to get both sides of the story. As the Supreme Court has accurately warned, a First Amendment distinction between the*

---

[24] *Obsidian Finance Group v. Cox*, 740 F.3d 1284 (9th Cir. 2014).

institutional press and other speakers is unworkable.

A. ANONYMITY

One major challenge with resolving defamation claims is anonymity. To date, neither social media providers nor the government has established a cost-effective method of verifying the identity of social media users. Some social media providers have a real-name user policy, which means that users must use a name supported by some form of offline identification i.e., mail, library card, driver's license, etc. This policy is generally enforced by the social media provider after one user reports another for not using their true identity. At times this will include users who, while not anonymous, use pseudonyms.

The one notable exception here is so-called "parody sites." These social media sites, primarily found on Twitter, are created and used to impersonate, lampoon, or parody others. However, even these generally require some type of disclaimer to ensure that the site is not taken seriously. Nonetheless, some of the targets of these sites don't see the humor and bring claims of defamation, invasion of privacy, and infliction of emotional distress.

There are a variety of reasons why people want to disguise their identity on social media. Some users engage in whistleblowing and worry about retaliation. Other users, like teachers, want to keep their professional and personal lives separate. A third group of anonymous users includes crime victims and members of groups that have been discriminated against in the past.

Unfortunately, not all social media users have benign reasons for remaining anonymous. Some do it in order to engage in crime, defamation, bullying, trolling, scams, and hate speech. These are the individuals that the social media providers, the general public, and occasionally law enforcement want to discover. The first step in that discovery process, at least with respect to defamation, is to identify or unmask the person who created the content. This assumes of course that the court hearing the matter first has jurisdiction, a topic discussed in depth in Section 10.02.

B. UNMASKING

When trying to unmask a party in a defamation lawsuit many jurisdictions adhere to the so-called Dendrite Test established in *Dendrite International, Inc. v. Doe No. 3.*[25] With the Dendrite test, courts follow a four-step procedure in order to determine whether or not to unmask a party. In Part one, the plaintiff must try to notify the poster that an order for disclosure is pending and that he or she can oppose the order. In Part two, the plaintiff must specifically identify the allegedly defamatory material. In Part three, the plaintiff must present a prima facie case of defamation against the anonymous poster. In Part four, the court balances the defendant's First Amendment right to

---

[25] *Dendrite Int'l, Inc. v. John Doe No. 3*, 775 A.2d 756 (N.J. App. Div. 2001).

anonymous speech against the strength of the plaintiff's prima facie case and the need to unmask the defendant.

Other jurisdictions, like Virginia, apply less stringent standards when determining whether to unmask a party in a defamation lawsuit. This point is illustrated in *Hadeed v. Yelp,* where the plaintiff, a carpet cleaning business, filed a defamation suit against several individuals who made critical posts about the plaintiff's business on Yelp.[26] In his complaint, plaintiff alleged that he tried to match the negative reviews with his customer database but could find no record that those who posted negative reviews were actual customers. The plaintiff then issued a subpoena duces tecum to Yelp seeking information about the authors. Yelp balked at the subpoena and the plaintiff moved to have it enforced by the court.

The trial court and the Virginia appellate court agreed with the plaintiff and ordered Yelp to turn over the information. In making their rulings, the Virginia courts did not apply the *Dendrite* test and instead used a "good faith basis" test. Thus, the plaintiff only had to have "a good faith basis" to believe that the comments were defamatory in order to receive the name of the anonymous posters, a much lower standard than *Dendrite.*

Yelp appealed the decision of the appellate court to the Virginia Supreme Court which overruled the

---

[26] *Yelp, Inc. v. Hadeed Carpet Cleaning, Inc.*, 770 S.E. 2d 440 (Va. Apr. 16, 2015).

lower court, finding that Yelp could not be forced to turn over the identities of the anonymous online reviewers. In overruling the two lower courts, the Virginia Supreme Court skirted the First Amendment issue and instead made its decision based on procedural grounds. The high court held that it could not order Yelp, a company headquartered in California, to produce documents located in California for an action that arose in Virginia.

It should be noted that the Virginia Supreme Court did not quash the initial subpoena because the plaintiff, if he so desired, could still try to enforce it under California law. It is unclear whether or not he would have been successful since the California courts have been split on whether to unmask an anonymous online commentator in a defamation lawsuit, see *Chevron v. Donziger*[27] and *Music Group Macao Commercial Offshore Limited v. Does.*[28]

C. STEP-BY-STEP PROCEDURES

Due to the variety of issues that can arise in a social media-related defamation lawsuit, the following step-by-step guidelines were created to provide general guidance to those involved in or considering a lawsuit in this area.

---

[27] *Chevron v. Donziger*, 2013 WL 4536808 CRB (NC) (N.D. Cal. Aug. 22, 2013).

[28] *Music Group Macao Commercial Offshore Ltd. v. Does*, 2015 WL 75073 (N.D. Cal. Mar. 2, 2015).

Step 1: pursue non-judicial alternatives discussed in Section 8.06

Step 2: review applicable anti-SLAPP statutes

Step 3: explore jurisdictional issues

Step 4: look at potential CDA immunity

Step 5: identify or unmask the social media user

Step 6: consider defamation defenses and privileges

§ 8.06 NON-JUDICIAL ALTERNATIVES

Not all tort related problems arising from social media require legal action or need to be litigated. In fact, in some instances, the litigation and ensuing publicity that arises from it can actually make matters worse. This point was illustrated in a 2003 right of privacy suit brought by Barbra Streisand.

In *Streisand v. Adelman* Streisand attempted to sue photographers for $50 million for an aerial photograph taken of her Malibu mansion.[29] The photographer took the photograph along with many others to document soil erosion along the Malibu coast. Prior to filing the lawsuit, the photo in question, "Image 3850," had been downloaded six times; two of those downloads were done by Streisand's attorneys. After the lawsuit was filed, Image 3850 was viewed over 420,000 times. The

[29] *Streisand v. Adelman*, Case No. SC 077 251 (Sup. Ct. Los Angeles Cty. Dec. 31, 2003).

lawsuit, which was ultimately unsuccessful, resulted in the creation of a new term entitled the "Streisand effect," whereby an individual's attempt to remove or censor online content has the unintended consequence of publicizing the information more widely.

A. STEP-BY-STEP PROCEDURES

Methods of resolving social media-related tort issues, short of litigation, will differ, of course, based on the particular problem and the facts presented. However, there are some general guidelines that can be followed. The following is a general step-by-step approach for dealing with potentially defamatory content found on social media.

Step 1: document the content

Step 2: consider the nature of the content and whether it will be supplanted or lowered in prominence by later postings

Step 3: ignore the content (remember the Streisand effect)

Step 4: consider whether to respond publicly or privately

Step 5: request that the poster remove the content

Step 6: request that the service provider remove the content (service provider's TOS may prohibit the content)

Step 7: request that major search engines such as Google remove the content from their search results

Step 8: contact law enforcement (depending on the nature of the content)

Step 9: institute civil proceedings (see Section 8.05)

CHAPTER 9

CRIMINAL LAW AND PROCEDURE

§ 9.01 INTRODUCTION

This chapter examines the impact of social media on criminal law and procedure. The first part of this chapter will look at criminal law. Here, the chapter will discuss the various ways in which criminal defendants use social media by examining crimes unique to social media e.g., revenge porn, online impersonation, and flash mobs. This section will also explore whether social media platforms can be held criminally liable for the actions of their users e.g., tweets by terrorists.

The second half of the chapter will delve into criminal procedure. The focus here is twofold. First, this section of the chapter will look at the legal questions that arise when the government employs social media to investigate others. Next, the section will explore the methods relied upon by the government, in the context of criminal law, to monitor and restrict an individual's use of social media.

§ 9.02 CATEGORIZING SOCIAL MEDIA CRIMES

Criminal defendants use social media to not only commit crimes, but also to organize, plan, discuss, and even brag about illegal activity. Generally speaking, these social media related crimes fall into one of two categories. Category I crimes involve defendants using social media to *relay* information to others. While most social media related crimes fall into Category I, some fall into Category II which involve the defendant using social media to *gather* information about victims. Certain criminal activity, like online impersonation, may cut across both Categories I and II.

Category II crimes are further divided into two subcategories. In the first subcategory, the criminal defendant uses the information gathered from social media to commit modern crimes that many associate with the Internet e.g., identity theft. In the second subcategory, the criminal defendant uses the information gathered from social media to commit traditional crimes that many do not necessarily associate with the Internet e.g., burglary.

United States v. Elonis serves as a typical Category I crime and is arguably the first social media case to reach the U.S. Supreme Court.[1] In *Elonis*, the defendant, Anthony Elonis, was charged in a five count indictment with violating the Interstate Communications Act (ICA). Specifically, he was alleged to have posted threats on his personal Facebook page. The threats were directed at the general public, law enforcement, co-workers, friends, and Elonis' soon-to-be ex-wife.

Elonis was ultimately convicted on four of the five counts and subsequently appealed. On appeal, Elonis argued that the trial court applied the wrong test to determine what constitutes a true threat on social

---

1 *Elonis v. United States*, 135 S. Ct. 2001 (2015).

media. Elonis claimed that the prosecution had to prove that he had a subjective intent to carry out his threats. This subjective intent standard is the law in a few jurisdictions. In contrast, the government argued that the lower court was correct and that it only has to show that a reasonable person would regard Elonis' Facebook posts as threatening. This reasonable person standard is followed by most jurisdictions.

The U.S. Supreme Court overturned the lower court's ruling; however, it side-stepped the key First Amendment question and did not directly accept either argument put forward by the parties. Instead, the Court based its decision on statutory grounds. The Court ultimately determined that a negligence standard was insufficient to support a conviction under the ICA. More specifically, the Court found that

> *[h]aving liability turn on whether a "reasonable person" regards the communication as a threat—regardless of what the defendant thinks—"reduces culpability on the all-important element of crime to negligence."*

For many, the Court's ruling did little to clarify the issue of what constitutes a true threat on social media. This in turn led to the introduction of Senate Bill S. 2552 (Interstate Threats Clarification Act) in 2016 which among others things helps clarify how the ICA applies to online threats.

With respect to Category I crimes, the term *relay* applies to any method by which an individual may deliver information to another. This includes such things as a Like or friend request. In one case from Tennessee, a radio host was criminally charged for improperly using the Like button. His charges stemmed from Liking a video on the Socialcam site of another person. Unfortunately for the radio host, the person in question, a former colleague/friend, had previously obtained a restraining order against him. In this case, the victim took screenshots of her video post and the defendant's subsequent Like. She then gave this information to the police who arrested the radio host for violating the protection order.

In relaying information to victims or the general public, criminal defendants take a variety of different approaches and use different techniques. Some communicate directly with the victim on social media, while others communicate indirectly by merely posting information on social media in a public or quasi-public place where the victims or the public can view it. In at least one case, discussed next, the defendant was convicted after the victim went to the defendant's social media site and actually sought out the offending information.

In *State v. Craig*, the New Hampshire Supreme Court upheld Brian Craig's convictions for criminal threatening, witness tampering, and stalking.[2] Craig's convictions arose, in part, from the Facebook comments that he made about a bartender who worked at a restaurant he frequented. Apparently, Craig thought that he was in a relationship with this

---

2 *State v. Craig*, 112 A.3d 559 (N.H. Feb. 12, 2015).

bartender despite the fact that the two had never been on a date or gone beyond polite social conversation.

In April of 2012, Craig sent the bartender a letter at her place of work in which he referenced his Facebook page and his belief that the bartender was trying to hurt him. Alarmed by the letter, the bartender went to the police. Shortly thereafter, the bartender received a second letter. The bartender again went to the police who served Craig with a warning letter informing him that future "stalking behavior" would result in prosecution. The next day a third letter arrived which led the victim to seek a temporary restraining order from the court.

Several days after obtaining a temporary restraining order from the court, the bartender decided to read Craig's Facebook page. She did so because Craig's initial letter to her referenced his Facebook page and her mother told her about "the extent and the severity" of Craig's posts. The posts about the bartender were contained in the defendant's Facebook "Notes," which could be read by opening the Notes section on Craig's Facebook profile page. After reading the posts, the victim was again alarmed and contacted the police who confronted Craig about the posts many of which were made after the defendant had notice of the initial temporary restraining order.

Craig was subsequently indicted for witness tampering, stalking, and criminal threatening. He was convicted and appealed the witness tampering and stalking convictions. The New Hampshire

Supreme Court ultimately affirmed the defendant's conviction on all three counts.

According to the New Hampshire Supreme Court, to convict for stalking the state had to prove that Craig,

> *by posting on his own public Facebook page after he had received a restraining order, engaged in a single act of conduct that constitutes: (1) an "act of communication"; and (2) "contact" pursuant to RSA 173–B:1, IV that violates the April 24th restraining order.*

Here, the court found that *any action to communicate with another either directly or indirectly constitutes contact*. According to the court,

> *[b]y posting messages addressing the victim on his public Facebook page, and directing the victim's attention to his page, the defendant both created a message and took steps to convey it to the victim.*

It did not matter to the court that the victim actually went to Craig's Facebook page to find the information. According to the court,

> *[w]e discern no meaningful difference between the defendant posting messages on Facebook with both the purpose and effect of communicating a message to her, and the defendant positioning himself on a street corner with the knowledge and expectation that the victim would pass by, and then shouting to her.*

For additional support for its position, the court looked to *Commonwealth v. Butler*.[3] In *Butler*, the defendant sent anonymous flowers to his ex-girlfriend and then was prosecuted for violating a restraining order. In upholding the defendant's conviction, the court in *Butler* determined that "[the defendant's] profession of anonymity merely invited inquiry." Upon receipt of the flowers, the ex-girlfriend contacted the florist and discovered that her ex-boyfriend had sent them.

State v. Craig illustrates the challenges that some courts face when applying current laws and cases to social media. In *Butler*, the defendant made contact and violated the restraining order as soon as the flowers were received by his ex-girlfriend. No contact means no contact regardless of whether one leaves a name or identifying information. With a no contact order in place, the defendant can't call the victim from an unregistered phone and then hang up before his voice is recognized. In addition, the defendant can't contact the victim through a third party. These scenarios, however, are different from what occurred in *Craig* where the victim on her own sought out the information.

Despite the ruling in *Craig*, it is not entirely clear whether someone can be convicted of stalking for merely posting information on a social media site without directing the victim to that particular site. In *Horowitz v. Horowitz*, the appellant successfully challenged a domestic violence protection order

---

[3] *Commonwealth v. Butler*, 661 N.E.2d 666, 667 (Mass. App. Ct. 1996).

issued against him on behalf of his estranged wife. The initial order stemmed from allegations of domestic violence in the form of cyberstalking. Specifically, Mrs. Horowitz complained that two Facebook posts by Mr. Horowitz demonstrated that he had "either 'hacked' her computer or was somehow spying on her because" his posts referenced information that "would have only been observable by accessing her personal Facebook account."[4]

In overturning the order, the appellate court found that appellant merely posted information to his own Facebook page and the posts were "not directed at a specific person" nor was the appellee tagged or mentioned in the posts. The court in *Horowitz* went on to draw a distinction between Facebook posts and email. With respect to the former, the court determined that they "are not directed at a specific person but are instead posted for all of the user's Facebook 'friends' to see, depending on privacy settings."

§ 9.03 IMPOSING CRIMINAL PENALTIES ON SOCIAL MEDIA PLATFORMS

In addition to Category I and II crimes, there is the potential that social media providers themselves could be held liable for the criminal conduct of their users. To date, there are no reported cases of a social media provider being prosecuted. However, this is not to say that they cannot be prosecuted or are immune from prosecution. Like any other

---

[4] *Horowitz v. Horowitz*, 160 So. 3d 530 (Fla. 2nd DCA April 1, 2015).

corporation, social media providers can face criminal charges. In the eyes of the law, corporations are "legal persons," capable of both engaging in civil legal actions and committing crimes.

One potential statute that may be used against social media providers is 18 U.S.C. § 2339B which prohibits anyone from providing material support to an entity designated as a "foreign terrorist organization (FTO)" by the State Department.[5] Pursuant to this statute, a social media provider could be prosecuted for granting an FTO a social media account. "Material support" includes "services" and "communications equipment." By providing an account, the social media provider is arguably offering the FTO an important "service" and extremely effective "communications equipment" to reach others.

The question here is whether the social media provider's service or communications platform can be deemed "communications equipment," which has been an undefined term to date. While no prosecutions of social media providers have occurred, despite the urging of some, the material support statute is so broadly written that it could conceivably encompass social media providers. Also, the Department of Justice has used this statute to prosecute individual users of social media and others who post terrorist content.

---

[5] 18 U.S.C. § 2339B prohibits "knowingly provid[ing] material support or resources to a foreign terrorist organization."

§ 9.04 NEW CRIMES

Despite the increased use of social media by criminal defendants, there has not been a widespread creation of new crimes. In fact, to date, only three new crimes have been created. Those three crimes, which will be discussed in depth next, are revenge porn, online impersonation, and flash mobs. However, this is not to say that criminal defendants do not regularly employ social media. Quite the opposite, criminal defendants, as previously mentioned, use social media to not only commit crimes, but also to organize plan, discuss, and even brag about criminal activity.

A. REVENGE PORN

Revenge porn, which is a Category I crime, involves the sharing, without consent, of another's private sexual images. The images are taken with consent by either the victim or a former intimate partner. However, they are later shared through electronic means with others without the consent of the victim. In certain instances, the images also include personal identifying information. For the purposes of this book, the discussion on revenge porn will be limited to instances where the victim, at least initially, allows the other person to possess the images in question.

Currently, a few states have enacted laws to target revenge porn directly. Among these states, most treat revenge porn as a misdemeanor but a few, like

Arizona, categorize it as a felony.[6] Some jurisdictions also require defendants convicted of revenge porn to register as a sex offender. For those states without specific laws on revenge porn, they combat the problem through traditional criminal statutes such as harassment, extortion, and stalking. In addition, many of these same states are in the process of and or considering enacting their own revenge porn laws.

California is one state that has enacted a law directly targeting revenge porn.[7] Initially, the California law did not include "selfies" or photos taken by the victim. This is because the victim retains ownership rights in selfies and could request that they be taken down. The law, however, was later amended to include selfies.

The California law as written does have some significant hurdles for the government to clear in order to successfully prosecute the criminal defendant. First, the prosecution must prove that the victim suffered serious emotional distress. This usually requires victim testimony, which is not always a straightforward proposition. Second, the prosecution must show that the parties agreed or understood that the image should remain private. Evidence to fulfill this element may be difficult to acquire. Finally, the law does not apply to redistributors only the person who makes the initial distribution or posting.

---

[6] Arizona Revised Statutes § 13–1425. It should be noted that this statute has been found unenforceable by at least one court.

[7] California Penal Code, § 647.

B. REVENGE PORN DEBATE

For a variety of reasons, laws targeting revenge porn have been both praised and criticized. First, some believe that the government should not be involved in the activities of two consenting adults. They see revenge porn, like defamation and invasion of privacy, as a civil not a criminal matter. Thus, they argue that the recourse for a revenge porn victim, like someone who has been defamed or had their privacy invaded, is in the civil court system.

Civil remedies include not only tort actions but also Digital Millennium Copyright Act (DMCA) take-down requests.[8] Pursuant to the DMCA, revenge porn victims can request that an online host site remove certain inappropriate photos.

In response to these arguments, those who favor criminalization claim that civil remedies are inadequate for the harm caused by revenge porn. Here, proponents note that many individuals who engage in revenge porn are judgment proof i.e., they don't have the economic resources to pay money damages. Another issue with civil lawsuits is the time and expense associated with bringing them.

With respect to the DMCA takedown notice, this remedy only works if the victim took the image. Moreover, just because the image is taken down on one site does not mean it won't appear on another. Thus, the victim gets caught up in a game of "Whack-a-Mole" where she spends a significant amount of

---

[8] Digital Millennium Copyright Act of 1998.

time tracking down the image wherever it might pop-up. Finally, there are some sites, especially those located beyond the borders of the United States, where running afoul of the DMCA is not a major concern for the owner or operator of the site.

Another option, which some find extreme, is to copyright one's anatomy. Here, the victim gives the U.S. Copyright Office a copy of the material, usually photos, that he wants protected—videos can be more challenging. Fortunately, these particular pictures are not put in the Library of Congress like other copyrights; however, the person's real name and the title of the image do appear in a public catalog.

A second argument put forward by opponents of criminalization is that the injuries suffered by the victims are self-inflicted. These critics distinguish revenge porn from other forms of harassment claiming that revenge porn victims are not real victims in the traditional sense because they allowed the images to be taken in the first place. Thus, rather than create new criminal laws, there needs to be more efforts at educating members of society about the long-term consequences of allowing or sending risque images online.

Proponents of revenge porn laws see this argument as blaming the victim for being a victim. They also claim that opponents of criminalizing revenge porn ignore the realities of the Digital Age where individuals, especially millennials routinely exchange sexually explicit photos. To illustrate how common sexting and electronic sharing of nude or semi-nude photos has become, proponents of revenge porn laws point to a Pew study which found that 20 percent of smartphone users reported receiving a nude photograph.

First Amendment concerns present the most compelling argument against criminalizing revenge porn. Here, opponents argue that revenge porn laws criminalize the publication of speech in the form of images. Opponents question why revenge porn should be criminalized when other forms of truthful but embarrassing speech revealed to the public is not criminalized e.g., gossip.

Other First Amendment advocates worry about the unintended consequences of criminalization. While most consider revenge porn in the context of relationships gone bad, these laws could be extended to other situations e.g., sharing or re-publishing images of nude celebrities that have been leaked online. Other situations that come to mind include sharing an image of a woman breastfeeding or the pyramid stacking of the half-naked prisoners at Abu Ghraib.

Proponents of revenge porn laws question these parade of horribles and argue that they can be avoided with a narrowly tailored statute. To show that a revenge porn law can be properly drafted, proponents point to the ACLU, an organization well known for its work in defending free speech. According to the ACLU, a revenge porn law can be constitutional if "[i]t. . . designate[s] that the perpetrator had malicious intent, that his or her action caused actual harm, that he or she acted knowingly without consent, and that the victim had an expectation of privacy."[9] The importance of requiring criminal intent was recently highlighted in Arizona where a federal judge determined that the state's revenge porn law was unenforceable. The judge reached this conclusion because Arizona's law did not require proof that the person distributing the images intended to harm or harass the person portrayed in the images.

In addition to the passage of criminal laws by states across the country, some social media providers have taken their own steps to prevent revenge porn. In 2015, Facebook modified its Community Standards to specifically address revenge porn. Facebook's policy now reads as follows:

> *To protect victims and survivors, we also remove photographs or videos depicting incidents of sexual violence and images shared in revenge or without permission from the people in the images.*
>
> *Our definition of sexual exploitation includes solicitation of sexual material, any sexual content involving minors, threats to share intimate images, and offers of sexual services. Where appropriate, we refer this content to law enforcement.*[10]

Twitter has made similar changes and now informs users that they "may not post intimate photos or videos that were taken or distributed

[9] Liz Halloran, *Race to Stop 'Revenge Porn' Raises Free Speech Worries*, NPR (March 6, 2014).

[10] Facebook Community Standards 2017.

without the subject's consent."[11] Finally, Google offers revenge porn victims their own form of the right to be forgotten. Here, the victims complete online forms to request that revenge porn content involving them no longer appear in Google searches. While this doesn't remove revenge porn from being online, it does help disassociate the image from the victim when someone runs online searches for him or her.

C. ONLINE IMPERSONATION

Online impersonation can be both a Category I and II crime. Unlike traditional identity theft, online impersonators are not motivated by economic gain. Instead, the defendant impersonates the victim for a variety of non-economic reasons.

While online impersonations arise in a number of different settings, they generally take one of three forms. The first method involves the impersonator pretending to be someone else in order to interact with or establish a relationship with a specific person who may or may not be a "victim" depending on how that term is defined. Examples here include "catfishing."

In 2014, the Oxford dictionary defined the term "catfish" as "lure someone into a relationship by adopting a fictional online persona."[12] This type of impersonation generally occurs over a period of time because the impersonator needs to connect and bond

---

[11] Twitter Rules 2015.

[12] Oxford English Dictionary 2014.

with the victim. The impersonator carries out the impersonation by creating a fake online identity. To date, the most famous catfishing incident involved Manti Te'o, a professional football player.

The second method of online impersonation involves the impersonator pretending to be someone else in order to interact with the general public rather than a specific person. The victim here can be both the general public and the person impersonated. Unfortunately, there are numerous instances of spurned individuals taking on the identity of their former significant other in order to cause embarrassment or harm to that person. However, a prior intimate relationship is not a prerequisite for this method of online impersonation, as illustrated next in *Commonwealth v. Johnson*.[13]

Here, the Massachusetts high court upheld the criminal conviction of a husband and wife who, among other things, used fake Craigslist ads to torment their neighbors (the Lyons family). Apparently, the defendants had a falling out with the Lyons family over a land development issue. The defendants went on a campaign to make life "miserable" for the Lyons family which included posting fake ads on Craigslist. These ads listed the phone number and address of the Lyons family and claimed that they had items for sale. As a result, the Lyons family was barraged with visits and phone calls from people looking to buy non-existent items.

---

[13] *Commonwealth v. Johnson*, 21 N.E.3d 937 (Mass. December 23, 2014).

At trial, the defendants argued that they could not be convicted under Massachusetts' anti-harassment statute because the ads on Craigslist were not directed to the Lyons family but rather to third parties. The Massachusetts Supreme Judicial Court rejected that argument, finding that "[t]he Craigslist postings were the equivalent of the defendants recruiting others to harass the victims." The court also noted that the "defendants cannot launder their harassment of the Lyons family through the Internet to escape liability."

The third form of online impersonation is not really impersonation in its truest sense. Here, the defendant maintains her own identity but claims to own, control, or be responsible for something belonging to another. For example, some young women have taken the photos of other people's children and claimed that they are the mother of the child. They have even gone as far as engaging in virtual role playing e.g., they pretend to participate in daily activities with the child. This has led to the creation of the term "digital kidnapping." At present, it does not appear as though any jurisdiction has criminalized this last form of online impersonation.

To combat the growing number of online impersonations, a few states have passed laws specifically targeting online impersonators. While all states and the federal government have laws combating identity theft and harassment, only a few states have specific laws that go after online impersonators.[14] California is one state that criminalizes this conduct through its penal code.[15]

One of the big challenges with online impersonation laws is defining the "harm" caused by the impersonator. This is because online impersonations, as discussed previously, are done for a variety of reasons. Some online impersonations are meant to invoke satire or humor. For example, an online impersonator took on the persona of the former CEO of Apple, Steve Jobs.[16] This person used the Twitter account (handle) "@ceoSteveJobs" and sent out tweets such as:

> *"It's official. The iPad now comes in greater variety than my clothing."*
>
> *"When Chuck Norris holds the iPhone 4 the signal increases,"*

To add clarity to what constitutes "harm," California's online impersonation law uses terms such as "intimidating, threatening or defrauding." Yet, even by adding these words, there is no clear picture on what makes-up "harm." Some believe that the harm must be significant and more than de minimis. Others see it differently and think that individuals should be prosecuted anytime they pretend to be someone else online and manifest bad

---

[14] See e.g., Connecticut, Hawaii, Mississippi, New York, Washington and Wyoming.

[15] California Penal Code § 528.5(a) (West 2014).

[16] Don Reisinger, *Twitter Suspends Fake Steve Jobs Account Then Backtracks,* CNET http://news.cnet.com/8301-13506_3-2003 8220-17.html.

intentions. In Texas, if the online impersonator has the intent to "intimidate or threaten" she potentially faces a felony.[17] Obviously, relying on a broad definition of harm will expose many more online impersonators to potential prosecution.

D. FLASH MOBS

A flash mob is a Category I crime where defendants use social media to communicate and orchestrate criminal activity. In 2004, the Oxford English Dictionary defined "flash mob" as "a sudden mass gathering, unanticipated except by participants who communicate electronically." In the world of criminal law, the flash mob takes a sinister twist as large groups of teens use social media to quickly gather at one location to vandalize, steal, and commit acts of violence in concert with one another. Flash mobs generate heightened concern among law enforcement and society as a whole because of the secretive (at times) and fluid nature in which they arise. Furthermore, flash mob participants disperse just as quickly as they assemble.

Some flash mobs involve unwitting co-conspirators. For example, a rapper, by the name of The Game, sent a tweet to his 580,000 followers alerting them to a possible internship in the music business. However, the contact number for the internship was not for anyone in the music industry but rather for the Los Angeles County Sheriff's Department. After sending out the tweet, the

---

[17] Texas Penal Code Annotated § 33.07(a).

Sheriff's line was bombarded with calls. In fact, law enforcement received so many calls that regular callers could not get through. After discovering the reason for the large number of calls, law enforcement contacted The Game, who then apologized for tweeting the wrong number. No criminal charges were filed against The Game who claimed that the inclusion of the phone number was a mistake.

To date, several cities and states have passed or are considering legislation to address the dangers flash mobs present. There has been no uniform approach to enacting such legislation. For example, in 2011, the Cleveland City Council passed an ordinance prohibiting the use of social media to incite people to riot, unlawfully congregate, or engage in disorderly conduct within the city's limits. This ordinance was met with stiff opposition from the ACLU, who viewed it as vague and an infringement on First Amendment rights. This in turn led the mayor of Cleveland to veto the ordinance.

In response to the mayor's veto, the city council passed another ordinance without the social media language. This new proposal classified electronic media devices as a criminal tool when used to incite riots. Since the mayor neither vetoed nor signed this new ordinance, it ultimately became law.

Another approach to addressing the dangers presented by flash mobs is to hold each person involved accountable for the damage done by the group as a whole. For example, if 30 teenagers show up at a convenience store and each one takes a beverage, each teenager could be charged with the total number of beverages stolen from the store. This change in the law would make it easier to charge misdemeanor petty theft offenses, which often occur during criminal flash mobs, as felonies. This idea of holding co-defendants liable for the actions of others within the flash mob is comparable to the crime of conspiracy and accomplice liability.

§ 9.05 CHALLENGES OF PREVENTING SOCIAL MEDIA CRIMES

Many believe that crimes involving social media are more difficult to prevent and prosecute than traditional crimes that occur entirely offline. For example, people point to the reach of social media and claim that it has made the physical proximity of the defendant to the victim less of an issue. Historically, the criminal defendant was limited in his choice of victims to those who were in close physical proximity to him. By knocking down these barriers, social media has provided the criminal defendant a much larger pool of victims. With social media, a criminal defendant can reach and interact with a victim that is thousands of miles away. Social media's reach also allows the criminal defendant to re-victimize the victim even when that person is no longer in the defendant's physical presence. This is because the criminal defendant can reach out and virtually "touch" the victim.

The second big challenge involves the identification of social media users. Anonymity flourishes on social media, which makes it difficult to confirm an individual user's true identity. This in turn makes accountability more challenging. For a more complete discussion on anonymity see Section 8.05.

Finally, there are concerns about the current laws and whether they adequately address the problems raised by social media. Some wonder whether new laws should be passed to deal with the ways in which criminal defendants employ social media. Others believe that the current laws need to be modified to address the constitutional questions that arise when social media is used in criminal activity.

§ 9.06 INVESTIGATING CRIMINAL ACTIVITY

A. SOCIAL MEDIA PROVIDERS

Due to a variety of factors, criminal investigations regularly occur on social media. These investigations are conducted by (1) social media providers, (2) the general public, and (3) law enforcement. At present, there is no requirement for social media providers to conduct these investigations. Furthermore, save for child pornography, social media providers have no legal duty to report any criminal conduct that they become aware of. However, many social media providers not only conduct investigations on their own sites, but also regularly report suspected criminal conduct to law enforcement.

Despite the efforts made by social media providers to root out criminal conduct, some members of Congress believe that they are not doing enough, especially with respect to investigating terrorists. As a result, there have been legislative efforts in Congress to require social media providers who conduct investigations to report suspected terrorist activity that they discover. Not surprisingly, several concerns arise with this type of legislation. First, many dislike the idea of social media providers becoming an arm of the government. They see this as a further erosion of user privacy. Second, the term "terrorist activity" is very broad and subject to various interpretations. As a result, some social media providers may err on the side of over reporting content to the government rather than underreporting. It remains to be seen whether these legislative proposals will actually become law.

B. GENERAL PUBLIC

Like social media providers, there is no requirement for the general public to investigate crime on social media. However, this has not stopped so-called virtual deputies from harnessing the power of social media to uncover illegal activity. At times, these investigations can prove quite helpful to law enforcement, which is why many police departments post pictures and videos of fugitives online and request the assistance of the general public.

Other times, the public can actually harm law enforcement's efforts. For example, certain public investigations take on a mob mentality, and when those involved rush to judgment, innocent people can see their lives turned upside down. In the race to find the perpetrators of the 2013 Boston Marathon bombing, social media sites like Reddit, 4chan,

Facebook and Twitter incorrectly identified an innocent person as a suspect in the bombing. This resulted in a barrage of unwanted attention unleashed on the man's family from both the media and the general public. This idea of "Justice and the Crowd" was previously discussed in Section 5.03.

C. LAW ENFORCEMENT

Like with offline investigations, citizens are not required to assist the police with their social media investigations. However, they also cannot interfere with those investigations to include using social media to expose a confidential informant. The following case illustrates what can happen to criminal defendants who attempt to disrupt ongoing police investigations through social media.

In *People v. Horton* a defendant was charged with selling a controlled substance.[18] His conviction stemmed primarily from a "controlled buy" from an informant which was videotaped. Prior to his plea on the charge of selling a controlled substance, the defendant publicly identified the informant to include providing a link to her Facebook page and uploaded a portion of the surveillance video to YouTube. Shortly after posting the information about the confidential informant online, a discussion was started on Facebook where the following comments were made: "snitches get stitches" and "I hope she gets what's coming to her."

---

[18] *People v. Horton*, 21 N.E.3d 207 (N.Y. 2014).

The defendant's actions led to him being charged and convicted of obstruction of justice and witness tampering. According to the appellate court that upheld the defendant's conviction,

> *[t]he evidence. . . is sufficient to establish that defendant knew that the confidential informant might testify in a proceeding, and that he wrongfully sought to stop her from doing so. After learning about Jackson's arrest and the confidential informant's role as a witness against Jackson and, potentially, himself, defendant immediately posted communications on the internet that the jury might have reasonably inferred were coded threats that were intended to induce the confidential informant not to testify.*

Horton is not an isolated case. To date, individuals across the country have turned to social media to profile and target government witnesses, undercover police officers, and prosecutors. Some social media sites include photos of the witnesses, their statements, and testimony. Many believe it is easier to conduct witness intimidation via social media than with traditional methods.

Due to the threat posed by outing or threatening someone on social media, courts have not been reluctant in upholding convictions for online witness intimidation. In *Commonwealth v. Casiano*, a criminal defendant was convicted of witness intimidation when he pointed a cellphone at an undercover police officer in a hallway who was waiting to testify against the defendant.[19] In addition, criminal defendants have been convicted of using social media to stalk prosecutors, see *State v. Moller*.[20]

Witness intimidation and obstruction of justice while important are not the biggest issues with respect to criminal investigations that occur on social media. The major concern here is the privacy rights of the individual being investigated. Or put differently, what constitutional limitations may be placed on the social media investigations conducted by law enforcement?

One of the first reported cases to apply the Fourth Amendment's expectation of privacy in the context of social media was *U.S. v. Joshua Meregildo*.[21] In this case, law enforcement was investigating a number of people to include Melvin Colon and Joshua Meregildo for their alleged involvement in illegal drug activities and possession of weapons. Like most people, Colon had a Facebook page. The general public could not view Colon's Facebook page but his Facebook Friends could see the messages and photographs that Colon and others posted. Working through a cooperating witness, who happened to be a Facebook friend of Colon, the government was able to see that "Colon posted messages regarding prior acts of violence, threatened new violence to rival gang members, and

---

[19] *Commonwealth v. Casiano*, 876 N.E. 2d 475 (Mass. App. Ct. 2007).

[20] *State v. Moller*, 846 N.W.2d 33 (Wis. Ct. App. June 26, 2014).

[21] *United States v. Meregildo*, 883 F. Supp. 2d 523, 525 (S.D.N.Y. 2012).

sought to maintain the loyalties of other alleged members of Colon's gang."

The government used this information to request and receive a search warrant for other portions of Colon's Facebook account.

Colon filed a motion to suppress, challenging the constitutionality of the government's warrant. Colon argued that the use of a cooperating witness by the government to uncover information about his personal Facebook page violated his Fourth Amendment rights.

The trial judge rejected Colon's argument finding that

> *Colon's legitimate expectation of privacy ended when he disseminated posts to his "friends" because those "friends" were free to use the information however they wanted—including sharing it with the government.*

The court also found that

> *[b]ecause Colon surrendered his expectation of privacy, the government did not violate the Fourth Amendment when it accessed Colon's Facebook profile through a cooperating witness.*

Ultimately, the court in *Meregildo* held that a criminal defendant, like in the offline world, loses his Fourth Amendment protections when he willingly reveals information to a friend who in reality is working or cooperating with the government.

In determining a defendant's expectation of privacy on social media, other courts have adhered to the holding of *Meregildo*. For example, in *United States v. Gatson*, a federal district judge, citing *Meregildo,* held that law enforcement can gather evidence against the defendant by creating fake Instagram accounts.[22] Gatson was a member of a burglary ring in the NY/NJ region that displayed photos of its stolen goods on Instagram. Somehow the police became aware of the photos and decided to create a fake Instagram account in order to see the photos on Gatson's account.

Once Gatson accepted the follow request from law enforcement, they were able to view photos and other information Gatson posted on his Instagram account. Gatson then tried to suppress the information discovered by law enforcement. The court denied the motion to suppress, finding that "[n]o search warrant is required for the consensual sharing of this type of information," even if the accepted friend is actually the police.

Another issue that arises when users of social media attempt to raise Fourth Amendment challenges is standing. Generally speaking, a defendant must have standing to raise any constitutional challenges like a reasonable expectation of privacy. This question of whether defendants have standing in the social media content

---

22 *United States v. Gatson*, 2014 WL 7182275 (D.N.J. Dec. 15, 2014).

they create, at least with respect to Twitter, was addressed in *People v. Harris*.[23]

Harris involved the named defendant, Malcolm Harris, and other Occupy Wall Street Protesters who were charged with illegally marching on a restricted portion of the Brooklyn Bridge. As part of their investigation, the prosecution sent a subpoena *duces tecum* to Twitter requesting, among other things, the email address and tweets for the Twitter account @destructuremal, which allegedly belonged to Malcolm Harris. According to the prosecution, they wanted this information to rebut a potential defense by Harris that law enforcement either led or escorted him onto the non-pedestrian part of the Brooklyn Bridge.

Shortly after receiving the subpoena, Twitter informed the defendant of the government's request. Harris then told Twitter that he would attempt to quash the subpoena. In his motion to quash, Harris argued that the subpoena: (1) violated the Stored Communications Act (SCA); (2) failed to comply with the procedural requirements of the Uniform Act to Secure the Attendance of Witnesses from Without a State in Criminal Procedures (Uniform Act); (3) was overbroad; and (4) was an unwarranted invasion of privacy infringing on the First and Fourth Amendments. Harris's motion to quash was denied.

In denying Harris's motion, the court determined that he did not have standing. The court also found

---

[23] *People v. Harris*, 945 N.Y.S. 2d 505 (N.Y. City Crim. Ct. 2012).

that even if Harris did have standing the SCA would not prevent the release of the information by Twitter. The decision by the court rested primarily on the premise that Harris did not have a proprietary interest in his tweets—they belonged to Twitter. To reach this conclusion, the *Harris* court analogized tweets to bank records. The court then found that in civil cases parties, who want to enforce a judgment, may serve information subpoenas on banks to determine whether the judgment debtor holds assets at those banks because customers lack a proprietary interest in the bank records.

The court also made note of Twitter's Terms of Service (TOS), in place at that time, in which users grant Twitter the following, "*a worldwide, non-exclusive, royalty-free license to use, copy, reproduce, process, adapt, modify, publish, transmit, display and distribute . . . Content in any and all media or distribution methods (now known or later developed).*" This inability to exclude Twitter's use of Harris's tweets, at least in the eyes of the court, further demonstrated that the defendant did not have a proprietary interest in his tweets. According to the court, *Twitter's license to use [his] Tweets means that the Tweets [Harris] posted were not his.*

After Harris's unsuccessful attempt at quashing the subpoena, Twitter filed its own motion to quash which was also denied. In making its motion, Twitter made the following arguments: (1) imposition of an undue burden; (2) the court incorrectly held that Harris did not have standing; (3) violation of federal law to disclose contents of a communication less than

180 days old without a warrant; and (4) New York does not adhere to the Uniform Act.

In addressing the first two issues raised by Twitter's motion, the court determined that the subpoena did not impose an undue burden because "every third-party respondent to a subpoena" must "choose between either providing user communications and account information in response to all subpoenas or attempting to vindicate. . . users' rights by moving to quash." Here, Twitter had argued that by denying the defendant standing the court had placed an undue burden on Twitter to either comply with all subpoenas or move to quash all subpoenas on behalf of all defendants.

As for the Fourth Amendment arguments, the court found that the defendant's tweets were not protected. According to the *Harris* court, there was no physical intrusion upon the defendant's tweets. They were obtained from Twitter. In addition, the defendant did not have a reasonable expectation of privacy, as established by *Katz v. United States*, in his tweets that were broadcasted to the world via the Internet. According to the court, sending a tweet is similar to "a man walk[ing] to his window, open[ing] the window, and scream[ing]." The court went on to say that Twitter is like the witness who heard the man yelling from the window.

In the eyes of the *Harris* court, Harris's circumstances were much different from those in *Katz* where the criminal defendant went into an enclosed pay phone to discuss his illegal bets with another person.[24] Harris desired his tweets to be disseminated and read by others. In contrast, the criminal defendant in *Katz* did not want the world to know about his phone call just the person on the other end of the telephone line. Thus, Katz took steps to ensure that his phone call was private.

The one bright spot for Harris and Twitter rested with the tweets that were less than 180 days old. Here, the court said that the government needed a search warrant to access them.

Not surprisingly, the *Harris* opinion has its share of critics, who, among other things, claim that just because a user sends a tweet does not mean that he loses standing to prevent that tweet from being subpoenaed. Other critics point to the fact that Twitter's TOS made no mention of users giving up ownership of their tweets. Finally, some question whether the judge was correct when he found that a non-exclusive license between the individual and the social media provider results in the loss of all proprietary interests for the individual.

As a result of *Harris*, some question whether other social media providers will follow in the footsteps of Twitter and change their policies to ensure that users maintain greater control and ownership of their information. Subsequent to the *Harris* court's initial decision denying the defendant's motion to quash, Twitter changed its TOS to read as follows, "[y]ou

---

24 *Katz v. United States*, 389 U.S. 347 (1967).

Retain Your Right To Any Content You Submit, Post Or Display On Or Through The Service."[25]

Additional questions have arisen about standing and what *Harris* means for other social media platforms. Put differently, was *Harris* limited to Twitter or does it apply to other social media platforms like Pinterest, Facebook, Craigslist, Reddit, etc.? In opinions prior to the *Harris* decision, courts have found that social media users do have standing to challenge subpoenas sent to social media providers. For example, in *Crispin v. Audigier*, a civil case involving copyright infringement, the court found that the plaintiff did have standing to object to subpoenas sent by defendants directly to Myspace and Facebook, see Section 10.04. Thus, it remains to be seen whether the *Harris* opinion will be limited to the specific facts of that case or if it will be followed by others. It should be noted, however, that even if the court in *Harris* had granted the defendant standing he still would have most likely had to turn over the tweets because the requested records were relevant to his anticipated defense.

Beyond the standing issue, some have questioned the logic in comparing tweets to bank records. Stripping protections from tweets as opposed to bank records appears to have much broader privacy implications. For example, allowing the government access to bank records is less likely to have the same chilling effect as granting the government access to someone's Twitter account. Furthermore, unlike

[25] Twitter Terms of Service (June 25, 2012).

bank records, tweets, in addition to the actual content, provide the government far more information e.g., IP addresses, user's browser types, operating system data, referring webpages, locations, pages visited, mobile carriers (if the system is accessed from a mobile device), device and application IDs, and search terms.

In contrast to *Harris* where the New York courts allowed Twitter to at least challenge the government's subpoena request, the court in *In re 381 Search Warrants Directed to Facebook* denied Facebook the opportunity to even contest the government's warrant request for user content. Here, the court held that "Facebook cannot litigate the constitutionality of the warrant pre-enforcement on its customers' behalf. . . because there is no constitutional or statutory right to challenge an alleged defective warrant before it is executed."[26]

In re 381 Search Warrants arose from a July 23, 2013 decision by a New York judge to issue 381 substantially identical digital search warrants to Facebook. The warrants were part of a large-scale investigation into the filing of false disability claims by retired police officers and firefighters. The warrants, which were supported by one 93-page affidavit, came with a gag order prohibiting Facebook from alerting its users about the warrant. Upon receiving the warrants, Facebook contacted the district attorney's office and requested that they

[26] *In re 381 Search Warrants Directed to Facebook, Inc. v. New York City District Attorney's Office*, 132 A.D. 3d 11 (N.Y. App. Div. 2015).

withdraw their request, which they declined to do. This in turn led Facebook to mount a legal challenge to the warrants.

Facebook made several arguments against the validity of the warrants. First, it argued that the warrants were overbroad. Next, Facebook claimed that since they were tasked with gathering the information for the government the warrants were more akin to subpoenas and should be treated as such. With a subpoena, the recipient generally has time to not only challenge it in court, but also share the existence of the subpoena with the target. The same cannot be said about warrants which are generally executed on the spot.

In response to the arguments put forward by Facebook, the district attorney categorized Facebook as an online depository that had no legal standing to raise constitutional concerns on behalf of its users. The district attorney also stated that Facebook could not alert its users about the warrants because doing so might cause the defendants to flee or lead to the destruction of evidence or witness tampering. Finally, the district attorney asserted that the warrants were a legitimate governmental action to assist in an expansive investigation.

In upholding the decision that Facebook had no right to litigate the constitutionality of the warrants pre-enforcement, the court discussed the ex ante and ex post protections in place to "ensure that the government does not exceed its authority when requesting or executing a search warrant." The emphasis here appeared to be on the motion to suppress which the court called "the most important ex post protection available to citizens." Another protection noted by the court was that a warrant can only be issued by a "neutral and detached judicial officer or magistrate." The take away from *In re 381 Search Warrants* is that legal challenges made to warrants issued to social media providers for a user's content are best made during a motion to suppress not prior to the execution of the warrant.

§ 9.07 GOVERNMENT RESTRICTIONS ON SOCIAL MEDIA USE

In addition to conducting undercover investigations, the government attempts to limit the criminal defendant's ability to exploit social media by monitoring and restricting use Regulation of social media occurs in a variety of ways. The first is an outright ban on social media. Presently, seven states have passed laws prohibiting certain criminal defendants from accessing or using social media. To date, social media bans have been deemed unconstitutional in whole or in part in three of the seven states that have them. Arguments for finding the bans unconstitutional range from freedom of expression to expressive association to prior restraint.

The second method of regulation involves government mandated social media disclosures, which occurs in one of two ways. The first approach requires the criminal defendant to reveal information to government officials. For example, the criminal defendant will have to provide his social media identifiers to the court, probation, or law enforcement. The second approach requires the criminal defendant to make information available to the general public. For example, the criminal defendant must list prior convictions on his personal social media site. Many classify this latter form of disclosure as a modern-day Scarlet Letter. The final method of social media regulation involves monitoring. Here, the defendant is required to grant the government access to his social media site which in turn allows the government to monitor the defendant's activities.

As will be discussed next, courts for the most part have been inclined to uphold these social media regulations when the criminal defendant has been convicted of a crime and is still under the jurisdiction of the court (parole, probation, or supervision). In contrast, courts are less inclined to uphold these regulations when the criminal defendant has completed his entire sentence and is no longer under the jurisdiction of the court. This section will look at several cases to see how far the government can go in regulating the use of social media by others in the criminal law context.

A. BAN

Social media bans, if imposed, normally occur after the defendant has been convicted but this is not always the case as demonstrated by *United States v. Collins*.[27] In *Collins*, the fourteen defendants,

[27] *United States v. Collins*, 2012 WL 3537814 (N.D. Cal 2012).

members of the group Anonymous, were alleged to have participated in a Distributed Denial of Services (DDoS) attack on PayPal for its suspension of WikiLeaks' account. They were charged with 15 counts of conspiracy to cause damage to a protected computer and aiding and abetting intentional damage to a protected computer, in violation of 18 U.S.C. § 1830.

On September 1, 2011, the defendants made their initial appearance and were arraigned. Each defendant consented to pretrial release under a number of conditions one of which prohibited them from using Twitter. Approximately one year later, the defendants again appeared before the court this time to address discovery issues and to challenge certain conditions of their pretrial release. With respect to the prohibition against using Twitter, the court ruled in favor of the defendants and removed it. In striking down the pre-trial prohibition against using Twitter the court wrote the following:

> *The indictment makes no mention of Twitter whatsoever. While the government's general proffer mentions Twitter, and courts regularly approve proceeding in detention proceedings by way of proffer, nothing proffered by the government sufficiently links any defendant's allegedly criminal activities to use of a Twitter account. In the absence of any indictment charge, any evidence, or even any specific proffer of such illicit activity by Twitter, the court is not persuaded that the restriction advances any legitimate interest in protecting the public's*

safety or prevent any defendant from fleeing. Under these circumstances, any illicit use of Twitter by any defendant may be adequately addressed by the monitoring approved elsewhere in the order.

Social media bans are most likely to be imposed in situations where the defendant has been convicted of a sex-related offense or a crime involving a child. At present, several states across the country have enacted laws that prohibit certain sex offenders from accessing or using social media. Generally speaking, these bans from social media have been upheld so long as the defendant was under parole, probation, or court supervision. However, once the court no longer has jurisdiction over the defendant imposing or maintaining such a ban becomes more difficult. This fact is reflected in the case of *John Doe v. Prosecutor, Marion County, Indiana.*[28]

In *Prosecutor, Marion County, Indiana* the plaintiffs (registered sex offenders no longer under the jurisdiction of the court) brought a class action lawsuit challenging the constitutionality of Indiana Code § 35–42–4–12(e). The statute, which was a Class A misdemeanor, prohibited certain registered sex offenders from knowingly or intentionally accessing a social networking site, instant messaging program, or chat room, if the offender knows that the site allows someone under the age of 18 to use or

---

[28] *John Doe v. Prosecutor, Marion County, Indiana*, 705 F.3d 694 (7th Cir. 2013).

access it. The statute defined a social networking site as follows:

> *[A]n Internet web site that: (1) facilitates the social introduction between two or more persons; (2) requires a person to register or create an account, a username, or a password to become a member of the web site and to communicate with other members; (3) allows a member to create a web page or a personal profile; and (4) provides a member with the opportunity to communicate with another person. The term does not include an electronic mail program or message board program.*

Here, plaintiffs argued that this ban as applied to those no longer on parole, probation, or supervised release violated their First Amendment rights. Specifically, the plaintiffs claimed that the statute affects three rights secured by the First Amendment: (1) the right to communicate; (2) the right to receive information; and (3) the right to associate.

On the initial question of what level of review to apply to the statute, the court agreed with the plaintiffs that intermediate scrutiny should be used since the statute was not content based. The court also acknowledged that the statute infringed on the plaintiffs' First Amendment rights. However, the trial court disagreed with the plaintiffs' assertion that the statute was invalid for being overly broad and not narrowly tailored.

The court made it clear that certain First Amendment infringements are permissible if narrowly tailored to serve a significant governmental interest and alternative forms of communication exist. As to the first prong, the court found that Indiana's interest in the statute was to protect children from potential online predators. The court went on to find that this harm was real and not merely conjecture. The court then found the ban narrowly tailored because it did not prevent plaintiffs from all social media sites; for example, the plaintiffs could still use LinkedIn, which, at the time, did not allow users under the age of 18.

As for the second prong, the trial court determined that the ban allowed for alternative channels of communication. The court pointed out that the plaintiffs could still

> *congregate with others, attend civic meetings, call in to radio shows, write letters to newspapers and magazines, post on message boards, comment on online stories that do not require a Facebook (or some other prohibited account), email friends, family, associates, politicians, and other adults, publish a blog, and use social networking sites that do not allow minors.*

On appeal, the Seventh Circuit Court of Appeals sided with the plaintiffs finding that the ban was not narrowly tailored. The appellate court determined that "illicit communication comprises a minuscule subset of the universe of social network activity." This finding is important because narrow tailoring must be examined in relation to the interest the state is attempting to fulfill.

Next, the appellate court determined that the ban was entirely too broad because it encompassed both protected speech and communication that had nothing to do with minors. Here, the appellate court noted that other methods existed by which the state could combat inappropriate communications between minors and sex offenders.

The Seventh Circuit Court of Appeals then went on to make it abundantly clear that, although it found the current ban unconstitutional, the court was not foreclosing future efforts by the legislature to restrict sex offenders from using social media. The court stated that a ban might be permissible if "appl[ied] to certain persons that present an acute risk—those individuals whose presence on social media impels them to solicit children."

Thus, one takeaway from the appellate court's ruling is that the state may restrict or ban individuals from social media. However, such bans must be drafted with precision to avoid being overly broad. The following are examples of ways a legislature may narrowly tailor social media bans:

Limit ban to high risk offenders

Apply the ban only to crimes involving children or the Internet

Narrow the definition of "social media" or "social network"

Create an appeal process for the defendant to have the ban removed

Establish an annual review of the ban to see if it is still necessary

Subsequent to the decision by the Seventh Circuit Court of Appeals, the state of Indiana reworked and significantly narrowed its ban. At present, it is unknown whether this new law will be found constitutional.

B. REVEALING INFORMATION TO THE GOVERNMENT

In addition to banning criminal defendants, the government can require them to disclose certain social media related information e.g., passwords, usernames, list of providers, etc. Unlike the ban, courts in this area have issued conflicting opinions on the constitutionality of requiring convicted defendants to disclose social media related information.

Several jurisdictions require sex offenders to turn over or register their online social media accounts and screen names with law enforcement. For example, the state of Montana recently passed a new law requiring registered sex offenders to reveal all of their email addresses and social media screen names. To some, this is an invasion of an individual's personal privacy and unlikely to improve public safety. Others see it differently and believe that such requirements serve as an extension of the sex offender registry. Those who support requiring criminal defendants to turn over such information claim that this information is beneficial to law enforcement and allows them to better track sex offenders.

At present, courts are still grappling with applying the proper constitutional framework for analyzing cases in this area. Some courts apply strict scrutiny to mandated social media disclosure laws. Thus, the government must show that the law serves a compelling governmental interest, is narrowly tailored to achieve that interest, and the provisions are the least restrictive means of advancing that interest.

In contrast, other courts treat these laws as content neutral and apply intermediate scrutiny. In these cases, the government need only show that the law is justified without reference to the content of the regulated speech and that the law is narrowly tailored to serve a significant governmental interest and leaves open alternative avenues of communication. Intermediate scrutiny is the most commonly adopted level of review by the courts today with respect to revealing social media information.

The intermediate scrutiny approach was used in *Doe v. Harris*.[29] Here, the Ninth Circuit Court of Appeals in a three-judge panel opinion affirmed a district judge's order that preliminarily enjoined provisions of the Californians Against Sexual Exploitation ("CASE") Act or Proposition 35. The panel found certain aspects of the CASE Act as applied to sex offenders, no longer under the

---

[29] *Doe v. Harris*, 2014 U.S. App. LEXIS 21808 (9th Cir. Nov. 18, 2014).

jurisdiction of the court, to be unconstitutional. Specifically, the panel affirmed the trial judge's decision to strike down the requirement that registered sex offenders provide law enforcement with all Internet names and addresses used in social media, instant messaging, and Web posts. This Ninth Circuit panel decision follows in the footsteps of other federal courts that have found similar laws unconstitutional.

C. REVEALING INFORMATION TO THE GENERAL PUBLIC

Due to the difficulty in banning criminal defendants from social media or requiring them to reveal social media information to the government, states are considering alternative ways in which to regulate a criminal defendant's use of social media. One state has decided to borrow from the past and require individuals to publicly acknowledge their prior crimes. While compelled speech does raise constitutional issues, it appears to be less restrictive than completely depriving someone of the opportunity to use social media.

Forcing a defendant to publicly acknowledge past criminal activity was made famous in Nathaniel Hawthorne's romantic novel, *The Scarlet Letter*. As some may recall, the main character in the book, Hester Prynne, was forced to wear a scarlet letter "A" on her chest for having a child out of wedlock. This letter "A" served to not only put the citizens of Hester's town on notice about her past misdeeds, but also to publicly shame her.

During the colonial period, public punishments were quite popular. Due to the close-knit communities in which people lived, many thought that the public display or acknowledgement of criminal activity deterred crime and reduced deviant behavior. This practice over time fell out of fashion for two main reasons. First, the migration from small towns to large urban areas allowed people to live more anonymously. Many individuals no longer knew their neighbors at least not intimately. Second, the creation of prisons as opposed to jails provided an alternative method of long term punishment for those who ran afoul of the laws. In fact, by the middle of the nineteenth century, incarceration had become a common, if not the dominant method for deterring and controlling deviant behavior.

The idea of publicly acknowledging past crimes as illustrated in the *Scarlet Letter* has been resurrected in the era of social media e.g., the state of Louisiana recently enacted the Digital Scarlet Letter Law. While similar to the original Scarlet Letter, this new law has undergone some slight modern-day modifications. Rather than make the defendant walk around with a sign or wear some form of clothing, this new law targets the defendant's online persona. The Louisiana law, the first in the country, requires sex offenders to indicate their criminal status on the social media site that they use. Failure to include a prior conviction on a social media site could result in incarceration and a monetary fine.

One major difference between the Digital Scarlet Letter and the original Scarlet Letter is the underlying reason for the law. The primary purpose of making Hester Prynne wear the letter "A" was public shaming. A secondary purpose was to safeguard the citizens of her town. With the letter "A" on her chest, residents were alerted to the fact that Hester was a criminal and potentially 'dangerous' at least to those trying to adhere strictly to the Puritan lifestyle. In contrast, the primary purpose for enacting the Digital Scarlet Letter is not public shaming but rather public safety, especially in regards to children. The Digital Scarlet Letter provides a form of notice to those interacting with others online.

Some view the Digital Scarlet Letter as an expansion of the sex offender registry. However, there are some marked differences between requiring an individual to register as a sex offender and requiring him to include a list of crimes on his social media site. First, the sex offender registry, as opposed to a Digital Scarlet Letter, is not readily identifiable with one individual. Furthermore, a registry requires the public to seek out information about sex offenders whereas the Digital Scarlet Letter does not require the public to go to an outside resource for information. Put another way, the Digital Scarlet Letter removes a step when attempting to determine an individual's sex offender status.

At first glance, one might view the Digital Scarlet Letter as one more draconian law targeting sex offenders. However, this law does offer a few benefits to the criminal defendant. First, unlike a traditional sex offender registry, the Digital Scarlet Letter allows defendants to discuss and explain their charges. In contrast, the sex offender registry does not allow an individual to elaborate or explain how the charges arose. In addition, the Digital Scarlet Letter does not totally cut off the defendant from social media like an outright ban.

For a variety of reasons, some question whether this new law will be effective or achieve its intended goals. As discussed earlier in this book, it is very easy to remain anonymous or impersonate someone else while using social media. Others also question whether states will allocate the resources necessary to enforce such laws because similar to other crime fighting measures this law will require the expenditure of resources for effective enforcement.

To date, the constitutionality of the Digital Scarlet Letter has not been challenged. Thus, it remains to be seen whether the law will be upheld by the courts. It should be noted at the outset that if the sole purpose of the Digital Scarlet Letter is to humiliate the criminal defendant then it will most likely be found unconstitutional. In contrast, if the proponents of the law can show that it is intended to rehabilitate, deter, or protect the public and the law is reasonably related to those goals, then it stands a good chance of being found constitutional.

The law appears to have a deterrent effect because it requires offenders to publicize their criminal activity to their self-created online communities. The rehabilitative impact is seen as soon as the criminal defendant self-reports his crime. For many, the first step for any criminal defendant's rehabilitation is the acknowledgement of the crime. Finally, the Digital Scarlet Letter places not only the criminal defendant's online friends on notice, but also society as a whole.

There is legal support for the Digital Scarlet Letter in the offline world. For example, some might compare Digital Scarlet Letters to the special license plates issued to those convicted of certain traffic offenses like driving under the influence. To date, the use of those specialized license plates has been upheld.

Other examples include cases where a judge orders a convicted defendant to publicly acknowledge their crimes. In *Lindsay v. State*,[30] a Florida trial judge required a defendant, as a condition of probation, to publish an advertisement in the local paper that included his mugshot, name, and the term "DUI—Convicted." The defendant's sentence was upheld on appeal. The appellate court determined that the sentence had a rehabilitative purpose and was logically connected to the defendant's criminal conduct.

Like with other concepts, it is sometimes difficult to draw a direct comparison between online and offline conduct. For example, one of the major distinctions between the Digital Scarlet Letter and special plates is the lack of permanency associated with the offline conduct. In contrast, with the Digital Scarlet Letter there is the potential to stigmatize the

---

[30] *Lindsay v. State*, 606 So. 2d 652 (Fla. Dist. Ct. App. 1992).

defendant for an extended amount of time or even for the rest of his life. Unlike the offline world, online information can exist in perpetuity; it has no shelf-life.

D. MONITORING

In addition to mandated disclosures and outright bans, some courts subject criminal defendants to social media monitoring. This is more likely to occur when the criminal defendant is under some form of supervision by the court. If a convicted criminal defendant is no longer on parole, probation, or any other form of supervised release, it is very difficult, constitutionally speaking, for the court to monitor his social media activities. Although the U.S. Supreme Court has not addressed this issue directly, several federal district courts have found these types of requirements unconstitutional.

CHAPTER 10
LITIGATION

§ 10.01 INTRODUCTION

This chapter will explore social media's impact on litigation. First, the chapter begins by examining how an individual's social media activities can result in the court obtaining personal jurisdiction over him or her. Next, the chapter explores the use of social media as a method of providing parties notice of upcoming legal matters e.g., service of process. Third, the chapter looks at social media as a discovery tool. Here, the book delves into the challenges of obtaining information from social media providers by discussing the Stored Communications Act (SCA). The last section provides a brief examination of the rules of evidence. The focus here is on the issues that arise when attorneys attempt to authenticate social media related information.

§ 10.02 JURISDICTION

A threshold question in all cases, both civil and criminal, is whether the court has jurisdiction to hear the case. In the civil context, jurisdictional issues are either personal or subject matter. Personal jurisdiction is the power of the court to direct that the defendant appear before it. Unlike subject matter jurisdiction, personal jurisdiction can be waived if not raised.

In examining personal jurisdiction, courts conduct a two-step analysis. In step one, the court looks to see whether there is an express statutory grant of authority which empowers it to exercise jurisdiction over the defendant. In step two, the court examines whether the exercise of jurisdiction over a particular non-resident defendant would violate Due Process as guaranteed by the Constitution. This section will focus on this second step.

In this second step, plaintiffs must demonstrate that the defendant has purposefully established such minimum contacts with the forum state that the defendant could reasonably anticipate being brought into court there. With respect to the Internet, courts generally rely on two different tests to determine if the defendant has purposefully availed himself of the forum state. First, the "Zippo test" from *Zippo Mfg. Co. v. Zippo Dot Com, Inc.* looks at how interactive the website is with the people in the forum state.[1] Second, the "Calder effects test" from *Calder v. Jones* looks at whether (1) the defendant intentionally committed a tortious action which was expressly aimed for dissemination in the forum state, and (2) the brunt of the effects of the actions are felt within the forum.[2]

A recent defamation case (*Jahmel Binion v. O'Neal et al.*), involving the former professional basketball player Shaquille O'Neal, illustrates how the courts have applied both the *Zippo* test and the *Calder* effects test to social media.[3] In *Binion v. O'Neal*, the

---

1 *Zippo Manufacturing Co. v. Zippo Dot Com, Inc.*, 952 F. Supp. 1119 (W.D. Pa. 1997)

2 *Calder v. Jones*, 465 U.S. 783 (1984).

3 *Binion v. O'Neal*, 95 F. Supp. 3d 1055 (E.D Mich. 2015)

defendant mocked the plaintiff by posting two photos side-by-side on his Twitter (8.50 million followers) and Instagram accounts (250,000 followers). One of the photos is of the plaintiff who suffers from ectodermal dysplasia, a rare genetic condition which causes cosmetic abnormalities. The other photo is of the defendant who contorts his face in an attempt to mimic the plaintiff. The post also contains the following caption:

SMILE PEOPLE

Upon learning of the post, the plaintiff brought suit against the defendant for invasion of privacy, intentional infliction of emotional distress, and general negligence. The suit was brought in the United States District Court of the Eastern District of Michigan. The plaintiff resides in Macomb County, Michigan. The defendant resides in Florida and Massachusetts.

Defendant filed a motion to dismiss plaintiff's claims arguing that he was not subject to the court's personal jurisdiction. In deciding the defendant's motion to dismiss for lack of personal jurisdiction the court applied both the *Zippo* test and the *Calder* effects test. In applying the *Zippo* test, the court found that merely posting information on social media is not sufficient to give the forum state jurisdiction. The defendant has to do more. Here, the court found that "the websites [Twitter and Instagram] are not owned or operated by O'Neal, were minimally interactive, and the posting were not intended to conduct business."

With respect to the *Calder* effects test, the court found the injury to a forum resident alone is not sufficient to grant jurisdiction. According to the court, the plaintiff failed to establish that defendant's posts were "expressly aimed for dissemination" in Michigan. The court went on to say that defendant's posts were directed at "a national or even international audience." Plaintiff's attorney argued that the defendant has business connections in the state; however, the court pointed out that the "[p]laintiff was not injured by O'Neal's business dealings in the state, and Plaintiff's cause of action is independent of any such business connection."

Ultimately, the court dismissed plaintiff's cause of action due to lack of personal jurisdiction. However, plaintiff refiled in federal district court in Florida (residence of the defendant) where the case is currently pending.

§ 10.03 NOTICE OF LEGAL PROCEEDINGS

At present, using social media to provide parties notice of pending legal matters has been more widely accepted outside of the United States than inside. For example, countries like Australia and the United Kingdom permit service of process via social media. Australia first allowed the practice in 2008 and the UK in 2012. While some American jurisdictions have become more willing to accept service of process via social media, others have not. At present, few American jurisdictions allow social media to serve as the primary method of service. Rather, service by social media, when allowed, serves as a supplemental or secondary form of service.

The following two family law cases (*In re Adoption of KPMA* and *Noel B. v. Anna Maria A.*) illustrate the conflicting views on providing notice by social media. In the case of *In re Adoption of KPMA*, the Oklahoma Supreme Court found notice by Facebook alone insufficient "to meet the requirements of the due process clauses of the United States and Oklahoma Constitutions because it is not reasonably certain to inform those affected."[4]

In this case, the biological father of KPMA was challenging the termination of his parental rights, arguing, among other things, that he had never received notice of the biological mother's pregnancy prior to the child being adopted. According to the father, he met the biological mother on July 4, 2011 and they engaged in sexual relations between August and October of 2011; however, they were not in any type of ongoing "romantic relationship." The last face-to-face interaction between the two occurred in November when the mother went to visit the father at his place of employment.

At some point prior to KPMA's birth, the mother sent the father a message via Facebook informing him that she was pregnant and planning to give the child up for adoption. The father claims he did not read the message until after the child's birth which occurred in June of 2012.

---

4 *In Re Adoption of K.P.M.A.*, 341 P.3d 38 (Okla. 2014)

KPMA was adopted shortly after her birth and the adoptive parents moved to terminate the rights of the biological parents. The mother willingly agreed but the father contested the termination proceeding. The father was unsuccessful at the trial court stage because the court found that he had previously waived his rights to challenge the adoption when he failed to take action upon "first learning" about the mother's pregnancy on Facebook. The trial court's ruling was ultimately overturned by the Oklahoma Supreme Court which found that the father's due process rights were violated. With respect to providing notice via Facebook, the Oklahoma Supreme Court held that,

> [it] *does not believe that attempts to provide notice via Facebook comport with the requirements of due process. While the adequacy of Facebook as a means of providing notice in a due process context is an issue of first impression in Oklahoma, to date only one federal court—of at least three that have considered the issue—has allowed service of process via Facebook and even then only as a supplementary means of providing notice.*

The Oklahoma Supreme Court then went on to discuss why notice via Facebook alone was insufficient to meet the requirements of due process. First, the court pointed out that the mother knew where the father worked and could have told him about the pregnancy face-to-face. Second, the court concluded that social media was not the best method to ensure that the father learned about the pregnancy. According to the court, "[Facebook] is an unreliable method of communication if the account holder does not check it regularly or have it configured in such a way as to provide notification of unread messages by some other means."

In contrast to *In re Adoption of KPMA*, the court in *Noel B. v. Anna Maria A.* was more willing to accept social media as a method of providing another party notice of a pending legal proceeding.[5] Here, the petitioner Noel B. was attempting to modify his child-support obligations; however, in order to do so he had to provide notice to the respondent, Anna Maria A, the mother of the child. He tried mailing the legal notice to her last known address but the respondent had since moved without a forwarding address. Petitioner also attempted to find out respondent's current address through her children. The petitioner even tried a Google search to find her, all without success.

Ultimately, petitioner requested permission from the court to provide legal notice to the respondent via social media. Petitioner knew that respondent had an active Facebook account because respondent had liked certain photos on the Facebook account of petitioner's wife. The court permitted service via Facebook finding that the respondent "maintains an active social media account on Facebook" and that service at her last known address would be "impracticable." The court also required the petitioner to follow up his service by Facebook with a

---

5 *Noel B. v. Anna Maria A.*, 201 N.Y. Misc. LEXIS 4708 (N.Y. Fam. Ct. Sept. 12, 2014)

mailing to respondent's last known address. While other courts have allowed social media as a secondary form of service, *Noel B. v. Anna Maria A.* appears to be one of the first cases to allow such service as a primary form.

In comparing social media to traditional forms of alternative notice like publication, social media appears to be a better tool if the ultimate objective is to make someone aware of a pending legal proceeding. Over the past twenty years, newspapers have faced a steady decline in readership, while social media has seen steady growth in its users. Of those who regularly read newspapers, few, if any, take the time to examine the legal announcements which are rarely, if ever, prominently displayed. In contrast, individuals routinely check their social media accounts and email. Furthermore, notice by publication presumes that the individual making the publication knows the physical whereabouts of the other party, which is not always the case. With social media, the physical location of the other party is irrelevant.

§ 10.04 OBTAINING INFORMATION

As a result of the vast amount of information available on social media, litigators, both civil and criminal, have made investigating social media an integral part of pre-trial preparation. In fact, some have gone so far as to say that failure to investigate social media is tantamount to malpractice. While this may sound somewhat hyperbolic, jurisdictions across the country increasingly require attorneys to be aware of and familiar with common social media platforms.

The process for obtaining information from social media can take a variety of forms such as conducting independent investigations, issuing subpoenas, and participating in discovery.

One of the big challenges in this area is obtaining information directly from social media providers. This is due in large part to the Stored Communications Act (SCA), which greatly restricts what information social media providers may reveal about their users.

A. SCA

The SCA imposes both criminal and civil penalties on entities and individuals including social media providers, who improperly reveal user information under their control to others. The SCA is a subsection of the Electronic Communications Privacy Act (ECPA); however, many people use the laws interchangeably. Congress's intent in passing the SCA in 1986 was to safeguard the confidentiality of new forms of communication and data storage that began to emerge in the 1980s.

Since Fourth Amendment protections can be somewhat lacking when applied to new forms of communication and data storage, the SCA was created to fill the gap. According to one court, "the SCA was enacted because the advent of the Internet presented a host of potential privacy breaches that the Fourth Amendment does not address.[6]" Similar to Section 230(c) in the Communications Decency Act, many believed at the time that SCA protections would allow new methods of communication to flourish.

The level of protection offered by the SCA varies depending on what is requested from the social media provider. For example, certain information may be obtained with just a subpoena (with or without prior notice to the user); other information requires a special court order (with or without prior notice to the user); and another category of information requires a search warrant.

One of the first courts to apply the SCA to social media providers was *Crispin v. Christian Audigier, Inc.*[7] In *Crispin*, the plaintiff, Buckley Crispin, an artist, was suing the defendant, Christian Audigier, Inc., for allegedly violating an oral license to use his art in the production of garments. In defense of the claims, the defendant sent subpoena requests to Facebook and Myspace seeking the plaintiff's subscriber information and private online communications that referenced the defendant. Although the subpoenas were sent to the social media providers themselves, the plaintiff became aware of the subpoenas and moved to quash them.

---

6 *Quon v. Arch Wireless Operating Co., Inc.*, 529 F.3d 892, 900 (9th Cir. 2008) (citing Orin S. Kerr, *A User's Guide to the Stored Communications Act, and a Legislator's Guide to Amending It*, 72 GEO. WASH. L. REV. 1208 (2004)).

7 *Crispin v. Christian Audigier Inc.*, 717 F.Supp. 2d 965 (C.D. Cal. May 26, 2010).

The court in *Crispin* made several key findings with respect to social media platforms and the SCA. First, the court found that the plaintiff, unlike in *People v. Harris*, did have standing to challenge the release of his information by Facebook and Myspace. According to the court, "an individual has a personal right in information in his or her profile and inbox on a social networking site and his or her webmail inbox the same way that an individual has a personal right in employment and bank records."

Next, the *Crispin* court determined that the SCA applies to social media platforms and that both Facebook and Myspace were Electronic Communication Service (ECS) providers because they provided message delivery services. The court also found that both were Remote Computing Service (RCS) providers because they offered message storage services. The distinction between ECS and RCS, which is somewhat of an anachronism, will be discussed later.

Finally, in addressing the merits of plaintiff's argument, the court granted plaintiff's motion with respect to subpoenas for his private email messages that were sent through the social media sites. The court deemed that the emails were private electronic communications protected from disclosure under the SCA. The court remanded for the magistrate judge to determine whether the plaintiff's privacy settings rendered the wall postings and comments public and therefore unprotected by the SCA.

The next section will delve into the actual structure of the SCA. One major byproduct of the statute, which was probably not foreseen when originally passed, is that criminal defense attorneys and civil attorneys are extremely limited in the amount of user information that they can obtain from social media providers. While prosecutors and law enforcement aren't as limited, they nonetheless must meet certain requirements to obtain user information from social media providers.

B. CONTENT[8]

As written, the SCA prevents defense counsel or civil practitioners from obtaining content information from a social media provider concerning a user's social media account absent permission from that user. This is true regardless of whether that information is subpoenaed directly from the social media provider. In certain limited situations, a social media provider may provide prosecutors and law enforcement content from an individual's social media account. To understand when this might occur, it is first necessary to classify the provider as either a RCS or an ECS.

RCS is "the provision to the public of computer storage or processing services by means of electronic communications system."[9] The statute covering RCS further defines an "electronic communications system" as "any wire, radio, electromagnetic, photo-optical or photo-electronic facilities for the transmission of wire or electronic communications,

---

8 "Content" is *any information concerning the substance, purport, or meaning* of a communication.

9 18 U.S.C. § 2711(2).

and any computer facilities or related electronic equipment for the electronic storage of such communications."[10] Also, a RCS is provided by an off-site computer that stores or processes data for a customer.

An ECS is, "any service which provides. . . users. . . the ability to send or receive wire or electronic communications."[11] "Electronic storage" is defined as, "any temporary, intermediate storage of a wire or electronic transmission thereof; and any storage of such communication by an [ECS] for purposes of backup protection of such communication."[12] Further, an ECS is any service which gives users the ability to send or receive wire or electronic communications.

Generally speaking, email, text messages and instant messages are sent via ECS providers. In contrast, RCS providers offer storage and processing services. While the ECS/RCS distinction made sense in 1986, technology has advanced so much that the terms have become anachronistic. For example, today the government might need to obtain a warrant to access a wall posting on a social media site that has not been viewed because the wall posting might be deemed an ECS. In contrast, if the posting is older than 180 days and has not been viewed, then the government may only need a subpoena because the wall posting might be deemed an RCS.

---

[10] 18 U.S.C. § 2510(14).

[11] 18 U.S.C. § 2510(17)(A).

[12] 18 U.S.C. § 2510(17).

This dichotomy is due to the technology in place at the time the SCA was originally passed. In 1986, social media and web-based e-mail was nonexistent. Rather, e-mail was kept on local intranets where users would download their messages from a server which rarely had a backup. Congress, in passing the SCA, presumed that any e-mails left on the server for more than 180 days would be similar to abandoned property. Obviously, this is no longer the situation today.

Another challenge with applying the ECS/RCS distinction to social media providers is that those providers might fall into both categories depending on how they are used. When that situation arises, many courts look at the specific service of the social media provider and classify it as either ECS or RCS. According to one federal court in Oregon, "[t]oday, most ISPs provide both ECS and RCS; thus, the distinction serves to define the service that is being provided at a particular time (or as to a particular piece of electronic communication at a particular time), rather than to define the service provider itself."[13]

If the provider or specific service is an ECS and the information requested has been stored for fewer than 180 days, the government needs a warrant to obtain the information. If the provider or specific service is an RCS or an ECS and the information requested has been stored for more than 180 days, the government

[13] *In re U.S.*, 665 F.Supp.2d 1210, 1214 (D. Or. 2009).

has the option of using a: (1) warrant, (2) court order (18 U.S.C. § 2703(d)), or (3) subpoena.

A warrant requires probable cause which is a higher evidentiary standard than either a 2703(d) court order or subpoena. When seeking a warrant for a social media account, the application submitted to the court should include a description of why law enforcement believes the account belongs to a particular individual and why they think the account contains evidence of a crime. In order to fulfill the Fourth Amendment's requirement of particularity, the search warrant must be clear enough to direct the social media platform to the correct profile. Therefore, the warrant should include the user's screen name, unique User ID, and profile page URL.

To obtain a 2703(d) court order, the government has to apply to the court and provide "specific and articulable facts" that the information requested is relevant and material to a criminal investigation. If law enforcement is able to make a sufficient factual showing, the judge signs the 2703(d) court order, which is served like a subpoena. A 2703(d) court order combines the requirements of a subpoena with the standard created in *Terry v. Ohio*.[14]

The requirements for a subpoena are even lower than the 2703(d) court order. Here, the government only has to show that the information sought is relevant and material to a criminal investigation.

---

[14] *Terry v. Ohio*, 392 U.S. 1 (1968).

Both the 2703(d) court order and the subpoena require social media providers to give account holders prior notice. Under certain conditions, this notice may be delayed. For example, the SCA permits delayed notice of up to 90 days if the government believes that "notification of the existence of the court order may have an adverse result."[15] The following constitute so-called "adverse results" (1) endangering the life or physical safety of an individual, (2) flight from prosecution, (3) destruction of or tampering with evidence, (4) intimidation of potential witnesses, and (5) otherwise seriously jeopardizing an investigation or unduly delaying a trial.

C. NON-CONTENT

For non-content information, the ECS or RCS distinction and 180-day threshold are irrelevant. The focus here is on the two subcategories of non-content information. Non-content transactional records, like a log, require either a warrant or a 2703(d) court order. In contrast, a subpoena is sufficient for information such as name and address of an account holder.

The SCA is silent on non-governmental entities requesting non-content information. Many social media providers, however, require that non-governmental entities obtain a subpoena in order to gain access to non-content information.

---

[15] 18 U.S.C. § 2705(a)(1)(A).

D. CRITICISM

Not surprisingly there have been numerous proposals put forward to improve or update the SCA. Members of Congress have introduced bills, and academics and practicing attorneys have written numerous articles on ways to modify or update the SCA. Many of these reform measures share similar traits. The following is a brief list of some of the more common updates suggested:

(1) Remove the arbitrary categories of RCS, ECS, and 180 days;

(2) Require a warrant for the disclosure of all content;

(3) Provide a suppression remedy when law enforcement violates the SCA;

(4) Strengthen the notice requirements;

(5) Require a warrant for GPS tracking; and/or

(6) Add simplicity and clarity to the SCA.

E. DISCOVERY

Both civil and criminal litigators may obtain information from opposing counsel through the discovery process. However, the methods used and the amount of information available is unique to both civil and criminal law. For starters, discovery in criminal law, due to a variety of factors, is far more limited than in the civil arena. In addition, discovery in criminal law is not necessarily a two-way street. Constitutional considerations may limit how much information the defense is required to reveal to the prosecution. One similarity found in both civil and criminal discovery is that failure to turn over discoverable information, social media related or otherwise, can result in a variety of court-imposed sanctions.

1. Criminal

The rules governing discovery in criminal law at least at the federal level are governed by Federal Rule of Criminal Procedure (FRCP) 16 and case law. Most states have created rules similar to FRCP. Under FRCP 16, the following must be disclosed by the prosecution upon request by the defense: (1) evidence that it intends to use in its case-in-chief, (2) items obtained from the defendant, and (3) relevant written and recorded statements of the defendant. Participation in the discovery process also subjects the defense to a reciprocal request from the prosecution under FRCP 16. Social media related information held by either prosecution or defense can be included in any discovery request.

In addition to the rules and rights created by the states and the federal government, attorneys may also make discovery requests based on applicable case law to include United States Supreme Court precedents such as *Brady v. Maryland* and *Giglio v. United States*[16] Pursuant to *Brady* and its progeny, the prosecution must provide the defense with any material information that would exculpate the

---

[16] *Brady v. Maryland,* 373 U.S. 83 (1963); *Giglio v. United States,* 405 U.S. 150 (1972).

defendant or reduce his sentence. Other requirements imposed on the prosecution relate to so-called *Giglio* material, which includes information that may be used to impeach a key government witness. Since *Brady* or *Giglio* material create a self-executing duty for the prosecution, the defense is not required to ask for this information. Moreover, information falling under *Brady* must be revealed at both the trial and sentencing stages. Similar to FRCP 16, the requirements of *Brady* and *Giglio* apply equally to social media related information.

Due to the limitations imposed on criminal defense attorneys by the SCA, one interesting issue has arisen with respect to whether the prosecution has to request information from social media providers on behalf of the defense. This situation might arise if the defense, through discovery, requests a prosecution witness's Facebook posts. The prosecution does not physically have the posts but could obtain them by making a request directly to Facebook. The defense, however, could not because of the SCA. This raises the question of whether or not the prosecutor has to request this information from the social media provider since the defendant cannot.

The general rule of discovery is that a party is only responsible for turning over information under their direct control. However, in this hypothetical situation, the defense may be able to make a Due Process argument that would require the prosecution to obtain the information if they planned to go forward with prosecuting the defendant. The success or failure of the defendant's argument may ultimately come down to whether or not the information sought is exculpatory in nature.

2. Civil

In civil litigation both plaintiff and defense attorneys may obtain pre-trial information from each other through the rules of civil procedure. Generally speaking, these rules allow for very broad discovery. For example, pursuant to Federal Rule of Civil Procedure (FRCP) 26(b)(1), "[p]arties may obtain discovery regarding any nonprivileged matter that is relevant to any party's claim or defense."

Due to the number of litigated disputes involving civil discovery, the topic has more developed case law than the criminal arena. However, this is not to say that the holdings of the cases in this area are either consistent or entirely clear. Courts struggle with determining the appropriate boundaries for granting access to an individual's social media account. At present, courts generally take one of four approaches in resolving discovery disputes related to social media information.

The first method may be deemed the "factual predicate approach." Here, the court requires the party seeking discovery to demonstrate a factual predicate before granting that party access to any private social media information. *Romano v. Steelcase Inc.*, illustrates how the factual predicate approach works. In *Romano*, the plaintiff claimed that the defendant's faulty chair caused her debilitating neck and back injuries. However, the photos on the public portion of plaintiff's Facebook and Myspace accounts told a different story. These photos, which portrayed a smiling plaintiff on vacation in Florida, served as the factual predicate to obtain full access to plaintiff's social media information. In granting the defendant access to plaintiff's social media sites, the court wrote that "[t]o deny [d]efendant an opportunity [to] access. . . these sites not only would go against the liberal discovery policies of New York favoring pre-trial disclosure, but would condone [p]laintiff's attempt to hide relevant information behind self-regulated privacy settings."[17]

The second method may be deemed the "wide-open or blanket approach." Under this approach, courts require the parties to exchange social media passwords. Here, there is little value placed on either the social media platform's Terms of Service or an individual's privacy rights. *McMillen v. Hummingbird Speedway, Inc.* illustrates the application of the blanket approach.[18]

In *McMillen*, the plaintiff, a race car driver, was rear-ended during a cool down lap following a stock car race. After filing suit against the defendants, the plaintiff posted several public comments on his Facebook page about recreational activities and attending the Daytona 500 race. Defendants discovered the comments and requested production of plaintiff's user names, log-in names, and passwords for his social media accounts. Plaintiff

---

[17] *Romano v. Steelcase, Inc.*, 907 N.Y.S. 2d 650 (N.Y. App. Div. 2010).

[18] *McMillen v. Hummingbird Speedway, Inc.* No. 113–2010 CD, 2010 WL 4403285 (Pa. Ct. Com. P1. Sep. 9, 2010).

objected to the request arguing that such information was confidential. The court overruled plaintiff's objection and granted defendants' motion to compel.

In *McMillen*, the court began its analysis by first pointing out that there is no general "social networking privilege." Next, the court applied a four-part test to determine whether a new privilege should be created. The stumbling block for creating a new privilege in this case was the first factor which addresses confidentiality of communications. According to the court,

> *Facebook, MySpace, and their ilk are social network computer sites people utilize to connect with friends and meet new people. That is, in fact, their purpose, and they do not bill themselves as anything else. Thus, while it is conceivable that a person could use them as forums to divulge and seek advice on personal and private matters, it would be unrealistic to expect that such disclosure would be considered confidential.*

The third method may be classified as the "reasonable particularity approach." Here, courts take a more limiting view on what is discoverable. *EEOC v. Simply Storage* offers an example of this method.[19] In *Simply Storage*, plaintiffs filed claims of sex discrimination and sexual harassment. In response to plaintiffs' complaint, defendants sought evidence related to one plaintiff's claim of depression and post-traumatic stress disorder allegedly caused

---

[19] *EEOC v. Simply Storage*, 270 F.R.D. 430 (S.D. Ind. 2010).

by the employer's harassment. In seeking this evidence, defendants made broad discovery requests of plaintiff's social media pages to include the following:

> *Request #1: All photographs or videos posted by [employee] or anyone on her behalf from April 23, 2007 to present*
>
> *Request #2: Electronic copies of [employee's] complete profile on Facebook and MySpace (including all updates, changes, or modifications to [employee's profile]) and all status updates, messages, wall comments, causes joined, activity streams, blog entries, details, blurbs, comments, and applications. . . .*

Plaintiffs objected to the discovery requests and the court was forced to step in and determine what would be discoverable. After weighing the interests and needs of both parties, the court found the defendants' discovery request somewhat overbroad and narrowed it as follows:

> *[T]he court determines that the appropriate scope of relevance is any profiles, postings, or messages (including status updates, wall comments, causes joined, groups joined, activity streams, blog entries) and [social media] applications for [the employees]. . . that reveal, refer, or relate to any emotion, feeling, or mental state, as well as communications that reveal, refer, or relate to events that could reasonably be expected to produce a significant emotion, feeling, or mental state.*

In *Simply Storage*, the court found that the requesting party must show relevancy. Furthermore, the court determined that the mere fact that "a claimant had social communications is not necessarily probative of the particular mental and emotional matters at issue in the case."

The fourth and final method may be classified as "the direct judicial approach." Here, the judge adopts a hands-on role and actually reviews the social media content personally to determine whether it needs to be disclosed to the opposing party. This judicial review occurs in one of three ways; some judges require the parties to friend the court; other judges require the parties to disclose their social media passwords to the court; and a final group of judges review the social media content *in camera* and then decide what will be released to each side.

F. SPOLIATION

Like in the offline world, parties involved in social media litigation have a duty to preserve litigation evidence. This duty arises when a party in "possession, custody, or control" of evidence knows that litigation by the party seeking the evidence is pending or probable and discarding the evidence would be harmful. If a party fails to preserve the evidence, she is deemed to have spoliated the evidence and may be subject to sanctions which include:

(1) dismissal of a claim,

(2) grant of judgment in favor of a prejudiced party,

(3) suppression of evidence,

(4) adverse inference,

(5) fines, and/or

(6) attorney's fees and costs.

The method by which individuals preserve evidence varies by the social media platform on which the content is found. For example, Facebook allows a user to download all of her information with one mouse click. The information provided includes, among other things, posts, messages, photos, clicked on ads, and IP addresses. In contrast, other social media platforms require more steps. For example, Twitter allows its users to download all tweets posted by requesting a copy of the user's Twitter archive. However, in order to access additional information like IP logs, users must contact Twitter via email.

In addition to these self-help measures, some parties employ third party vendors to ensure complete preservation. These companies have tools specifically designed for searching and collecting information on social media.

G. INVESTIGATING JURORS

Besides using social media to discover information about parties and witnesses, attorneys also rely on it to investigate jurors. Through social media investigations of jurors, attorneys are able to;

(1) confirm juror answers during voir dire,

(2) discover which jurors are favorable or unfavorable to their clients,

(3) bond with jurors,

(4) monitor juror behavior, and

(5) discover grounds for appeal.

One threshold question that arises in this area is whether attorneys must investigate jurors. At present, no jurisdiction requires attorneys to investigate the social media sites of jurors before, during, or after trial. Furthermore, while most jurisdictions overwhelmingly approve of the practice, a few judges prohibit attorneys from investigating jurors, believing that it is an invasion of privacy. As juror investigations continue to gain in popularity, they may become standard practice which may lead to claims of malpractice or ineffective assistance of counsel for those who fail to conduct them. Another consequence of failing or waiting to investigate jurors is that an attorney may be foreclosed from later raising claims of juror misconduct.

The final question with respect to investigating jurors concerns disclosure. More specifically, must an attorney disclose the information discovered to either opposing counsel or the court. Generally speaking, such information is deemed attorney work-product and thus not subject to the rules of discovery. As for an attorney's ethical obligation that only arises when the information uncovered involves fraud, crime, or misconduct. Section 11.04 discusses in-depth an attorney's ethical obligation to reveal information discovered on a juror's social media site.

§ 10.05 EVIDENCE

Like with other aspects of litigation, social media has had an impact on how evidence is accepted and admitted in the courtroom. This section will examine the influence of social media on the rules of evidence. To date, the most influential case on the topic of admission of electronically stored information (ESI) to include social media is *Lorraine v. Markel Am. Ins. Co.*[20] In this well-written opinion, Judge Paul W. Grimm provides a thorough discussion of the evidentiary issues most relevant to ESI to include the following:

(1) relevancy under FRE 401,

(2) authentication under FRE 901(a),

(3) prohibitions on the admission of hearsay exceptions or exclusions,

(4) whether ESI is an original or duplicated under the original writing rule and if not, whether there is admissible secondary evidence to prove the content of the ESI under FRE 1001–1008, and

(5) probative value.

The five evidentiary requirements discussed in *Lorraine* can also be viewed as three distinct hurdles

---

[20] *Lorraine v. Markel American Insurance Co.*, 241 F.R.D. 534 (D. Md. 2007).

that must be cleared prior to getting any content from social media admitted into evidence. The first hurdle concerns relevancy. The second hurdle involves authentication. The final hurdle relates to the exclusionary rules like character and hearsay. Due to the nature of social media, especially with respect to anonymity and online impersonation, the focus in evidence will be on authentication.

A. RELEVANCE

To be relevant, evidence must "make the existence of any fact that is of consequence to the determination of the action more probable or less probable."[21]

Generally speaking, establishing the relevancy of evidence is not a difficult burden.[22] To be relevant, the evidence must pertain to an element of the case, an affirmative defense, or be used to impeach or undermine the credibility of a witness. At times, however, this initial evidentiary threshold is not met. The following two cases will illustrate how courts have addressed the issue of relevancy in the context of content from social media.

In *Quagliarello v. Dewees*,[23] the plaintiff brought a civil rights action against a police officer for the

---

[21] Norman M. Garland, *An Overview of Relevance and Hearsay: A Nine Step Analytical Guide*, 22 S.W. U. L. REV. 1039 (1993).

[22] *Lorraine v. Markel,* 241 F.R.D. 534 (D. Md. 2007) ("Once Evidence has been shown to meet the low threshold of relevance . . . .").

[23] *Quagliarello v. Dewees*, 2011 WL 3438090 (E.D. Pa. Aug. 4, 2011).

officer's actions during a stop and arrest of the plaintiff. Prior to trial, plaintiff filed a motion in limine to preclude the introduction of photos from her Facebook and Myspace pages. The pictures in question depicted plaintiff with her friends, playing with a dog, drinking at a party, and riding a mechanical bull.

Plaintiff argued that the photographs she posted had no relevance to the ongoing litigation and may impute to her a negative character trait. In contrast, defendants argued that plaintiff put her mental and physical condition at issue by alleging past and future physical and mental pain, anguish, severe emotional trauma, embarrassment, and humiliation resulting from her arrest.

The court ultimately decided that some of the photographs posted on social media could be relevant to plaintiff's claim for emotional distress. Thus, the court held that if plaintiff testifies about her emotional distress after the arrest, the defense may show up to three photographs on cross-examination. The court also held that the plaintiff could rebut defendant's photos with three of her own from the same time period.

In contrast to *Quagliarello*, a federal judge in *Webb v. Jessamine County Fiscal Court*[24] found that eight photos purported to be from the plaintiff's Myspace account "bear no relation at all to the extreme humiliation and mental anguish" the plaintiff

---

[24] *Webb v. Jessamine County Fiscal Court*, 2011 WL 3652751 (E.D. Ky. 2011).

suffered at the hands of the defendant. Here, the plaintiff filed a civil rights action against the local jail and its employees for failing to provide her medical care while she gave birth in their custody and control. Plaintiff claimed that she was refused proper medical treatment during the birth of her child and as a result suffered extreme humiliation, mental anguish, and emotional distress.

In an effort to minimize or weaken plaintiff's argument, defendants attempted to introduce eight photos of the plaintiff to show that "a reasonable person would be embarrassed if such photographs were placed in a public view." Apparently, the defendants wanted to argue that the photos made it less probable that plaintiff would experience humiliation and mental anguish by being in a jail cell delivering a baby without any assistance. The plaintiff argued that "being ignored, or called a child and a liar, during labor and delivery can certainly be considered humiliating and embarrassing in a fashion totally different than taking photographs like those at issue here." Ultimately, the court found the plaintiff's argument more persuasive and prohibited the admission of the photos.

B. AUTHENTICATION

Historically, the bar for getting evidence authenticated had not been set very high. Social media, however, has raised the traditionally low authentication hurdle to new heights. This is because evidence derived from social media, unlike those derived from other forms, can be more easily altered or forged. In addition, individuals can create entirely bogus social media sites or pretend to be others on social media. This concept of online impersonation was previously discussed in Sections 8.05 and 9.04.

There are two primary authentication requirements a proponent of social media evidence must be prepared to address. The first and more basic requirement is simply demonstrating that the evidence being admitted is from the social media site in question. This can be accomplished by having someone with personal knowledge of the social media site testify that the evidence being offered is from that specific site.

The second and more complex requirement is attributing the social media evidence to a specific person. Put differently, the proponent of the evidence must demonstrate that "the person to whom any words are attributable is actually that person and not another person."[25] Absent an admission from the individual who created the social media evidence, the practitioner must rely on circumstantial evidence to fulfill the second requirement of authentication.

At present, the law in this area is not entirely clear. To date, states have taken varying approaches to authenticating social media related evidence.

---

[25] Byron L. Warnken, Social Networking Sites and Criminal Litigation, PROF. BYRON L. WARNKEN'S BLOG (Jan. 3, 2011), http://www.professorwarnken.com/2011/01/03/social-networking-sites-and-criminal-litigation.

Parker v. State, a Delaware Supreme Court case, illustrates this fact.[26]

In *Parker*, two women (Tiffany Parker and Sheniya Brown) were involved in a physical altercation that arose over Facebook messages regarding a mutual love interest. Ultimately, Parker was indicted on one count of Assault in the Second Degree and one count of Terroristic Threatening.

As part of its case-in-chief, the prosecution introduced Facebook entries made by Parker after the fight to discredit the defendant's theory of self-defense. The Facebook entries were as follows:

> *bet tht bitch didnt think was going to see her ass. . . bet she wont inbox me no more, #caughtthatbitch*
>
> *. . . [ctfu]. . . this girl is crazy. . . she really got these ppl thinkin that was on some nut shit. . . first of all she hit me first. . . if you really want to put it out there since you shared i. . . See more*
>
> *. . . told you go head and you inboxed me back still being disrespectful. . . told you say no more . . . seen you today. . . we said our words you put your hands on me. . . hit you back. . . WE. . . See more*

The Facebook entries also included Parker's picture, the name "Tiffani Parker," and a time-stamp for each entry, indicating that they were posted on December

---

[26] *Parker v. State*, 85 A.3d 682 (Del. 2014).

2, 2011, the same day as the fight. The victim shared Parker's Facebook posts on her own page.

The defendant claimed self-defense. She was acquitted on the Threat charge but convicted on the Assault charge. She subsequently appealed to the Delaware Supreme Court, which ultimately upheld her conviction.

One of the main issues before the Delaware Supreme Court was whether the court properly admitted the defendant's Facebook posts. Since this was a case of first impression for the Delaware Supreme Court it looked to other jurisdictions to see how they addressed the issue. Specifically, the Delaware Supreme Court looked at *Tienda v. State* ("Texas Approach") and *Griffin v. State* ("Maryland Approach").[27]

In *Griffin,* which was decided before *Tienda,* the state introduced printouts of alleged Myspace postings made by Jessica Barber, the defendant's girlfriend. One of the postings read as follows:

> *I HAVE 2 BEAUTIFUL KIDS... FREE BOOZY!!!! JUST REMEMBER SNITCHES GET STITCHES!! U KNOW WHO YOU ARE!*

The state did not call Barber to testify in order to introduce the evidence. Instead, the state relied on a police officer who testified that he knew the printouts belonged to Barber because the Myspace profile where he obtained the information: (1) had a picture

---

[27] *Tienda v. State*, 358 S.W.3d 633 (Tex.Crim.App.2012); *Griffin v. State*, 192 Md. App. 518 (Md. Ct. Spec. App. 2010).

of Barber and the defendant, (2) referenced her children, (3) had her birthdate, and (4) referenced the defendant's nickname, Boozy.

In overturning the defendant's murder conviction, the Maryland Court of Appeals (state high court) determined that the trial judge "failed to acknowledge the possibility or likelihood that another user could have created the profile in issue or authored the 'snitches get stitches' posting." The appellate court further found that "the picture of Ms. Barber coupled with her birthdate and location were not sufficient 'distinctive characteristics' on a Myspace profile to authenticate its printout." According to the appellate court, the trial court should have: (1) asked Barber if she created the post, (2) searched the Internet history and hard drive of Barber, or (3) obtained information directly from Myspace to establish the identity of the person who posted the information. To date, several jurisdictions have followed the Maryland Approach.[28]

In contrast to *Griffin* stands *Tienda*. Here, the state introduced evidence from the defendant's Myspace profiles (he had several) that intimated that he had knowledge of or was responsible for the death of the victim, David Valadez.[29] The state did not rely

---

[28] *People v. Beckley*, 185 Cal. App. 4th 509 (Cal Ct. App. 2010); *State v. Eleck*, 130 Conn. App. 632 (Con, App. Ct. 2011); *Commonwealth v. Williams*, 456 Mass. 857 (Mass. 2010).

[29] Examples of the posts made by the defendant include the following:

If you ain't BLASTIN, You ain't Lastin

I live to stay fresh!! I kill to stay rich!!

on Tienda to get his Myspace profile admitted into evidence. Instead, the state relied on Valadez's sister who was the one who actually found the Myspace profiles. The defendant was convicted of Valadez's murder and subsequently appealed, arguing, among other things, that the trial judge improperly admitted the Myspace profiles.

The Texas Court of Criminal Appeals upheld Tienda's conviction finding that the trial judge had properly admitted the Myspace profiles. The court found that there was enough circumstantial evidence "to support a finding by a rational jury that the MySpace pages that the State offered into evidence were created by the [defendant]." Examples of the circumstantial evidence included the fact that: (1) the Myspace pages were registered to a person with the defendant's nickname and legal name, (2) the photographs on the Myspace profile were clearly of the defendant, and (3) the defendant's profile referenced the victim and his murder along with the defendant's home monitoring which was imposed as part of his pre-trial bail.

The Maryland and Texas approaches may be summarized as follows. Under the Maryland approach, the court sets a high bar for the admissibility of evidence by refusing to admit the exhibit unless the court definitively determines that the evidence is authentic. Under the Texas approach, the court determines the admissibility of evidence based on whether there is sufficient evidence of

---

RIP, David Valadez

authenticity for a reasonable jury to conclude that the evidence was authentic.

In deciding which approach to adopt, the Delaware Supreme Court went with the Texas approach, which has been followed by states like Arizona and New York. In upholding the defendant's conviction for assault, the Delaware Supreme Court held that[30],

> *the substance of the Facebook post referenced the altercation that occurred between Parker and Brown. Although the post does not mention Brown by name, it was created on the same day after the altercation and referenced a fight with another woman. Second, Brown's testimony provided further authenticating evidence. Brown testified that she viewed Parker's post through a mutual friend. Thereafter, Brown "shared" the post and published it on her own Facebook page.*

On the federal level, *United States v. Vayner* illustrates the approach taken by some federal courts.[31] Here, a three-judge panel from the U.S. Court of Appeals for the Second Circuit overturned Aliaksandr Zhyltsou's conviction for unlawful transfer of a false identification document. This decision was based on the fact that the trial judge hearing the case erred in admitting a printout of the defendant's alleged profile on VK.com (Russian equivalent to Facebook).

---

[30] *State v. Assi*, 2012 WL 3580488; *People v. Clevenstine*, 68 A.D. 3d 1448 (N.Y. App. Div. 2009).

[31] *United States v. Vayner*, 769 F.3d 125 (2d Cir. Oct. 3, 2014).

In this case, Vladyslav Timku testified that the defendant sent him a bogus birth certificate for an "invented infant daughter," which Timku used to avoid compulsory military service in the Ukraine army. Timku claimed that he had received the bogus birth certificate from the following email address: azmadeuz@gmail.com. The prosecution supported Timku's testimony, the only evidence directly connecting Zhyltsou to the Gmail address used to transmit the forged birth certificate, with testimony from Robert Cline, a Special Agent with the State Department's Diplomatic Security Service. Through Cline, the prosecution admitted Zhyltsou's purported profile page from VK. The profile page included the defendant's profile, an alternative spelling of his name ("Alexander Zhiltsov"), and other facts about which Timku had testified. Cline also acknowledged, however, that he was not very familiar with VK and only had a cursory understanding of the website.

The court acknowledged that a document's "contents" or "distinctive characteristics" can at times provide sufficient grounds to authenticate; however, neither was sufficient here. According to the court,

> *[T]he information contained on the VK page allegedly tying the page to Zhyltsou was also known by Timku and likely others, some of whom may have had reasons to create a profile page falsely attributed to the defendant. Other than the page itself, moreover, no evidence in the record suggested that Zhyltsou even had a VK profile page, much less that the page in question*

> *was that page. Nor was there any evidence that identity verification is necessary to create such a page with VK, which might also have helped render more than speculative the conclusion that the page in question belonged to Zhyltsou.*

To help explain the appellate court's ruling, the panel attempted to draw a comparison between the printout profile from VK to a random flyer found on the street. Here the court wrote:

> *Had the government sought to introduce, for instance, a flyer found on the street that contained Zhyltsou's Skype address and was purportedly written or authorized by him, the district court surely would have required some evidence that the flyer did, in fact, emanate from Zhyltsou. Otherwise, how could the statements in the flyer be attributed to him?. . . . ("[A] mere assertion of identity by a person talking on the telephone is not in itself sufficient to authenticate that person's identity. . . ."). And contrary to the government's argument, the mere fact that a page with Zhyltsou's name and photograph happened to exist on the Internet at the time of Special Agent Cline's testimony does not permit a reasonable conclusion that this page was created by the defendant or on his behalf.*

C. EXCLUSIONARY RULES

1. Hearsay

Hearsay as defined by Federal Rule of Evidence (FRE) 801(c) is "a statement, other than one made by the declarant while testifying at the trial or hearing, offered in evidence to prove the truth of the matter asserted."[32] In the context of social media, hearsay can take the form of updates, messages, and photograph captions. Unlike authentication, the hearsay inquiry for social media evidence is fairly straightforward.

The first step in any hearsay analysis is to determine whether the evidence is a statement made by a person. Information generated automatically by machines is ordinarily not considered a statement. By way of example, certain social media providers use a time-stamp whenever an individual posts information on an account. This time stamp would not be a statement so long as it was automatically computer generated. However, the other information in the post would be a statement.

Next, the court has to consider whether the statement is offered for the truth of the matter asserted. In *People v. Valdez*, the government introduced pages from the defendant's Myspace account that included, among other things, his gang moniker ("Yums"), a photograph of the defendant making a gang hand signal, and written notations including "T.L.F.," "YUM $ YUM," "T.L.F.'s '63 Impala," "T.L.F., The Most Wanted Krew by the Cops and Ladiez," and "Yums. You Don't Wanna F wit this Guy."[33] According to the government, these posts were admitted for two reasons: (1) corroboration of

---

[32] Fed. R. Evid. 801(c).

[33] *People v. Valdez*, 201 Cal. App. 4th 1429 (4th Dist. 2011).

the victim's identification of the defendant from his Myspace site, and (2) foundation for the government's gang expert.

The defendant was ultimately convicted of two counts of attempted murder, four counts of assault with a firearm, and two counts of street terrorism arising from two separate drive-by shootings. On appeal, the defendant argued, *inter alia,* that the content from his Myspace page should not have been admitted into evidence because it was hearsay. The appellate court found defendant's hearsay challenge to the Myspace posts to be without merit. According to the appellate court, "the trial court did not admit the Myspace material for the truth of any assertion on the page."

If the evidence is both a statement and offered for the truth of the matter asserted, then the judge must determine whether the statement is excluded from the definition of hearsay. For example, certain prior witness statements are excluded from the definition of hearsay pursuant to FRE 801(d)(1). In addition, certain statements by party opponents are excluded from the definition of hearsay pursuant to FRE 801(d)(2).

At least one legal commentator has suggested that a "Like" on Facebook could be deemed an admission and thus could be excluded from the definition of hearsay. According to this individual, "Facebook 'likes' are most properly viewed as manifestations of belief in an existing statement rather than independent statements, and therefore "likes" constitute adoptive admissions under the Federal Rules of Evidence."[34]

If all the above requirements are met and the statement fits the definition of hearsay, the judge would finally look at whether an exception to the general prohibition against admitting hearsay evidence exists. There are numerous exceptions to the hearsay rule. The more commonly used exceptions for admitting hearsay evidence derived from social media include present sense impression, excited utterance (e.g., tweets and status updates), public record, and business record.

It should be noted that some legal commentators have expressed concern with the continued use of the present sense impression in the age of social media. The fear here is that with tweets and status updates there could be a wholesale admission of "social media hearsay."[35] This concern, however, appears overblown because the present sense impression exception to the ban on hearsay has several requirements which serve to limit such evidence. For example, there must be: (1) a determination that the event or condition described by the statement occurred or existed, (2) the declarant must have personal knowledge of the event or condition, and (3) the declarant must make the assertion while

[34] Molly D. McPartland, *An Analysis of Facebook "Likes" and Other Nonverbal Internet Communication Under the Federal Rules of Evidence*, 99 Iowa L. Rev. 445, 448 (2013).

[35] Jeffrey Bellin, *Facebook, Twitter, and the Uncertain Future of the Present Sense Impressions*, 160 U. PA. L. REV. 331 (2012).

perceiving the event or condition or immediately thereafter.

2. Best Evidence Rule

FRE 1002, the best evidence rule also known as the original writing rule, states that "[a]n original writing, recording, or photograph is required in order to prove its content unless these rules or a federal statute provides otherwise."[36] The best evidence rule arises when an attorney attempts to prove the contents of a writing, recording, or photograph. This typically occurs when the writing is itself the item a proponent wants to prove or a proponent wants to prove a matter by using a writing as evidence of that matter. To properly apply the best evidence rule, the judge must "determine when 'the contents' of a writing, recording or photograph actually are being proved, as opposed to proving events that just happen to have been recorded or photographed, or those which can be proved by eyewitnesses, as opposed to a writing or recording explaining or depicting them."[37]

People v. Vilton illustrates an unsuccessful attempt by a criminal defendant to raise a best evidence argument with respect to evidence admitted from social media.[38] Here, the defendant was convicted of felonious assault and possession of a firearm during the commission or attempt to commit

---

[36] Fed. R. Evid. 1002.

[37] *Lorraine v. Markel American Ins. Co.*, 241 F.R.D. 534, 576 (D. Md. 2007).

[38] *People v. Vilton,* No. 318626 (Mich. Ct. App. Feb. 3. 2015) (unpublished).

a felony. On appeal, the defendant argued, *inter alia,* that his attorney provided ineffective assistance for failing to object to the admission of Facebook exchanges that occurred with the defendant and two complaining witnesses. The defendant pointed to two specific examples in which each complaining witness testified about taking some specific action based on a Facebook post or message to them from the defendant.

In upholding the defendant's conviction, the appellate court determined that the defendant was not disputing the contents of the writing but rather just the form in which they were presented i.e., on Facebook. Furthermore, the court found that the evidentiary value of the defendant's Facebook posts were not in their truth, but in describing what motivated the meeting between the defendant and the two complaining witnesses. The court stated that "[b]ecause the contents of the Facebook messages were not an issue and were not an operative fact, the best evidence rule did not apply."

3. Character Evidence

FRE 404(b) reads as follows:

> *Evidence of a crime, wrong, or other act is not admissible to prove a person's character in order to show that on a particular occasion the person acted in accordance with the character.*
>
> *. . . This evidence may be admissible for another purpose, such as proving motive, opportunity,*

> *intent, preparation, plan, knowledge, identity, absence of mistake, or lack of accident.*[39]

United States v. Phaknikone and *Harden v. State* provide examples of how the issue of improper character evidence arises with respect to social media.[40] In *Harden,* the defendant Larry Harden was convicted of sexual battery, false imprisonment, and domestic battery. Harden allegedly committed these crimes against his then girlfriend, K.W. At trial, the defendant wanted to admit certain messages sent from K.W. to Kayla, who was Harden's current girlfriend at the time. The defense planned to use these messages to support its theory that K.W. was a jealous ex-girlfriend who was making up these charges to get back at the defendant. The messages included statements such as:

> *I'm too beautiful for you to compete, you look like a F'g gorilla, for real dog*
>
> *Larry's ladies, you hoes don't stand a chance*

The trial disallowed the admission of these statements finding among other things that the prejudice outweighed the probative value of the messages. The appellate court overruled the trial court finding that the messages should have been admitted. According to the appellate court, which ultimately overturned the defendant's conviction on other grounds, "the MySpace messages were relevant because they demonstrated bias and supported the

---

[39] FED. R. EVID. 404 (b)(1)–(2).

[40] *United States v. Phaknikone*, 605 F.3d 1099 (11th Cir. 2010); *Harden v. State*, 87 So.3d 1243 (Fla. Dist. Ct. App. 2012).

defense theory that [K.W.] was a jealous ex-girlfriend with a motive to lie. . . . while [K.W.] may be embarrassed that she sent the messages, we fail to see how the messages were unfairly prejudicial to the state."

In *Phaknikone*, the defendant, Souksakhone Phaknikone, was charged, along with others, with the armed robbery of several banks. According to the government, these banks were robbed in a "gangster style" to include the manner by which the defendants held their weapons. In order to demonstrate that Phaknikone committed the robberies, the government admitted his Myspace page into evidence. The Myspace page included the following posts and photographs:

(1) *The defendant's profile page that listed the name "Trigga" with "$100 bills . . . float[ing] down the screen.",*

(2) *His subscriber report, listing the full name "Trigga FullyLoaded" and email address gangsta_trigga@yahoo.com., and*

(3) *Two photographs, including one of the defendant bearing a tattoo, holding a handgun sideways (apparently gangster style), with a child and another man as passengers.*

The prosecution claimed that this evidence not only proved Phaknikone's identity, but also the method by which he robbed the banks. According to the prosecution, Phaknikone was "an individual [with] access to . . . a gun, as shown and evidenced by the brazen nature with which he publishes it to every single person on the internet through a MySpace account." The defense objected to the evidence but the trial judge still allowed it in.

The case eventually made it to the Eleventh Circuit Court of Appeals which sided with the defendant with respect to the admissibility of the Myspace evidence. In the eyes of the appellate court, Rule 404(b) was created exactly for situations like *Phaknikone*. According to the appellate court,

> *[t]he Myspace evidence is not evidence of identity. . . . The subscriber report proved nothing more than Phaknikone's nickname. . . . The photograph of a tattooed Phaknikone, his face completely visible, in a car, holding a handgun sideways in his right hand, and with a child as a passenger, proves only that Phaknikone, on an earlier occasion, possessed a handgun in the presence of a child. Although the photograph may portray a "gangster-type personality," the photograph does not evidence the modus operandi of a bank robber who commits his crimes with a signature trait. The Myspace evidence is not evidence of a modus operandi and is inadmissible to prove identity.*[41]

Ultimately, however, the appellate court did not overturn Phaknikone's conviction. This was due in large part to the overwhelming evidence of his guilt, including his own confession.

---

[41] *Id.*

CHAPTER 11
ETHICS

§ 11.01 INTRODUCTION

This chapter delves into the intersection of ethics and social media. The chapter begins with a brief discussion of why attorneys need to stay abreast of technological changes to include advancements in social media. Next, the chapter examines the attorney-client relationship. The focus here is on what advice attorneys can and cannot give their clients regarding social media. This section will be followed by a brief discussion of client confidentiality.

This chapter also looks at the ethical missteps that can arise when attorneys use social media to communicate with and investigate jurors, witnesses, and parties. The chapter concludes with a discussion of the ethical problems that occur when attorneys use social media to interact with the general public. The last section explores inadvertent attorney-client relationships, attorney advertising, and attorney commentary on pending litigation.

§ 11.02 COMPETENCE

In 2012, the ABA modified the Model Rules of Professional Conduct to emphasize that lawyers have a duty to be competent in both the law and technology.[1]

---

[1] *See* ABA Model Rule 1.1 Comment 8.

To date, at least 26 states have adopted this model rule and/or acknowledged its importance by issuing advisory and formal ethics opinions in support of it. While this new rule does not require attorneys to become experts in the field of technology, it does suggest that lawyers, at a minimum, need to have a basic level of competency with new and emerging technologies. Arguably, this includes familiarity with common social media platforms. *Womack v. Yeoman*[2] illustrates the problems that emerge when attorneys don't have at least a rudimentary understanding of popular social media platforms and how they operate.

Womack involved a motor vehicle accident in which the plaintiff alleged that she suffered a traumatic brain injury. In response to the claims asserted by the plaintiff, defense counsel conducted an in-depth online investigation of the plaintiff and her family which included reviewing their social media sites. Through this investigation, defense counsel discovered relevant information about the plaintiff including photographs and text postings.

In contrast, counsel for plaintiff merely asked his client "about the nature of her accounts." Plaintiff's counsel claimed that his client informed him that she did not have a social media account and the accounts of her family members were private. Plaintiff's counsel also claimed that plaintiff's sister informed him that her account was private. However, counsel for plaintiff did not verify this information nor did he thoroughly research the SCA, which, as discussed in

---

[2] *Womack v. Yeoman*, 2011 WL 9330606 (Va. Cir. Ct. 2011).

Section 10.04, regulates how social media providers may release user information.

Upon learning about the photographs and text postings that defense counsel discovered through her social media research, plaintiff's counsel presumed that she had "hacked" plaintiff's or her family members' accounts or violated someone's privacy rights in order to obtain the information. This, in turn, led plaintiff's counsel to file a motion for sanctions arguing, among other things, that the information discovered by defense counsel "violate[d] [p]laintiff's and her families (sic) right to privacy under the Stored Communications Act." It appears that plaintiff's counsel, at the time he filed his motion for sanctions, was unaware of the various privacy settings available on social media.

Not surprisingly, the court overruled plaintiff's sanctions motion finding that defense counsel did not engage in hacking but instead conducted diligent and thorough research. Thus, rather than grant sanctions against defense counsel, the court ordered plaintiff's counsel to pay defense counsel for her costs in defending this meritless motion. Arguably, had plaintiff's counsel better understood social media and how it worked, he would have been less inclined to request sanctions and accuse another attorney of hacking into his client's account.

§ 11.03 CLIENTS

A. ADVICE

Attorney advice to clients regarding social media is either proactive or reactive. When done proactively, the attorney attempts to limit any potential harm that might arise from the client's future use of social media.

At a minimum, proactive advice includes discussing the attorney-client privilege, which can be waived when the client discloses information about his case to others. In *Lenz v. Universal Music Corp.*, the plaintiff used various forms of social media, including a blog, to discuss prior conversations she had with her attorney regarding possible defenses to claims, the impetus for filing her lawsuit, and case strategy.[3] Plaintiff's online statements and comments ultimately led the court to find that she had waived her attorney-client privilege and that the defendants were entitled to discovery of attorney-client communications related to plaintiff's motivations for pursuing litigation, legal strategy, and other factual issues.

Proactive advice also includes informing clients about the risks associated with using social media accounts owned or operated by third parties like employers. For example, an employee's communication with her attorney might not be

---

[3] *Lenz v. Universal Music Corp.*, No. 5:07–cv–03783 JF, 2010 WL 4789099 (N.D. Cal. Nov. 17, 2010).

confidential if conducted on a social media account created or owned by her employer.

Some attorneys have gone so far as to provide their clients warnings about using social media in the initial client engagement letter. Here is a sample social media warning notice to a client:

> *We recommend that all of our clients refrain from posting content on social media (Facebook, Twitter, Tumblr, Snapchat, Instagram, and the like) during the course of representation. We make this recommendation because social media content is not private, can be discoverable, and may be potentially damaging to your interests. Information shared with others be it verbally; in writing via email, text message or letter; or even posted online could harm your interests in a number of different ways to include the loss of attorney-client privilege.*

In certain instances it is not the client who posts the confidential information on social media but rather a third party. In *Gulliver Schools Inc. v. Snay*, a confidential settlement agreement was found void because the defendant disclosed the terms.[4] In this case, Patrick Snay told his daughter that he had settled his age discrimination lawsuit with Gulliver Preparatory School. This in turn led the daughter, who had attended Gulliver, to post the following on her Facebook page:

---

[4] *Gulliver Schools, Inc. v. Snay*, 137 So. 3d 1045 (Fla. 3rd DCA 2014).

> *Mama and Papa Snay won the case against Gulliver. . . Gulliver is now officially paying for my vacation to Europe this summer. SUCK IT.*

This comment went to 1200 of the daughter's friends some of whom were current or former students at Gulliver. Once the attorneys for Gulliver became aware of the daughter's post, they went to court and had the settlement terms vacated. The appellate court ultimately found in favor of Gulliver. According to the court, "Snay violated the agreement by doing exactly what he had promised not to do. His daughter then did precisely what the confidentiality agreement was designed to prevent, advertising to the Gulliver community that Snay had been successful in his age discrimination and retaliation case against the school."

In contrast to proactive advice is reactive advice. Here, the attorney advises clients about information that has already been posted on social media. Attorneys must be careful about what they tell their clients regarding reactive advice. Unlike proactive advice, which may involve a discussion about the perils of future use of social media, attorneys may be foreclosed from providing certain reactive advice, especially in the criminal arena.

An attorney may be subject to criminal prosecution for obstruction of justice or tampering with evidence for offering improper reactive advice. Generally speaking, an attorney may provide his client or a witness advice about increasing privacy settings. It is less clear if an attorney can advise a client to deactivate an account, especially if the content on that account is no longer accessible. Complete destruction of an account or the content on that account may run afoul of both ethical and legal rules, especially if the content or the account itself could be deemed evidence in a criminal matter.

Attorneys advising on purely civil matters face a different set of concerns than those in the criminal arena. To date, several jurisdictions have determined that it is ethical for attorneys in the civil context to instruct clients to "clean-up" potentially damaging information on a social media account. The New York County Lawyers Association went so far as to say that a competent lawyer should "review a client's social media pages, and advise the client that certain materials posted on a social media page may be used against the client for impeachment purposes."[5]

When offering advice on cleaning-up a social media account, attorneys have to remind clients to follow all applicable rules and preserve content where required. In addressing this topic of cleaning up a social media account, the Florida Bar determined that:

> *[p]rovided that there is no violation of the rules or substantive law pertaining to the preservation and/or spoliation of evidence, a lawyer also may advise that a client remove information relevant to the foreseeable proceeding from social media*

[5] New York County Lawyers Association Committee on Professional Ethics in July 2013, Formal Opinion 745.

pages as long as an appropriate record of the social media information or data is preserved.[6]

While it may appear that the rules are straightforward here, they are not. It is very easy for lawyers to find themselves subject to sanctions and on the wrong side of an ethics opinion if they are not careful in the advice they offer to clients about cleaning-up social media accounts. *Lester v. Allied Concrete Company* serves as a shining example of what can go wrong when an attorney provides his client with the wrong advice about social media.[7]

In 2007, Isaiah Lester and his wife Jessica were involved in a car accident with a driver from Allied Concrete Company. The truck driver crossed the center line, tipped over, and crushed Lester's car resulting in the death of Jessica. Since the truck driver had previously pled guilty to manslaughter, liability in *Lester* was a foregone conclusion. The real dispute in this case was the awarding of damages.

Prior to trial, during discovery, counsel for defendants obtained partial access to Lester's Facebook page (apparently Lester, for some unknown reason, sent defense counsel a message via Facebook) and found a picture of him holding a beer can while wearing a t-shirt with the following inscription:

I ♥ hot moms.

Defense counsel sent the photo along with a discovery request to plaintiff's counsel. The request dated

---

[6] Florida Bar Ethics Opinion 14–1 (June 25, 2015).

[7] *Allied Concrete v. Lester*, 736 S.E.2d 699 (Jan. 10, 2013).

March 25, 2009 sought "screen print copies on the day this request is signed of all pages from Isaiah Lester's Facebook page including, but not limited to, all pictures, his profile, his message board, status updates, and all messages sent or received." Upon receipt of this request, counsel for plaintiff directed his paralegal to inform Lester that he needed to "clean up" his Facebook account.

On April 14th, one day before scheduled interrogatories, Lester, while working with plaintiff's counsel, deactivated his Facebook account. Thus, when responding to defendants' interrogatories plaintiff's counsel was able to submit the following statement on behalf of his client "I do not have a Facebook page on the date this is signed, April 15, 2009." This response led defendants to file a Motion to Compel Discovery. Prior to a hearing on the defendants' Motion to Compel Discovery, counsel for plaintiff provided the defendants additional documents from Lester's Facebook page.

On or around May 11, 2009, Lester reactivated his Facebook page; however, it did not have 16 prior photos which had been deleted by Lester presumably in an effort to clean up his page. All but one of the photos were later recovered by the defense's computer forensic expert. Approximately six months later, Lester was deposed and claimed, among other things, that he never deactivated his Facebook page.

Defense filed a Motion for Sanctions for Spoliation of Evidence on August 18, 2010. The court found that spoliation had occurred and directed that an adverse inference be given to the jury and that Lester and his attorney would be subject to sanctions.

After a three-day trial in December 2010, a jury awarded Lester $8.6 million, later reduced by the judge to $4.1 million. The following year the court granted the defendants' Motion for Monetary Sanctions for Spoliation of Evidence. The court sanctioned Lester $180,000. Lester's attorney received a $542,000 sanction which at the time was a record amount. In issuing the sanctions, the court stated that the actions of both Lester and his attorney displayed "an extensive pattern of deceptive and obstructionist conduct[.] . . ." Two years later, the Virginia state bar suspended Lester's attorney from the practice of law for five years.

Lester offers several key takeaways for attorneys. First, telling a client to clean up a social media account raises a potential ethical minefield. Therefore, attorneys should go beyond generic advice like clean-up your account and delve into specific topics with clients such as spoliation. Second, social media evidence, although persuasive, is not always as impactful as some attorneys think. In *Lester*, neither the photo of the plaintiff nor the adverse instructions by the court prevented the jury from granting the plaintiff a substantial award.

When dealing with attorneys who run afoul of the rules regarding spoliation of social media content few courts have been as punitive as *Lester*. For example, in *Katiroll, Inc. v. Kati Roll and Platters, Inc., No. 10–3620,* the court refused to impose sanctions or apply an adverse instruction even though spoliation occurred with defendant's Facebook page. This case arose from a trademark infringement lawsuit in which two restaurants sold a similar type of food called katirolls.[8]

At some point during the litigation, plaintiff went to defendant's Facebook page to print off evidence proving that defendant had infringed on plaintiff's trademark. However, by the time plaintiff took this action, defendant had already updated his page. Thus, the allegedly infringing content was gone. This in turn led the plaintiff to request sanctions claiming that defendant failed to preserve his Facebook page and profile in its original state i.e., displaying the original trade dress at issue.

While the trial court agreed with plaintiff that spoliation had occurred, it was viewed as unintentional. Plus, the defendant had acted in response to an earlier take down request by the plaintiff. Ultimately, the court fashioned its own remedy, one that did not require either an adverse inference or an imposition of monetary sanctions. The court in *Katiroll* simply ordered the defendant to repost the allegedly infringing content on Facebook for a specific amount of time to allow the plaintiff to make copies of whatever information he deemed relevant for his lawsuit.

---

[8] *Katiroll Co., Inc. v. Kati Roll & Platters, Inc.*, No. 10–3620 (GEB), 2011 WL 3583408 (D.N.J. Aug. 3, 2011).

B. CONFIDENTIALITY

Another area of concern with respect to the attorney-client relationship and social media is confidentiality. Here, problems can arise in a variety of different circumstances. Sometimes confidentiality issues come to light when the attorney uses social media to highlight successful case outcomes on social media. To safeguard against revealing private information, attorneys should limit all discussions regarding clients, even positive outcomes, to generalities and avoid using any personal identifiers. The topic of client confidentiality will be revisited later in this chapter in the discussion on attorney advertising.

Other problem areas with confidentiality can spring up from attorney-client disagreements that either start on social media or spill over to social media. In *the Matter of Skinner*, a Georgia attorney faced disciplinary action for, *inter alia,* revealing client information online.[9] In this case, a client was dissatisfied with how her attorney was handling her divorce. Thus, the client requested a refund, retained another attorney and went online to make less than flattering reviews about the attorney. This in turn led the attorney to respond with online postings of her own which happened to include the following information:

(1) client's name,

---

[9] *In the Matter of Margrett A. Skinner*, 295 Ga. 217, 758 S.E.2d 788 (Ga. 2014).

(2) how much the client had paid her,

(3) county in which the divcrce had been filed, and

(4) the fact that the client had a boyfriend.

As a result of her online conduct, the attorney was found to have violated the rules on client confidentiality and was issued a public reprimand and instructed to take advantage of the state's Law Practice Management services. Fortunately for the attorney, she accepted the petition for voluntary discipline and had several mitigating factors in her favor that the bar took under consideration to include no prior disciplinary issues, the absence of a dishonest or selfish motive for her improper online conduct, and repayment of a substantial portion of her fee even after doing work for the client.

Unfortunately, the example from Georgia is not an isolated event. *In the Matter of Tsamis* an Illinois attorney was disciplined for posting private information about her former client on Avvo (a social media site that allows individuals to rate an attorney's performance).[10]

In this case, the attorney represented a flight attendant who was contesting the denial of his unemployment benefits. Apparently, the flight attendant lost his job after he assaulted a fellow employee during an actual flight. The attorney met with the client a couple of times and then represented him in a telephonic hearing before the Illinois

---

[10] *In the Matter of Tsamis*, No. 2013PR00095 (2013).

Department of Employment Security ("IDES"), the state agency that regulates unemployment benefits.

Shortly after the hearing, the client both terminated his relationship with the attorney and learned that IDES had denied him benefits. Approximately one month later, the flight attendant decided to use Avvo to comment on his attorney's performance. Specifically, he made the following post about his attorney:

> *She only wants your money, claims "always on your side" is a huge lie. Paid her to help me secure unemployment, she took my money knowing full well a certain law in Illinois would not let me collect unemployment. [N]ow is billing for an additional $1500 for her time.*

The attorney contacted the flight attendant and asked him to remove the post. The flight attendant agreed if the attorney fully refunded his money ($1500) and provided him with a copy of his file.

The attorney then turned to Avvo and asked for the post to be removed which it did. However, this led the client to post a second review, which Avvo did not take down. The second review reads as follows:

> *I paid Ms.* [redacted] *$1500 to help me secure unemployment while she knew full well that a law in Illinois would prevent me from obtaining unemployment benefits.*

After seeing the second review, the attorney felt the need to respond on Avvo and wrote the following:

> *This is simply false. The person did not reveal all the facts of his situation up front in our first and second meeting. [sic] When I received his personnel file, I discussed the contents of it with him and informed him that he would likely lose unless the employer chose not to contest the unemployment (employers sometimes do is [sic]). Despite knowing that he would likely lose, he chose to go forward with a hearing to try to obtain benefits. I dislike it very much when my clients lose but I cannot invent positive facts for clients when they are not there. I feel badly for him but his own actions in* ***beating up a female coworker*** *are what caused the consequences he is now so upset about* (emphasis added).

Upon discovering the attorney's post, the Illinois bar took action and issued the attorney a public reprimand for failing to maintain client confidentiality.

Not surprisingly, some in the legal profession were bothered by the public reprimand issued to the attorney. Those opposing the reprimand believe that similar to the offline world an attorney has a right to defend herself in the online world. Other attorneys, however, were not necessarily troubled by the reprimand. They acknowledge that an attorney has a right to defend herself online but this particular attorney went too far when she revealed private information about the client.

Those who think that the attorney had a right to defend herself online point to ABA Model Rule 1.6 *Confidentiality of Information*, which contains a self-defense exception in sub-paragraph 5 that allows for disclosure by the attorney of confidential information in order to establish a defense to a "controversy" that arises with the client. However, "controversy" as defined by the Pennsylvania State Bar Ethics Committee (Opinion 2014–200) does not include an online disagreement about the lawyer's services. This same opinion went on to say that no "proceeding" is pending or imminent merely because a client impugns a lawyer's character in an online review.

Pennsylvania Ethics Opinion 2014–200 also addresses the question of what action if any a lawyer should take when confronted with online criticism. According to the opinion, lawyers should consider posting the following generic response to any negative online review.

> *A lawyer's duty to keep client confidences has few exceptions and in an abundance of caution I do not feel at liberty to respond in a point-by-point fashion in this forum. Suffice it to say that I do not believe that the post presents a fair and accurate picture of the events.*

A few attorneys, like other professionals, believe that the best way to prevent unfair online criticism is to have clients sign an anti-disparagement clause as discussed in Section 8.04. To date there are no reported cases of attorneys using anti-disparagement clauses. Furthermore, it is not entirely clear whether such a clause would be upheld by either the courts or the local bar, especially after passage of the Consumer Review Fairness Act. An attorney, like anyone else, also has the option of filing a defamation lawsuit, but as discussed in Section 8.05, that raises its own set of concerns.

Another approach for attorneys is to follow the advice of Avvo's general counsel:

> *Negative commentary can be a golden marketing opportunity. By posting a professional, meaningful response to negative commentary, an attorney sends a powerful message to any readers of that review. Done correctly, such a message communicates responsiveness, attention to feedback and strength of character. The trick is to not get defensive, petty, or feel the need to directly refute what you perceive is wrong with the review. . . . [A] poorly-handled response to a negative review is much worse than no response at all. It makes you look thin-skinned and defensive. Worse yet, if you argue and reveal client confidences (or even potential harmful non-confidences), you may be subject to discipline.*

§ 11.04 JURORS, WITNESSES, AND PARTIES

Another area ripe for ethical problems is attorney investigations. For the most part, attorneys are free to view any public social media site belonging to a juror, witness, or party. In fact, ethical opinions from the ABA and state bar associations from around the country have endorsed the practice. While there are a small number of judges who don't allow the practice with respect to jurors and/or require attorneys to disclose in open court that they plan to investigate the jurors, these judges are few and far between. The real area of concern here is when attorneys go beyond merely viewing and actually use social media to interact with jurors, witnesses, or parties.

A. NO CONTACT

As a general rule, attorneys may not contact jurors or represented persons. Most, if not all, courts hold that "contact" can occur both offline and online. Thus, if an attorney sends a friend request or uses instant messaging, that constitutes contact and violates the ethical rules. This prohibition is imputed to those working for and/or on behalf of the attorney. ABA Model Rule 5.3 (Responsibilities Regarding Nonlawyer Assistants).

Recently, two defense attorneys from New Jersey were cited by their state bar for instructing their paralegal to become Facebook Friends with a plaintiff during an ongoing personal injury case.[11] The actions of the paralegal and defense attorneys came to light during a deposition when one of the defense attorneys asked the plaintiff questions about traveling, dancing, and other physical activities that related to the seriousness of his injuries. The defense team also later amended their interrogatories to include conversations, photos, and a video of the plaintiff wrestling with his brother. All of this information was obtained by defense counsel through their paralegal who had improperly friended the

[11] *Robertelli v. New Jersey Office of Atty. Ethics*, 2015 N.J. Super. Unpub. LEXIS 213 (App.Div., Feb. 3, 2015).

plaintiff and thus gained access to his private Facebook page and those of his friends.

One exception to the no contact rule involves contact initiated by the client. In 2013, the New Hampshire Ethics Committee in an advisory opinion determined that an attorney's client may friend a represented party and then reveal the information uncovered. N.H Ethics Committee Advisory Opinion #2012–13/05. However, the client's attorney cannot direct the client's actions, and the attorney must comply with all other ethical obligations.

Subsequent to the New Hampshire opinion, the New York State Bar Association (NYSBA) has added further clarity to this topic. According to NYSBA's 2014 Social Media Ethics Guidelines of the Commercial and Federal Litigation Section (March 18, 2014):

> *A lawyer may review the contents of the restricted portion of the social media profile of a represented person that was provided to the lawyer by her client, as long as the lawyer did not cause or assist the client to: (i) inappropriately obtain confidential information from the represented person; (ii) invite the represented person to take action without the advice of his or her lawyer; or (iii) otherwise overreach with respect to the represented person.*[12]

---

[12] NYSBA's 2014 Social Media Ethics Guidelines (March 18, 2014).

B. INADVERTENT CONTACT

At present, there is a split of opinion on whether the no contact rule includes inadvertent contact or contact automatically generated by the social media provider itself. For example, many users of Twitter read tweets by subscribing to or following a sender's Twitter account. When an individual follows someone's tweets or subscribes to someone's tweets, Twitter, in certain circumstances, generates an automated message alerting the sender that she is now being followed by a specific person.

In examining this type of indirect contact with a juror, the New York City Bar held that the automated response, if the attorney was aware of it, may be an ethical violation.[13] Thus, if an attorney decides to follow the tweets of a juror and the juror receives the automated response from Twitter that she is now being followed by a certain attorney, this might be an ethical violation, according to the New York City Bar, so long as the attorney understood how Twitter functioned. Interestingly, the New York City Bar took no position with respect to situations where the attorney was ignorant or unaware of the automated response procedures of the social media platform.

As support for its opinion, the New York City Bar relied on Opinion 743 by the New York County Lawyers' Association (NYCLA) which stated, among

---

[13] The Association of the Bar of the City of New York Committee on Professional Ethics Formal Opinion 2012–2: JURY RESEARCH AND SOCIAL MEDIA.

other things, that "[i]f a juror becomes aware of an attorney's efforts to see the juror's profiles on websites, the contact may well consist of an impermissible communication, as it might tend to influence the juror's conduct with respect to the trial."[14]

In contrast to the two ethical opinions from New York, the ABA has issued an opinion (April 24, 2014 Lawyer Reviewing Jurors' Internet Presence) stating that contact automatically generated by the social media provider does not constitute an ethical violation because the lawyer is not communicating directly with the juror. Instead, the opinion states that it is the social media platform that communicates with the juror. The ABA opinion analogizes automatic contact by the social media provider to a juror's neighbor recognizing an attorney's car driving down the juror's street. If that neighbor later told the juror that he saw the lawyer's car drive down the juror's street that would not violate the rules on ethics.[15] It is the third party neighbor, not the lawyer, who is communicating with the juror. The ABA opinion went on to say that the problem raised in the prior NYCLA opinion can be fixed if jurors are told beforehand that the attorneys might investigate them online. Other states, like Pennsylvania, have adhered to the ABA rule on this issue.

---

[14] NYCLA Committee on Professional Ethics Formal Opinion No.: 743 (May 18, 2011).

[15] ABA Formal Opinion 466 April 24, 2014 (Lawyer Reviewing Jurors' Internet Presence).

The aforementioned no contact rule is inapplicable to witnesses who are *un*represented by counsel. Here, attorneys, generally speaking, may contact or friend these witnesses. However, in making this contact, the rules of ethics require that attorneys be truthful and non-deceptive. Most, but not all, jurisdictions also prohibit pretexting by attorneys, which will be discussed next.

C. PRETEXTING OR DECEPTION

The definition of pretexting varies by jurisdiction but generally involves disguising one's identity and purpose when interacting with an individual, usually the defendant, in order to obtain information. Only a few jurisdictions allow pretexting by attorneys. It is generally limited to the civil arena and involves circumstances where the attorney has no other method of obtaining crucial information, e.g., civil rights (housing discrimination) or intellectual property (patent infringement). Also, some jurisdictions like Oregon allow attorneys to supervise certain deceptive activities. For example, Oregon RPC 8.4(b) permits an attorney to "advise clients and others about or to supervise lawful covert activity in the investigation of violations of civil or criminal law or constitutional rights, provided the lawyer's conduct is otherwise in compliance with these Rules of Professional Conduct."[16] "Covert activity" is defined as "an effort to obtain information on

---

[16] Oregon RPC 8.4(a)(3).

unlawful activity through the use of misrepresentation or other subterfuge."

The topic of pretexting has received renewed interest in the Digital Age because it is fairly easy to remain anonymous or impersonate someone on social media as discussed in Section 8.05. Any attorney who plans to engage in pretexting or deception should thoroughly research the law in her specific jurisdiction and obtain an advisory ethics opinion before taking such action. In Ohio, a prosecutor was terminated from his position and sanctioned by the bar for creating a bogus Facebook profile and pretending to be the defendant's ex-girlfriend. The prosecutor carried out this impersonation in order to interact with the criminal defendant's alibi witnesses both of whom were female. The prosecutor wanted to dissuade them from testifying for the defendant whom he was prosecuting for aggravated murder.

D. DISCLOSURE

While most jurisdictions prohibit attorneys from directly lying to unrepresented witnesses, it is not entirely clear what information, if any, the attorney must share with the witness. For example, must the attorney reveal any information about himself to the witness? The answer to that question is not clear-cut because jurisdictions across the country generally take one of two approaches known as either the New York City Rule or Philadelphia Rule. The New York City Rule is derived from a New York City Bar opinion (Committee on Professional and Judicial Ethics—Opinion 2010–2 Sept. 2010) which determined that an attorney contacting a witness through social media need not disclose the reasons why she is contacting the unrepresented party. The opinion, among other things, states that "an attorney or her agent may use her real name and profile to send a 'friend request' to obtain information from an unrepresented person's social networking website without also disclosing the reasons for making the request[.] . . ."[17] The New York City Rule places a high value on informal discovery by attorneys. At present, the New York City Rule has not been widely adopted by other jurisdictions.

In contrast to the New York City Rule is the Philadelphia Rule, which derives from an ethics opinion by the Philadelphia Bar Association Professional Guidance Committee.[18] This opinion prohibits an attorney from contacting an unrepresented witness through social media without first revealing the purpose for the contact. The Philadelphia Rule, unlike the New York City Rule, greatly values, even more so than informal discovery, candor to the public.

The opinion by the Philadelphia Bar stressed that failure to reveal why the attorney was making contact would violate Pennsylvania Rule of Professional Conduct 8.4 (deceit, misrepresentation, dishonesty, and fraud). The attorney would be

---

[17] The Association of the Bar of the City Of New York Committee on Professional and Judicial Ethics, Opinion 2010–2 (Sept. 2010).

[18] The Philadelphia Bar Association Professional Guidance Committee, Opinion 2009–02 (March 2009).

omitting a highly material fact—namely, that the attorney asking to be allowed access to the witnesses' social media site is doing so only for a pending or future legal proceeding. The opinion further states that it is irrelevant whether the witness allows almost anyone access to her social media site, i.e., friends them. Of the jurisdictions that have addressed the question of whether or not an attorney must reveal information to an unrepresented witness, most follow the Philadelphia Rule. For example, the San Diego County Bar Association, (SDCBA) in examining the ethical ramifications of attorneys friending witnesses, stated:

> *We agree with the scope of the duty set forth in the Philadelphia Bar Association opinion, notwithstanding the value in informal discovery on which the City of New York Bar Association focused. Even where an attorney may overcome other ethical objections to sending a friend request, the attorney should not send such a request to someone involved in the matter for which he has been retained without disclosing his affiliation and the purpose for the request.*[19]

For those jurisdictions adhering to the Philadelphia Rule, the next question becomes how much information must be revealed to the unrepresented witness. The SDCBA states that, if it is merely the client making the request, then she need only reveal her name because, presumably, the witness would recognize the reason for the request.

[19] SDCBA Legal Ethics Opinion 2011–2.

In contrast, this same ethics opinion also states that if it is the attorney making the request, she must disclose her affiliation and the purpose of the request.

Similarly, in New Hampshire, the lawyer must "inform the witness of the lawyer's involvement in the disputed or litigated matter," disclose the "lawyer by name as a lawyer," and provide "identification of the client and the matter in litigation."[20] While not as specific as New Hampshire or San Diego, Oregon requires the lawyer to provide "additional information" if the person being friended "asks for additional information. . . or if [the l]awyer has some other reason to believe that the person misunderstands her role.[21] The takeaway from these various ethics opinions is that, depending on the jurisdiction, the attorney may have to make significant disclosures to an unrepresented witness prior to sending a friend request.

Since attorneys are prohibited from ex parte contact with jurors, the question of what information the attorney must reveal to a juror would rarely, if ever, come up. Instead, the concerns involving disclosure here center on whether the attorney has to disclose to opposing counsel or the court information uncovered during an investigation of the juror's social media site. ABA Model Rule 3.3 Comment 12

---

[20] New Hampshire Ethics Committee Advisory Opinion #2012–13/05.

[21] Oregon State Bar Committee on Legal Ethics, Formal Opinion 2013–189 (2013).

only requires that an attorney turn over juror information that is either criminal or fraudulent.

Some jurisdictions have adopted this Model Rule completely, while others have created their own rule or made minor changes. For example, many jurisdictions require attorneys to report jurors when they are not only involved in some type of criminal or fraudulent activity but also when they commit misconduct. Thus, an attorney's ethical obligation to disclose information from a juror's social media site varies by jurisdiction but should at minimum include anything related to crime or fraud.

In addition to issues that arise with jurors and witnesses, attorneys must also be cognizant of how they interact with unrepresented parties on social media. The safest course of action for any attorney is to limit contact with an unrepresented party and avoid offering any type of advice except to suggest that the person seek counsel. *In re Gamble* illustrates the ethical problems that arise when attorneys provide unrepresented parties advice via social media.[22]

In re Gamble involved a disciplinary action taken against an attorney for ex parte communication via Facebook with an unrepresented party during an adoption proceeding. In this case, the attorney represented the biological father who was contesting the adoption of his child. The attorney sent the biological 18-year-old mother of the child an emotional Facebook message encouraging her not to

[22] *In re Gamble*, 338 P. 3d 576 (Kan. 2014).

consent to the adoption. The message contained statements such as the baby "deserves to know that you love her," she could still "make things right," and that she was making a mistake that she would "live with the rest of . . . [her] life."

In reviewing the actions of the attorney, the disciplinary hearing panel found that the attorney did not violate the state's rule on contacting an unrepresented party because he did not imply or state to the young woman that he was disinterested. However, the panel did find that the attorney's actions adversely reflected on his fitness to practice law and were prejudicial to the administration of justice. According to the panel, the attorney's conduct amounted to "emotional blackmail" and was designed to "embarrass, burden and create guilt." As a result, the attorney, who self-reported his actions to the bar, received a 6-month suspension from the practice of law.

§ 11.05 GENERAL PUBLIC

As demonstrated by the earlier parts of this chapter, attorneys have run afoul of the rules of ethics when they use social media in connection with specific individuals or groups such as clients, jurors, parties, and witnesses. Unfortunately, these are not the only examples of ethical missteps by attorneys. As illustrated next, some attorneys get in trouble when they direct their social media activity at the general public.

A. INADVERTENT ATTORNEY-CLIENT RELATIONSHIP

Due to the interactive nature of social media, attorneys run a potential risk that they may create unintended attorney-client relationships by responding to questions or posts made by the general public to their social media sites. The ABA Model Rules do not directly address the question of how attorney-client relationships are formed. However, *Restatement (Third) of Law Governing Lawyers § 14* (2000) does. The restatement reads as follows:

> *A relationship of client and lawyer arises when:*
>
> *(1) A person manifests to a lawyer the person's intent that the lawyer provide legal services for the person; and either*
>
> *(a) the lawyer manifests to the person consent to do so; or*
>
> *(b) the lawyer fails to manifest lack of consent to do so, and the lawyer knows or reasonably should know that the person reasonably relies on the lawyer to provide the services*[.] . . .

Attorneys generally take two different approaches to decrease the likelihood of creating an unintended attorney-client relationship through social media. The first approach involves prominently featuring disclaimers on all social media sites. Here is a sample disclaimer relied upon by some attorneys for their blogs.

All content on this blog is for informational purposes only. Nothing on this blog should be viewed as legal advice. The law constantly evolves and varies by jurisdiction. Thus, any reader who requires legal advice should seek out a licensed attorney. No attorney-client relationship is formed through this blog nor should any relationship be implied.

Attorneys should avoid burying the disclaimer in fine print or on a Terms and Conditions page that is rarely read. Also, attorneys should try to get the reader to click on an "acceptance" of the disclaimer prior to any exchange of information.

The second approach involves attorneys keeping all information on social media very general in nature and avoiding any content that could be deemed legal advice by the public. Of course, it can be difficult sometimes to distinguish between legal advice and general information, especially when examined from the layperson's point of view.

B. ADVERTISING

Due to the nature of social media, attorneys can easily find many of their daily online activities labeled as advertising by the state bar. For instance, a LinkedIn profile that merely contains an attorney's education and past employment would not constitute advertising, at least in the state of New York. However, if that same LinkedIn profile added practice areas or certain skills, recommendations, or endorsements, it could be deemed advertising, which in turn, depending on the jurisdiction, imposes additional duties on the attorney such as pre-approval, retention, and disclaimers.

Jurisdictions also vary on the type of disclaimers required for attorney advertising. Some jurisdictions require attorneys to label the content "attorney advertising." Other jurisdictions require statements such as "prior results do not guarantee a similar outcome." Since it would be difficult to place all this information on certain social media platforms that have a character limit, e.g., Twitter, some jurisdictions like New York, allow attorneys to utilize commonly recognized abbreviations in the disclaimer.

The leading case involving attorney advertising and social media is *Hunter v. Virginia State Bar*.[23] In *Hunter*, a criminal defense attorney had a blog entitled *This Week in Richmond Criminal Defense*. Hunter maintained and edited the blog on his firm's website. The blog did not permit comments nor did it have any disclaimers. Hunter used his blog to both comment on various legal issues of the day and to highlight the favorable results he obtained for his clients.

Upon learning about the blog, the Virginia State Bar conducted an investigation and determined that it constituted advertising and thus required a disclaimer. Hunter saw it differently and refused to post a disclaimer. According to Hunter, the disclaimer violates his First Amendment rights

---

[23] *Hunter v. Virginia State Bar, ex rel. Third District Comm.*, 285 Va. 485, 744 S.E.2d 611 (2013).

because "it's not what I want to say. It cheapens the speech when I have to put in front of it, 'Oh, by the way, this is for advertising.' "

Ultimately, the bar found that Hunter, through his blog, had violated Virginia Rules of Professional Conduct 1.6 (client confidentiality), 7.1 (advertising), and 7.2 (disclaimer). As a result of its findings, the bar gave Hunter a public admonition and required him to remove case-specific information from his blog and to post a disclaimer. Hunter appealed to the Virginia Supreme Court.

Hunter found partial success at the Virginia Supreme Court which found Rule 1.6 unconstitutional as applied to Hunter's blog. However, the same court found Rules 7.1 and 7.2 constitutional. With respect to Rule 1.6, the Virginia Supreme Court held that "[t]o the extent that the information is aired in a public forum, privacy considerations must yield to First Amendment protections. In that respect, a lawyer is no more prohibited than any other citizen from reporting what transpired in the courtroom."

A few legal commentators believe that the Virginia Supreme Court in *Hunter* created a public records or public knowledge exception to client confidentiality that other states don't or have yet to recognize. Other commentators believe that the court might have reached a different outcome on this question had the attorney blogged about pending cases rather than completed ones.

With respect to Rules 7.1 and 7.2, the Virginia Supreme Court found them constitutional as applied to Hunter's blog. Hunter argued that his posts were more political than commercial and therefore deserved the highest level of protection under the First Amendment. The court saw it differently and found that the majority of Hunter's posts were commercial in nature. The court offered a number of reasons for why it reached this conclusion.

(1) Attorney's motivation for the blog was partially economic.

(2) Most of the posts pertained to positive case results; and thus advertised the attorney's lawyering skills.

(3) The blog was maintained on the firm's website rather than an independent website.

(4) The blog was non-interactive and did not allow for public discourse.

After determining that the posts were commercial speech, the court then found the required disclaimer, as applied to Hunter's blog, constitutional. The court went on to say that Hunter's posts had the *potential* to be misleading as opposed to calling them *outright* misleading, which is what the bar had claimed.

Other states, like California, have taken a similar approach to Virginia in determining whether an attorney's blog constitutes advertising. In a recent ethics opinion from the State Bar of California, the Standing Committee on Professional Responsibility and Conduct determined that blogging by an attorney may be subject to the requirements and restrictions relating to lawyer advertising if the blog "expresses the attorney's availability for professional employment directly through words of invitation or offer to provide legal services, or implicitly through its description of the type and character of legal services offered by the attorney, detailed descriptions of case results, or both." Proposed Formal Opinion Interim No. 12–0006 (Attorney Blogging).

This same opinion also noted that a blog placed on a law firm's website is subject to the same rules regulating the website. Finally, the opinion states that a standalone blog, even if linked to the attorney's website, is not subject to the rules of advertising if unrelated to the practice of law or otherwise used to express the attorney's availability.

C. ENDORSEMENTS

Another topic somewhat related to advertising is endorsements. Issues have arisen in the past with how endorsements are both obtained and maintained. Most jurisdictions allow attorneys to solicit endorsements. The Connecticut Bar in Informal Opinion 2012–03 (2012) determined that it is ethical for attorneys to seek positive reviews from clients and direct them to applicable websites. However, attorneys, at least in Connecticut, can't offer anything in kind for the endorsement. Other jurisdictions that allow paid endorsements require disclosures stating that compensation has been provided for the endorsement.

The final issue with respect to endorsements is maintaining accuracy. Lawyers can't request or suggest that clients submit bogus or false reviews. Nor can attorneys or those acting on their behalf submit bogus claims. This includes a prohibition against "Astroturfing" which was previously discussed in Section 3.03. In fact, attorneys must take steps to ensure their social media sites only include accurate endorsements. This includes removing, if necessary, references to skills or expertise that the attorney does not have or are prohibited in that particular jurisdiction. For example, some jurisdictions do not allow attorneys to be classified as "specialists" or "experts." Others require attorneys to obtain proper certification in order to be classified as a "specialist."

D. PENDING LITIGATION

To date, attorneys have effectively used social media to influence people both inside and outside of the courtroom. For example, when the focus is on people outside the courtroom some criminal attorneys have turned to social media as a way to tell their client's story in order to shape and galvanize public opinion. Through social media, both prosecutors and defense attorneys are able to reach the public on their own terms without going through the media or some other third party.

Any attorney who takes to social media to discuss her case must be cognizant of ABA Model Rule 3.6a, which prohibits lawyers associated with a particular matter from making extrajudicial statements that have a substantial likelihood of materially affecting the proceeding. In addition to the general ethical provisions that apply in ABA Model Rule 3.6, prosecutors also have to be cognizant of ABA Model Rule 3.8(f), which cautions prosecutors about making extrajudicial statements that increase the possibility of public condemnation of the defendant. *Missouri v. Polk* illustrates the application of this rule to an overzealous prosecutor in St. Louis.[24]

In *Polk*, the government was trying a twenty-year-old cold case that involved the rape of a young girl. Before and during the trial, the St. Louis Circuit Attorney, made several tweets related to the trial.

> Before jury selection: *David Polk trial next week. DNA hit linked to 1992 rape of 11yr old girl. 20 yrs later, victim now same age as prosecutor*
>
> During trial: *I have respect for attys who defend child rapists. Our system of justice demands it, but I couldn't do it. No way, no how.*
>
> During deliberations: *Jury now has David Polk case. I hope the victim gets justice, even though 20 years later.*

Once the defendant became aware of the tweets, he used them as a basis for a new trial arguing that they violated the Missouri Rules of Professional Conduct and prejudiced the jury against him. While the appellate court did determine that the prosecutor's tweets were troubling, it did not find any evidence that jurors were influenced by them or that the

---

[24] *State v. Polk*, 415 S.W.3d 692 (Mo. Ct. App. 2013).

fairness of the trial had been comprised. The court wrote that:

> *We doubt that using social media to highlight the evidence against the accused and publicly dramatize the plight of the victim serves any legitimate law enforcement purpose or is necessary to inform the public of the nature and extent of the prosecutor's actions. Likewise, we are concerned that broadcasting that the accused is a "child rapist" is likely to arouse heightened public condemnation. . . Though we do foresee how comments like Joyce's could taint a jury, we cannot conclude that the jury in this case was substantially swayed based on the mere potential for prejudice.*

In a few instances, prosecutors have gone too far in their efforts to influence the public. This was illustrated in *United States v. Kenneth Bowen*, which involved the prosecution of several Louisiana law enforcement officers for abusive conduct that occurred shortly after Hurricane Katrina.[25] During the prosecution of these officers, federal attorneys, while using aliases, made numerous inflammatory statements in the comments section of a local paper about the case. Ultimately, the efforts by the attorneys were uncovered and led to the dismissal of numerous counts against the officers. According to the trial judge, the convictions had to be dismissed due to the "deliberate and especially egregious pattern of prosecutorial misconduct."

---

[25] *United States v. Bowen*, 969 F.Supp.2d 546 (E.D. La. 2013).

One of the main concerns with attorneys commenting on pending litigation, whether civil or criminal, is that one party may somehow unduly prejudice the jury through comments made on social media. This has led some attorneys to request the issuance of gag orders, which prevent attorneys from publicly discussing the case outside of the courtroom.

Courts for the most part are hesitant to issue a gag order and infringe on an individual's First Amendment rights. In George Zimmerman's trial for the death of Trayvon Martin, the prosecution made repeated attempts to prevent Zimmerman's attorney, Mark O'Mara, from using social media both before and during trial to discuss the case. Prosecutors tried three different times to get the judge to issue a gag order on all parties in the case. Prosecutors claimed that the information provided by defense counsel would unduly prejudice the jurors and possibly taint their decision making. The presiding judge saw it differently. According to the judge, "[t]here has not been an overriding pattern of prejudicial commentary that will overcome reasonable efforts to select a fair and impartial jury."[26]

Examples of civil attorneys requesting gag orders for extrajudicial references on social media include *Ex parte Wright*.[27] In *Ex parte Wright,* plaintiffs sued defendants for, among other things, fraud and breach of warranty and contract. The dispute arose from a warranty in which the defendants, A-1

---

[26] Lizette Alvarez, *Judge in Trayvon Martin Case Denies Request for Silence,* NY TIMES (October 29, 2012).

[27] *Ex parte Wright*, 166 So. 3d 618 (Ala. 2014).

Exterminating, agreed to protect plaintiffs' residences from termites.

During the litigation, A-1 filed a protection order forbidding plaintiffs from, *inter alia*, referencing the case on Facebook and other social media platforms. Defendants had claimed that plaintiffs had made numerous online comments about the case. Defendants further asserted that these comments were not only defamatory, but also "intended to influence prospective jurors."

The trial court granted the defendant's request and issued the following order:

> *Plaintiff's counsel shall remove all mention of the above styled cases and the surrounding circumstances of the above styled cases from its website, Facebook page, social media (including electronic social media), and related web search engines. Plaintiffs and Plaintiffs' counsel are otherwise ordered to refrain from referencing this case and/or its surrounding circumstances outside of court.*

The order was subsequently amended to clarify that plaintiffs' counsel could use electronic communication to include social media to discuss the case with clients and other members of the law firm. The amended order also broadened the scope of the social media sites covered to include LinkedIn. In addition, the amended order added the personal social media accounts of plaintiffs' counsel.

Plaintiffs subsequently appealed to the Alabama Supreme Court. At the Alabama Supreme Court, plaintiffs argued that the trial court's order acted as an impermissible prior restraint on speech in violation of the First Amendment. In contrast, A-1 argued that the protective orders were necessary to safeguard its right to a fair trial. Ultimately, the Alabama high court sided with the plaintiffs finding that the protective orders were overbroad and not narrowly tailored. The state high court noted that the orders as written prohibited plaintiffs from using electronic communication to discuss the case with potential clients, putative class members, state regulators, non-expert witnesses, and anyone who might be of assistance with the discovery of evidence.

Some attorneys, as discussed next, have gone so far as to use social media as a medium by which to pressure or influence a judge about a pending legal matter. *In re McCool* involved a Louisiana attorney (McCool) who represented Raven Boyd in a very contentious family law matter in which Boyd, among other things, alleged that her husband was sexually abusing their two minor children.[28] The first Mississippi judge who heard the case in 2007 determined there was no merit in the sexual abuse claims. However, he passed away, and Judge Deborah Gambrell inherited the case in 2011.

Judge Gambrell ultimately decided to reintroduce the father to his children through supervised visitation in 2011. This led Boyd's new husband, Dustin Maurer, to file an intra-family adoption in the Louisiana courts. Judge Dawn Amacker, who was

---

[28] *In re McCool*, No. 2014–OB–0366, 133 So.3d 669 (La. 2014).

assigned to hear the Louisiana case, denied an emergency custody motion and stayed the matter pending the outcome of the proceedings in Mississippi.

On August 16, 2011, someone sent Judge Gambrell an online change.org petition which, among other things, asked the judge to give up her jurisdiction in the case. McCool acknowledged creating the petition and a website to facilitate the online petition. In addition, McCool admitted that the online petition was intended to provide information and elicit reaction from others and have them voice their thoughts directly to the judge.

McCool also used Twitter to distribute audio recordings of the minor children being interviewed by their mother about sexual abuse, as well as to communicate her opinion on how Judges Gambrell and Amacker were handling the underlying cases.

Twitter was not the only social media platform relied upon by McCool to influence public opinion. For example, on the blog sheeplessinamerica. blogspot.com McCool created a blog post entitled "Justice for H (REDACTED) and Z (REDACTED)." In the post, she discussed the underlying case and stated "**Horrified? Call the judges and let them know**."

Ultimately, the Louisiana Attorney Disciplinary Board suspended McCool for a year and a day. In addition, she was required to attend Ethics School. In comparison to other attorneys who have been punished for similar conduct, McCool's punishment appeared to be on the high end, especially in light of the fact that she had no prior disciplinary infractions. However, the Board pointed to the fact that "she used the internet and social media to facilitate her misconduct. Consequently, the offending language remains present and accessible on the internet today."

CHAPTER 12

JUDGES

§ 12.01 INTRODUCTION

This chapter explores the impact of social media on the judiciary. The first part of the chapter looks at ways in which judges use social media to interact with attorneys, witnesses, parties, and the general public. The second part of the chapter examines the methods by which judges regulate the use of social media inside their courtrooms. The focus here will be on jurors and the media.

§ 12.02 INTERACTING WITH OTHERS

A. NON-ATTORNEYS

Like attorneys, judges must be careful with how they use social media to interact with others. The two big areas of concern are comments about ongoing cases and less than judicious posts. To date, a small number of judges have been reprimanded for their conduct on social media. *In re Dianna Bennington* serves as an example of how judges can find themselves in trouble even when they post personal comments about matters unrelated to judicial decision making.[1] In this case, the judge and the biological father of her children (J.W.) were in a dispute over child support. The judge, after noticing a photo of J.W. and his girlfriend on vacation, posted a comment on the Facebook page of J.W. The post,

---

1 *In re Dianna Bennington*, 24 N.E.3d 958 (Ind. 2015)

which was visible to others who had access to the page, reads as follows:

> *Must be nice to take such an expensive trip but not pay your bills. Just sayin*

According to the Indiana Supreme Court, the comment was contrary to the judge's duty to "act at all times in a manner that promotes public confidence in the. . . integrity. . . of the judiciary." This post, in addition to other misconduct by the judge, ultimately led the Indiana Supreme Court to ban her from serving in any future judicial capacity.

To prevent judges from running afoul of ethical rules or judicial canons several jurisdictions have issued opinions reminding judges about the importance of maintaining judicial decorum while using social media. Ohio's Supreme Court of Commissioners on Grievances and Discipline wrote that "[a] judge must maintain dignity in every comment, photograph, and other information share on the social network."[2] Similarly, a commission in California noted that "[w]hile it may be acceptable for a college student to post photographs of himself or herself engaged in drunken revelry, it is not appropriate for a judge to do so."[3]

As for discussing ongoing cases, similar to the offline world, judges are prohibited from making online comments about cases or issues before them or

---

[2] Ohio Board of Commissioner's Grievances & Discipline, Advisory Opinion 2010–7.

[3] California Judges Association Ethics Committee Opinion 66 (2010).

likely to come before them. Generally speaking, any statement about a case from a judge should come in the form of an official order or opinion. Commentary also includes endorsements. Thus, if a judge is prohibited from putting up a yard sign endorsing a political candidate or local business, the judge may not Like a particular candidate or business on Facebook. Finally, judges, similar to attorneys, must monitor the comments made on their social media accounts by others.

In re: Hon. Michelle Slaughter illustrates the problems that arise when judges take to social media to discuss pending cases.[4] This judicial disciplinary proceeding arose from the case of *Texas v. Wieseckel.* In *Wieseckel,* the defendant was charged with unlawful restraint of a child. The defendant allegedly required his 9-year-old son to use a 6 foot by 8 foot wooden enclosure as his so-called "bedroom." This led the media to reference the defendant's trial as the "Boy in the Box" case. Once the jury was selected, the judge hearing the case provided the jurors the following instructions:

> *During the trial of the case, as I mentioned before, you cannot talk to anyone. So make sure that you don't talk to anyone. Again, this is by any means of communication. So no texting, emailing, talking person to person or on the*

---

4 Special Court of Review, Appointed by the Supreme Court. In re Honorable Michelle SLAUGHTER, Presiding Judge of the 405th Judicial District Court, Galveston County, 480 S.W.3d 842. Decided: September 30, 2015.

> *phone or Facebook. Any of that is absolutely forbidden.*

This admonition, however, did not stop the judge from making her own online comments about the case. After the first day of testimony, the judge posted the following on her Facebook page:

> *Opening statements this morning at 9:30 am in the trial called by the press 'the boy in the box.'*
>
> *After we finished Day 1 of the case called the 'Boy in the Box' case, trustees from the jail came in and assembled the actual 6'×8' 'box' inside the courtroom!*
>
> *This is the case currently in the 405th! [post included a link to a Reuters news article discussing the case].*

Upon learning about the posts, defense counsel moved for a mistrial and asked that the judge be recused, both of which were granted.

When confronted about her actions, the judge claimed that she made her comments to promote "transparency" and to "encourage individuals to come watch the proceedings." The Texas State Commission on Judicial Conduct was unconvinced. Instead, the Commission determined that the posts by the judge were inconsistent with the proper performance of her duties. This was because the posts cast reasonable doubt on her impartiality and violated her own admonition to jurors.

In addition, the commission noted that the posts went beyond explaining court procedures and actually highlighted evidence that had yet to be introduced into court. The Commission also noted that the judge's social media activity had led to her recusal from the case. In light of the judge's conduct, the Commission publicly admonished the judge and required her to obtain additional instruction on the proper and ethical use of social media.

The judge appealed the decision of the Commission to a Special Court of Review where, after a two-day trial, she was exonerated. Nonetheless, the judge had to endure the costs of defending herself and see her reputation, at least temporarily, impugned for her use of Facebook.

B. ATTORNEYS

Most jurisdictions permit judges to interact with attorneys through social media. However, there is a sharp split in opinion as to whether this interaction should continue if the attorney has a case or will appear before the judge. At present, jurisdictions take one of four approaches in addressing this issue.

The first approach, adopted by states like Florida, Massachusetts, and Oklahoma, is an outright ban on judges interacting via social media with attorneys who appear before them. Jurisdictions relying on this approach fear that judges may favor one attorney over another or that people may perceive a potential for favoritism. In the eyes of the Massachusetts Committee on Judicial Ethics, "[a] judge's 'friending' **attorneys** on social networking sites creates the impression that those attorneys are in a special position to influence the judge. Therefore, the Code does not permit you to 'friend' any attorney who may appear before you[.]"[5]

The second approach, followed by states like Kentucky, Maryland, New York, and Ohio, is the complete opposite of the first. These states permit judges to interact via social media with attorneys that appear before them. Judges, however, are instructed that although permissible such relationships may become problematic. For example, the state of New York warns judges to:

> *[B]e mindful of the appearance created when he/she establishes a connection with an attorney or anyone else appearing in the judge's court through a social network. In some ways, this is no different from adding the person's contact information into the judge's Rolodex or address book or speaking to them in a public setting. But, the public nature of such a link (i.e., other users can normally see the judge's friends or connections) and the increased access that the person would have to any personal information the judge chooses to post on his/her own profile page establish, at least, the appearance of a stronger bond. A judge must, therefore, consider whether any such online connections, alone or in combination with other facts, rise to the level of a*

[5] The Massachusetts Judicial Branch, Supreme Judicial Court, CJE Opinion No. 2011–6: Facebook: Using Social Networking Web Site, (Dec. 28, 2011).

"close social relationship" requiring disclosure and/or recusal.[6]

The third approach, followed by California, is a hybrid of the first two approaches. In California, judges may friend attorneys who appear before them only if those attorneys don't have active cases before that judge.

The last approach, followed by states like South Carolina and Tennessee, is to remain silent on the issue. Both of these jurisdictions permit judges to use social media. However, neither state has affirmatively prohibited nor allowed judges to friend the attorneys that appear before them.

The topic of judges friending attorneys has even grabbed the attention of the ABA which recently issued an advisory opinion on the matter. According to the opinion by the ABA's Standing Committee on Ethics and Professional Responsibility, it is ethical for judges to not only use social media, but also to friend attorneys, so long as they adhere to the judicial conduct rules.[7]

The opinion also discusses the following six rules of the Model Code of Judicial Conduct that all judges should keep in mind when using social media. First, act in a manner promoting public confidence in the judiciary (Rule 1.2). Second, avoid ex parte

---

[6] N.Y. Advisory Committee on Judicial Ethics, Opinion 08–176 (Jan. 29, 2009).

[7] ABA Committee on Ethics & Professional Responsibility, Judge's Use of Electronic Social Networking Media, Formal Opinion 462 (Feb. 21, 2013).

communication (Rule 2.9(A)). Third, do not comment on pending or impending matters (Rule 2.10). Fourth, do not form relationships with persons or groups that may convey an impression that these people and entities are in a position to influence the judge (Rule 2.4(C)). Fifth, do not offer legal advice (Rule 3.10). Sixth, do not use social media to conduct independent investigations into pending matters (Rule 2.9(C)).

Finally, the ABA opinion warns judges about the differences between online and offline communication. Here, the opinion mentions both the permanency of online information and the absence of physical cues that occur in traditional face-to-face conversations. These cues are important because they give context to communication and reduce the risk of misinterpretation.

For those jurisdictions that permit judges to friend attorneys, judges must consider whether or not they must disclose that friendship to others. The aforementioned ABA opinion says that a judge who employs social media is not necessarily required to disclose to the litigants or counsel that the judge has an online connection to a person involved with the case. This viewpoint is similar to Kentucky and New York. In contrast, California, which at present does not allow judges to friend attorneys who have cases before them, does require judges to disclose social media relationships as a general matter. According to a California Judge's Association Ethics Committee Opinion:

> *[If] the online interaction were permitted, a judge would have to disclose not only the fact that*

> *interaction took place in the first instance, but also that it is going to continue. This continuing contact could create the impression that the attorney is in a special position to influence the judge simply by virtue of the ready access afforded by the social networking site.*[8]

In addition to concerns about ethical violations, certain judge-attorney social media relationships have been grounds for recusal and retrial in both civil and criminal cases. To date, at least one criminal defendant has had the trial judge on his case recused because of the judge's social media relationship with the prosecutor.

Pierre Domville v. State, a criminal case from Florida, illustrates how a judge can be removed from a case because of his social media relationship with one of the parties.[9] In *Domville*, the defendant sought recusal of the judge hearing his case after discovering that the prosecutor and judge were friends on Facebook. In denying the defendant's request, the judge claimed that his social media friendship with the prosecutor did not prevent him from treating the defendant fairly or acting impartially.

The defendant appealed and the Florida Court of Appeals agreed with him. According to the appellate court, the defendant alleged sufficient "facts that would create in a reasonably prudent person a well-

---

[8] California Judges Association Ethics Committee Opinion 66 (2010).

[9] *Pierre Domville v. State of Florida*, 103 So.3d 184 (Fla. 4th Dist. Ct. App. Sept. 5, 2012).

founded fear of not receiving a fair and impartial trial[.]" The appellate court went on to say that "when a judge lists a lawyer who appears before him as a 'friend' " on Facebook this "reasonably conveys to others the impression that these lawyer 'friends' are in a special position to influence the judge."

C. PARTIES AND WITNESSES

Attempts to overturn judicial decisions because of a judge's social media relationship with a witness, rather than an attorney, have been less successful. In *Onnen v. Sioux Falls Independent School District*, a civil case, the plaintiff sought a new trial based on a witness's "Happy Birthday" post on the judge's Facebook Wall. The judge, however, did not personally know the witness nor did he request the post. Thus, the judge ultimately concluded that this one post from a witness, albeit a main witness, would not cause him to favor one side over the other and; therefore, was insufficient grounds for a new trial. The plaintiff appealed to the South Dakota Supreme Court, which upheld the trial judge's ruling.

In upholding the judge's decision, the South Dakota Supreme Court found that the Happy Birthday post had no connection to the facts of the case and, thus, did not unduly sway the judge. Specifically, the South Dakota Supreme Court held that "where an ex parte communication is not invited or initiated by the judge, reversible error occurs only if the adverse party is prejudiced by an inability to rebut the facts communicated and if improper influence appears with reasonable certainty."[10]

In contrast to witnesses, social media interaction between judges and parties is more problematic, especially if initiated by the judge. In *Chace v. Loisel*, a divorce proceeding in Florida, the judge sent a friend request to the plaintiff, Sandra Chace, prior to the final judgment.[11] Upon advice from counsel, Chace did not respond to the invitation. However, once the final judgment was entered, Chace moved to disqualify the trial judge, claiming that the final judgment was "disproportionately excessive" and the judge had retaliated against her for not accepting the friend request.

On appeal, the appellate court agreed with Chace, finding that "[t]he 'friend' request placed the litigant between the proverbial rock and a hard place: either engage in improper ex parte communication with the judge presiding over the case or risk offending the judge by not accepting the 'friend' request." The court went on to make several insightful observations about Facebook friendships. According to the court,

> *The word "friend" on Facebook is a term of art. A number of words or phrases could more aptly describe the concept, including acquaintance and, sometimes, virtual stranger. A Facebook friendship does not necessarily signify the existence of a close relationship. Other than the*

---

[10] *Onnen v. Sioux Falls Indep. Sch Dist.*, 801 N.W. 2d 752, 758 (S.D. 2011).

[11] *Chace v. Loisel*, 170 So.3d 802 (Fla. Dist. Ct. App. 2014).

public nature of the internet, there is no difference between a Facebook "friend" and any other friendship a judge might have.

§ 12.03 REGULATING THE COURTROOM

As for judges regulating or controlling how others use social media in the courtroom, a sharp divide exists between jurors and non-jurors. For the most part, judges have significant leeway in regulating the conduct of jurors. For example, judges can sequester jurors and completely cut them off from all forms of communication including social media. The same, however, cannot be said for other individuals who might be in the courtroom, like court personnel, media, the public, and attorneys. Here, the judge has far less power.

A. NON-JURORS

The use of social media by non-jurors in the courtroom arises in a variety of different circumstances. As discussed in Section 10.04, attorneys increasingly rely on social media to investigate jurors. Another example of social media used inside the courtroom includes real-time reporting by both new and traditional media. This generally occurs in high-profile trials that generate significant public interest.

Some courts permit real-time reporting or create a presumption in favor of such activity. The jurisdictions that allow such reporting do so provided that the methods used do not disrupt the proceedings. While a few courts attempt to draw distinctions between new and traditional media, these distinctions, as discussed in Section 8.05, are increasingly meaningless in the Digital Age.

Courts that allow social media in the courtroom for reporting purposes contend that it:

(1) increases public understanding of the legal system,

(2) brings greater openness to the process,

(3) allows more people to follow legal proceedings,

(4) facilitates real-time reporting, and

(5) instills confidence in the legal system.

Utah was one of the first jurisdictions to provide social media specific rules regarding real-time reporting. Under the Utah court rules, amended in 2012, "news reporters" in the courtroom have a presumptive right to use electronic media. The Utah rules also provide a broad definition of "news reporters" to include "any person who gathers, records, photographs, reports, or publishes information for the primary purpose of disseminating news and information to the public." In fashioning this new rule, Utah examined the impact of electronic media coverage on the court system and determined that the use of electronic media had no detrimental impact on the parties, jurors, counsel, or courtroom decorum.

Courts that prohibit social media in the courtroom for reporting purposes contend that it:

(1) disrupts the sanctity of the courtroom,

(2) distracts jurors,

(3) allows for sequestered witnesses to learn about the testimony of other witnesses,

(4) facilitates juror misconduct,

(5) creates a potential for tainting prospective jurors, and

(6) runs the risk of intimidating witnesses and jurors.

Witness and juror intimidation are often cited as the main reasons for disallowing real-time reporting. According to the Cook County Chief Judge, these prohibitions are necessary

> *to provide safety within the courts, prevent pictures from being taken with electronic devices and help to protect innocent individuals and those testifying in court. We want to do everything we can to ensure that justice is properly done by preserving the integrity of testimony and maintaining court decorum. We understand this may be an inconvenience to some, but our primary goal is to protect those inside our courthouse and perhaps save lives in the process.*[12]

---

[12] Kevin Davis, *Intimidated: Witness Harassment Has Gone Digital, and the Justice System is Playing Catch-Up*, 99 ABA J. 54, 56 (2013).

B. JURORS

In the Digital Age, jurors increasingly use social media to either discuss or research the case even though such conduct is generally prohibited. To prevent jurors from using social media in connection with the case on which they sit judges have tried a number of remedies to include: imposing penalties on jurors, allowing jurors to ask questions, improving jury instructions, and requiring juror oaths.

The penalties imposed on jurors for violating the court's rules on using social media range from fines to public embarrassment to sequestration to incarceration (in the rare case). The common thread with all juror penalties is that, once imposed, they make citizens less inclined to want to serve as jurors.

The next method relied upon by judges is allowing jurors to ask questions. Some judges believe that jurors who are permitted to ask questions will be less inclined to seek alternative avenues for information like social media. While most states today allow juror questions, they leave the practice up to the discretion of the trial judge.

The most common remedy for preventing jurors from improperly using social media is improving jury instructions. Many jurisdictions have or are in the process of updating their instructions to reflect how society communicates in the Digital Age. The most important update to these instructions is telling jurors "why" they should not discuss or research the case on social media.

The final and least common method relied upon by judges is the jury oath. Here, the court requires jurors to sign a written pledge or take an oath in which they promise to abide by the court's rules and not discuss or research the case on social media. Some believe that memorializing and emphasizing certain instructions, such as not disclosing or researching the case on social media, makes jurors more likely to adhere to them.

INDEX

References are to Pages
